TEACH YOURSE

D0199946

ORIGAMI

Robert Harbin

To Neal Elias and Fred Rohm

Long renowned as the authoritative source for self-guided learning – with more than 30 million copies sold worldwide – the *Teach Yourself* series includes over 200 titles in the fields of languages, crafts, hobbies, sports, and other leisure activities.

British Library Cataloguing in Publication Data
A catalogue record for this title is
available from the British Library

Library of Congress Catalog Card Number: 92-80886

First published in the UK 1992 by Hodder Headline Plc, 338 Euston Road, London NW1 3BH

First published in US 1992 by NTC Publishing Group, 4255 West Touhy Avenue, Lincolnwood (Chicago), Illinois 60646 – 1975 U.S.A.

Copyright © 1968 Robert Harbin
Copyright © 1992 and 1980 Trustees of The British Origami Society

'A Short History of Origami' and 'Bibliography'
Copyright © Hodder and Stoughton Ltd 1980 and 1992

In UK: All rights reserved. No part of this publication may be reproduced or transmitted in any form or by any means, electronic or mechanical, including photocopy, recording, or any information storage and retrieval system, without permission in writing from the publisher or under licence from the Copyright Licensing Agency Limited. Further details of such licences (for reprographic reproduction) may be obtained from the Copyright Licensing Agency Limited, of 90 Tottenham Court Road, London W1P 9HE.

In US: All rights reserved. No part of this book may be reproduced, stored in a retrieval system, or transmitted in any form, or by any means, electronic, mechanical, photocopying, or otherwise, without prior permission of NTC Publishing Group.

Typeset by Rowland Phototypesetting Ltd, Bury St Edmunds, Suffolk.
Printed in England by Cox & Wyman Ltd, Reading, Berkshire.

First edition 1968
Second edition 1992

Impression number	14 13 12 11 10 9 8 7 6 5 4 3
Year	1999 1998 1997 1996 1995

CONTENTS

Preface	iv
A Short History of Origami	1
The Essentials of Origami	7
A Note on Symbols	9
Symbols	10
Reverse Folds	14
Feet	16
Bird's Head	17
House	18
G.I. Cap	22
Boat	24
Salt Cellar	26
Colour Changer	31
Spanish Box	32
Turban	38
Samurai Hat	43
Sampan	48
Water Bomb	53
Sanbow 1	58
Sanbow 2	63
Basket	68
Multiform	73
Gondola	78
Bird Base	83
Flapping Bird	90
Pigeon	93
Praying Moor	99
Frog	102
Bat Mask	113
Penguins	116
Penguin 1	121
Penguin 2	124
Rabbit	127
Tropical Bird 1	129
Tropical Bird 2	132
Xmas Tree	134
Mother Hubbard's Dog	137
Mother Hubbard	138
Friar Tuck	142
Squirrel	144
Printer's Hat	147
Decoration 1	150
Decoration 2	153
Japanese Gentleman	158
Japanese Lady	161
Fish	163
Ornithonimus	167
Aladdin's Lamp	170
Ostrich	175
Church	177
Pink Elephant	181
Swans	185
Bibliography	187

PREFACE

Writing a book, whatever the subject, is always a laborious task for me. But writing this addition to the *Teach Yourself* series has been a real pleasure, because I am anxious to introduce as many as possible to the world of origami, which has given me so much enjoyment.

The main task has been to design the illustrations, because without them there could not be a book. Diagrams take a long time to prepare because, fold by fold, the three-dimensional paper model must be reduced to a two-dimensional drawing on a flat sheet of paper. And the drawing must be clear and accurate if the student is to understand how to produce the finished model from it.

It could be argued, I suppose, that origami has an end product that is not worth keeping. Nothing could be further from the truth. At the time of writing, I have a delightful collection of the world's best paper folds, carefully stored in transparent envelopes, which are in turn mounted on a sheet of black board. This way, they are ready to be produced and shown quickly – and they *are* produced and shown, at the slightest provocation!

If this art form captures you, as it has certainly captured me and many others, you will discover that it brings with it a new dimension in enjoyment, which is infinite in its variety and unrivalled in its capacity to make you relax and forget everything else.

Robert Harbin

A SHORT HISTORY OF ORIGAMI

'Origami' is a Japanese word which simply means 'paper-folding' and it was adopted first in English and then in other languages in recognition of the long tradition of the Japanese people for folding paper.

The Chinese invented paper, probably before the birth of Christ, and we can only guess that they were the first to fold paper. But we do know that by the twelfth century A.D. paper was used in Japan for folding ceremonial wrappers ('tsutsumi') for storage of household goods, such as herbs, and for gifts, especially gifts of flowers, where each kind of flower had its special wrapper. The present-day Japanese custom of attaching to gifts small tokens of folded paper called 'noshi' is a relic of this ceremonial paper-folding and there remain some other survivals.

Apart from occasional far-from-clear references to paper animals, birds and flowers, the earliest informative records we have of recreational, as opposed to ceremonial, paper-folding are two Japanese books the *Senbazuru Orikata* and the *Chushingura Orikata* both dating from 1797. The first describes how to fold connected groups and chains of paper cranes (very similar to the classic flapping bird on page 90) and the second shows how to fold a series of characters from a popular play. These paper dolls resemble somewhat Robert Harbin's Japanese Lady and Gentleman on pages 158 to 162. The folding in these two books is much more advanced than the simple folds familiar to children round the world and it presupposes a long tradition of paper-folding in Japan before 1800.

The little paper dolls appear again in the *Kan no mado,* a manuscript encyclopedia believed to date from the middle of the nineteenth century. This contains several ceremonial folds and also some elaborately folded animals and insects which use extensive cutting: something which would not be acceptable today.

As modern creative origami avoids cutting it does not derive directly from the tradition of the *Kan no mado* and it is the flapping bird itself which lies at the heart of the modern development of the art. This remarkable folded toy was brought to Europe from Japan about 1880. Japanese stage magicians and also educationalists are believed to have been involved. The flapping bird was quickly absorbed into the small European repertoire of children's folds which already had a long tradition. European folds were, however, for the most part, restricted to a few simple hats, boxes and boats, together with the salt cellar (page 26) and what Robert Harbin called the 'multiform' series of folds (pages 73 to 83). Another multiform figure not included in this book is the curious 'hobby horse', which is known in Spain as the *pajarita,* meaning 'little bird'. The Spanish philosopher Miguel de Unanumo (1864–1936) took a delight in childish things, including paper-folding, and was fascinated by the pajarita. Later, by manipulating the bird base (pages 83–89), which was the foundation for the flapping bird, he created a series of somewhat angular birds and animals which nevertheless greatly extended the possibilities of paper-folding. His most significant discovery was the sideways twist of the flaps of the bird base which is also used in Yoshizawa's pigeon (page 93). A small group of followers of Unanumo came into being and the Praying Moor (page 99) is an example of their work. The Spanish tradition spread to South America and culminated in the vast analytical work of Dr. Solorzano Sagredo and the delicately creative work of his pupil, the late Ligia Montoya of Argentina, two of whose simpler models are the Tropical Birds on pages 129 to 133.

In Japan, Isao Honda made collections of traditional and modern origami and new books began to appear, notably those by Michio Uchiyama and his son Kosho Uchiyama. Then, quite independently of Unanumo, Akira Yoshizawa made similar discoveries about the possibilities of the bird base. Some of his work was published by Isao Honda in 1944. After the

Second World War, Yoshizawa began to publish his own books and articles and Japanese paper-folding entered a new period of creativity. Akira Yoshizawa's ingenuity is matched by his incomparable skill in bringing his models to life and he continues to dominate the art in Japan.

Before the war, paper-folding in English-speaking countries had been limited to the traditional children's folds, but in the 1950s it began to develop through the efforts of three people: Gershon Legman and Lillian Oppenheimer of the United States and Robert Harbin of Britain. Curiously none of them claimed to be a creative folder. Gershon Legman compiled a bibliography and also established contacts with both Akira Yoshizawa and Ligia Montoya. Lillian Oppenheimer publicised origami and founded the Origami Center of America in New York. She put folders in touch with one another and made many books available, including some in Spanish and Japanese. Robert Harbin demonstrated paper-folding on television for the first time in 1955, and in 1956 he published his excellent book *Paper Magic* which summarised the art and for a time became the standard manual in English.

The work of these three people brought together for the first time many people who had been folding paper for their own amusement in isolation and the newly available books inspired a generation of creative folders, especially in America where Fred Rohm, Neal Elias, Robert Neale, George Rhoads and Jack Skillman devised new techniques and basic folds which opened up possibilities for paper-folding undreamed of even in Japan. For a time the bird base and its related folds, the fish base and frog base, remained the foundations for folding but they were soon joined by more complex versions including multiple and 'blinzed' bird and frog bases. Before long entirely new ideas emerged including the 'box-folding' of Dr. Emanuel Mooser of Switzerland and 'box-pleating' developed especially by Neal Elias.

Despite the influence of Robert Harbin, paper-folding in Britain lagged behind until the British Origami Society was formed in 1967 from a group of folders whom Lillian Oppenheimer had put in touch with each other. The Society developed slowly but its membership grew following the original publication of *Teach Yourself Origami* in 1968. Since then the Society's magazine *British Origami* has become one of the world's leading journals on the subject.

In the 1970s, just when some began to think that the limits of folding had been reached, members of the British Origami Society broke new ground and produced a large number of greatly varied models of remarkable ingenuity, widely differing in style, sometimes mechanical, sometimes artistic. The classic bird and frog bases were now abandoned by creative folders and new, specialised bases were developed uniquely appropriate for the model to be folded.

The new Western techniques were taken back to Japan, where a younger generation of Japanese have combined the mechanical virtuosity of the West with the delicate artistry of the East. Dokvohtei Nakano and Yoshihide Momotani were two of the best-known among many new Japanese folders. Another Japanese, Shuzo Fujimoto, made new discoveries about the geometrical possibilities of folding, which he developed with great ingenuity. Many of his ideas await exploration by other folders.

In the 1980s Nakano's complex bases were further developed in the United States by John Montroll, Robert Lang, Stephen Weiss and Peter Engel and in Japan by Jun Maekawa. While their style was too technical for some people's tastes, their folding of anatomically correct insects and sea creatures, complete with all their legs and other appendages, finally proved that the possibilities of an uncut square of paper were limitless.

Contrasted with the 'technical school', the British Paul Jackson's minimalist style uses creases to tension the paper and create a kind of uncut paper-sculpture. Another Briton, John S. Smith, devised 'Pure-land' folding, which used only simple mountain and valley folds. It began as an attempt to find simple folds for children and handicapped people and ended as an intellectual exercise. Folding does not have to be complex to retain its beauty and fascination.

The 1980s showed the continuing vitality of paper-folding in other ways. 'Modular origami' (the linking of many identical folded units to form composite models) became popular and was exemplified by the immaculate work of Miss Tomoko Fuse of Japan. The First International Meeting of Origami Science and Technology was held at Ferrara in Italy in 1989, at which a distinguished gathering of scientists and mathematicians explored the awesome depths of origami geometry. There has also been a revived awareness of the value of paper-folding as a therapy for the disabled and handicapped and in child education, where it is employed not only as a manual exercise and for stimulation of geometrical awareness in the tradition of Friedrich Fröbel (1782–1852), the originator of the kindergarten, but also in less obvious fields such as the development of language ability and as an aid to conceptualisation.

The happiest thing about paper-folding is that it has grown as a truly international movement and folders in North and South America, Britain, France, Italy, Germany and many other countries are in regular contact and frequently travel long distances to visit the conventions of each other's societies. New discoveries are shared and exhibitions are held to which contributions are sent from all over the world. Groups have now been formed in eastern Europe and paper-folders from Russia have already visited England.

When we practise origami we pay tribute to the memory of Robert Harbin, the master stage-magician, who became so enthralled by the world contained in a mere square of paper that he decided to tell everyone about his discovery. He freely admitted that conjuring tricks depended on deception, but said that paper-folding really was magic. He would surely have been happy to watch the continuing growth of his 'paper-magic' and its spread to the far corners of the Earth. It was Robert Harbin's heartfelt wish that his beloved origami should ever continue to bring peace and friendship to all people and by sharing in that hope, paper-folders will honour his memory in the way that he himself would have cherished.

David Lister

Information on membership of the British Origami Society and about supplies of books and paper for folding can be obtained from:

The Secretary
The British Origami Society
253 Park Lane
Poynton
Stockport
Cheshire SK12 1RH

The Society has published a series of booklets of very varied aspects of folding, including the advanced work of some of the world's leading creative folders. There is also available for members a wide selection of books in English and other languages including Japanese. Write to the Secretary for information.

Residents of other countries may wish to get in touch with other paper-folding societies. Among them are:

The Friends of the Origami Center
71 West 77th Street
New York NY 10024-5192
USA

Mouvement Français des Plieurs du Papier (MFPP)
56 rue Coriolis
75012 Paris
France

Origami Societeit Nederland (OSN)
Postbus 35
9989 ZG Warffum
Nederlands

Belgische Nederlandse Origami Societeit (BNOS)
Postbus 100
B-2400 MOL
Belgium

Centro Diffusione Origami (CDO)
Casella Postale 225
40100 Bologna
Italy

Association Española de Papiroflexia
C/Pedro Teixeira No 9
Esc 1sq - 90 Dcha
28020 Madrid
Spain

Origami Deutschland
Postfach 1630
Mittlerer Graben 4
8050 Freising
Germany

The New Zealand Origami Society
79 Dunbar Road
Christchurch 3
New Zealand

THE ESSENTIALS OF ORIGAMI

Most beginners are not able to follow diagrams and instructions easily and successfully, however carefully they may have been planned. As a rule, origami illustrators try to cram into each page as much information as possible. This practice is welcomed by the enthusiast and the expert, because it means that the book will be able to explain a large number of models. Unfortunately, though, a page filled with diagrams completely bewilders most beginners.

I have borne this in mind while preparing this book, and you will see that the earlier pages have been designed with no more than two or three diagrams on each page. All the diagrams are clearly drawn, and contain instructions and symbols to give you all possible help, and to explain the mainly standard models which bring you in touch with most of the Basic Folds.

A Basic Fold is a fold from which many models can be made. There are many Basic Folds, both ancient and modern, but this book will introduce you to just enough to give you a good groundwork on which to begin.

Look at the first fold illustrated in the book, and notice how the instructions are placed on the parts to be folded: FOLD THIS SIDE DOWN, and then TO HERE, and so on. The instructions are made to work for you. Later in the book, the instructions are placed next to the diagrams, and not on them, because it is assumed that by then you will have become familiar with the different processes.

Always fold carefully, accurately and neatly. If you fold carelessly, the result will be disastrous.

Study each diagram showing the complete folded model, and only then, place your origami paper in front of you and make your first fold.

When you make a fold, always crease the paper firmly with the back of your thumbnail. Good creases make folding easy, and are an invaluable guide later in the model, when you are making a series of folds.

Pre-creasing is an important feature. Consider, for example, the Japanese Lady (page 161). This model was sent to Samuel Randlett, who immediately used the idea to produce his fine Fish (page 163). Notice how he pre-creases the paper he uses so that everything folds into place at the right moment.

Before you make a Reverse Fold, pre-crease the paper by folding the whole thickness before opening the paper and making the fold (see Reverse Folds).

Notice how paper coloured on one side is used to get the maximum effect for each model. The subject of paper is an important one. Origami paper should be strong, thin and suitably coloured. But if you cannot find special origami paper, almost any paper may be used.

If you are instructed to use a square of paper, make sure that it really is square, and that a rectangle is a true rectangle. Most of the models in this book are based on squares of paper, but there is no regular rule about this, as all shapes of paper can be used, according to the model's needs. See, for example, the Ornithonimus (page 167) and Aladdin's Lamp (page 170).

Origami is not a simple art. To the expert, it is a challenge to the eye, the brain and the fingers – a wonderful mental and physical therapy.

When you fold one of the decorations explained in this book, you will find that by altering this or that fold you can invent endless shapes. In fact, you can improvise for hours.

When you have mastered the Basic Folds, you will then be equipped to produce figures and shapes of your own inventions. Have something in mind, and then consider the best Base from which to start. You will notice that there are three different ways in which to make a penguin. The penguin seems to be a favourite subject, and almost every folder has a go at it.

Watch out for terms like Squash Fold. It is so named because you do just that – squash the part indicated so that the sides bulge and it flattens, in most cases symmetrically.

Study the Petal Folds, the Rabbit's Ears and the various Bases, and try to remember what they are. If you get stuck, have a look at the Contents and refer to the pages concerned.

You will notice that certain procedures are used over and over again. You will soon get used to these and be able to carry them out automatically.

When you have folded everything in the first half of the book, you will find that more and more diagrams begin to appear on each page, and that the symbols begin to play a bigger part than the instructions. Decoration 2 (page 153) has been included as an exercise so try to make this up using the symbols only.

Finally – take it slowly; fold carefully, neatly and accurately. And START AT THE BEGINNING!

A note on symbols

The symbols used in this book are based on Akira Yoshizawa's code of lines and arrows. Symbols will become second nature to you when folding as they are easy to acquire.

The moment you see a line of dashes, you know that the paper must be Valley Folded along that line. When you see a line of dashes and dots, you recognise the sign for a Mountain Fold. To make a Mountain Fold, you naturally turn the paper upside down and make a Valley Fold.

Arrows show the directions in which you must fold: left, right, up, down, in front, behind and into.

You will notice one arrow which shows that a drawing has been enlarged for clarity. Another arrow indicates that a model must be opened out (see Samuel Randlett's Fish, page 163). My own little black arrow indicates that you must sink, press, squeeze or push in at certain points.

The symbols are in fact self-explanatory. They are simple common sense, and can be learnt in about ten minutes.

Try to use the symbols only and ignore explanations. This will help you when you come to read Japanese origami books.

INTERNATIONAL ORIGAMI SYMBOLS

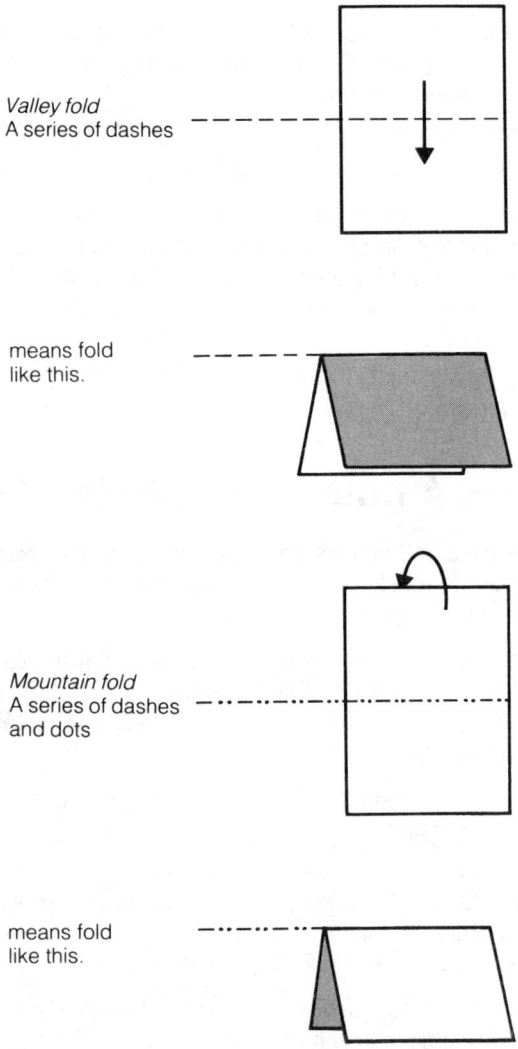

STUDY THE SYMBOLS CAREFULLY

If a drawing
was marked
with these symbols

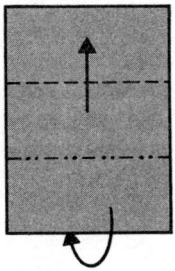

the result
should be
this.

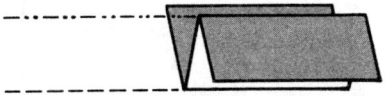

When a drawing
is followed by
this little looped
arrow

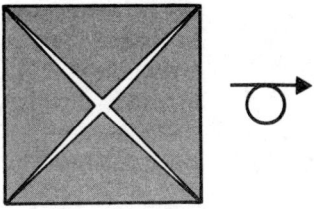

turn the
model over
so.

SYMBOLS TAKE THE PLACE OF INSTRUCTIONS

This black arrow

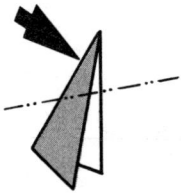

means push in.

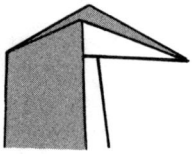

Thin lines mean creases.

This symbol

means

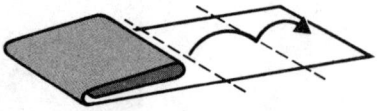

fold over and over.

MAKE THIS WATER BOMB BASE AND PRELIMINARY FOLD

If a drawing is
marked like this

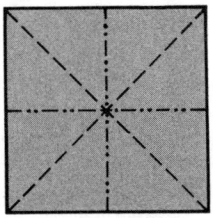

you make this
water bomb base.

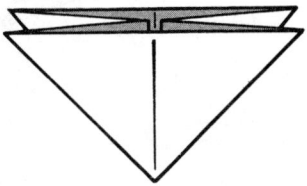

If you turn this
fold inside out
you will get this

preliminary fold.

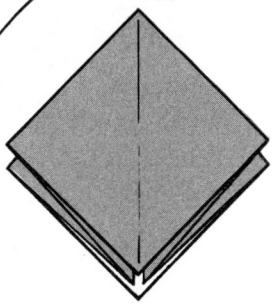

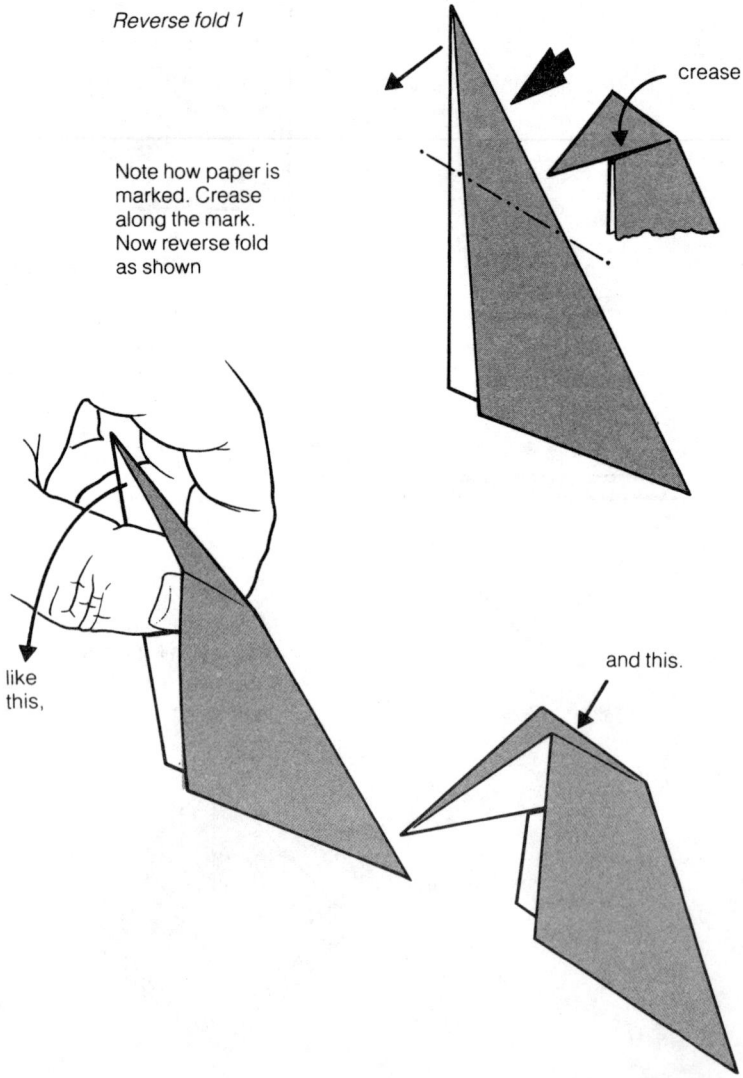
Reverse fold 1
crease
Note how paper is marked. Crease along the mark. Now reverse fold as shown
like this,
and this.

Reverse fold 2

Note how paper is marked. Crease along the mark. Now reverse fold as shown.

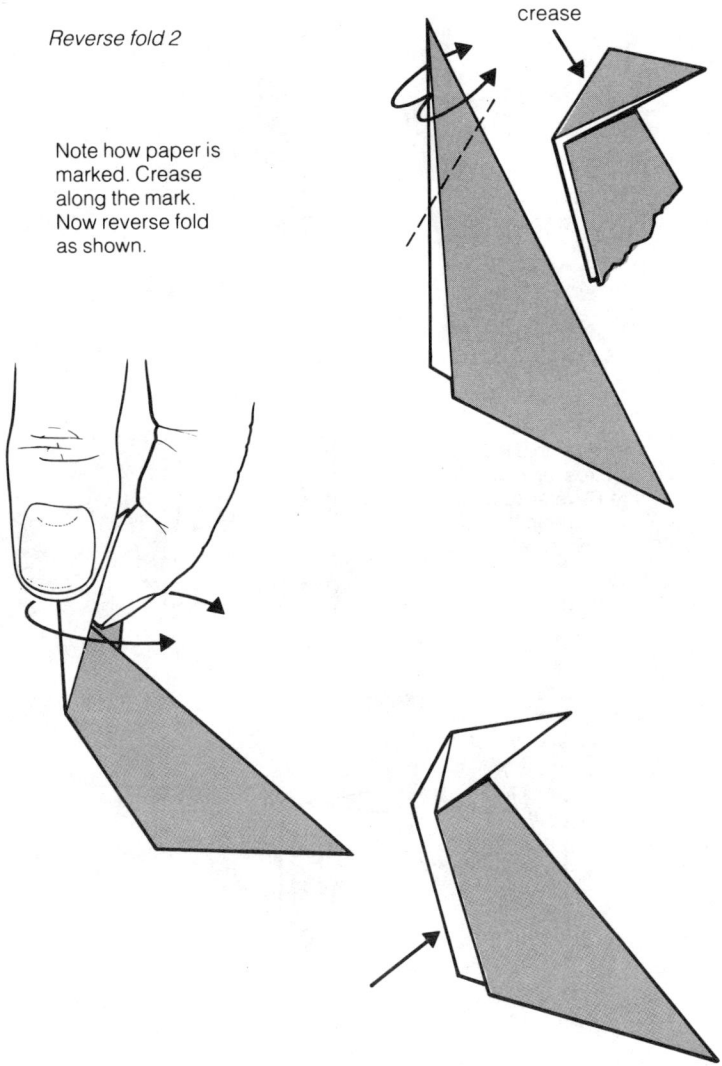

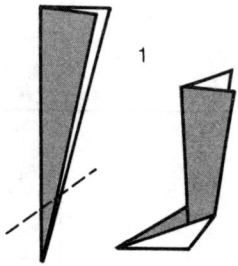

How to fold feet
(birds, animals, people).
1 Reverse fold 2.
2 Reverse fold 1.
3 Two reverse folds.

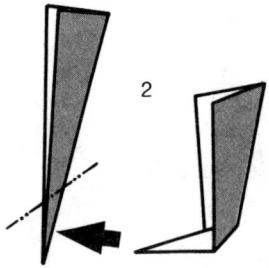

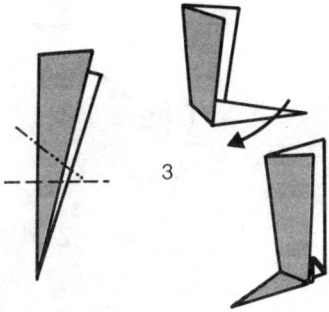

HOW TO MAKE A BIRD'S HEAD

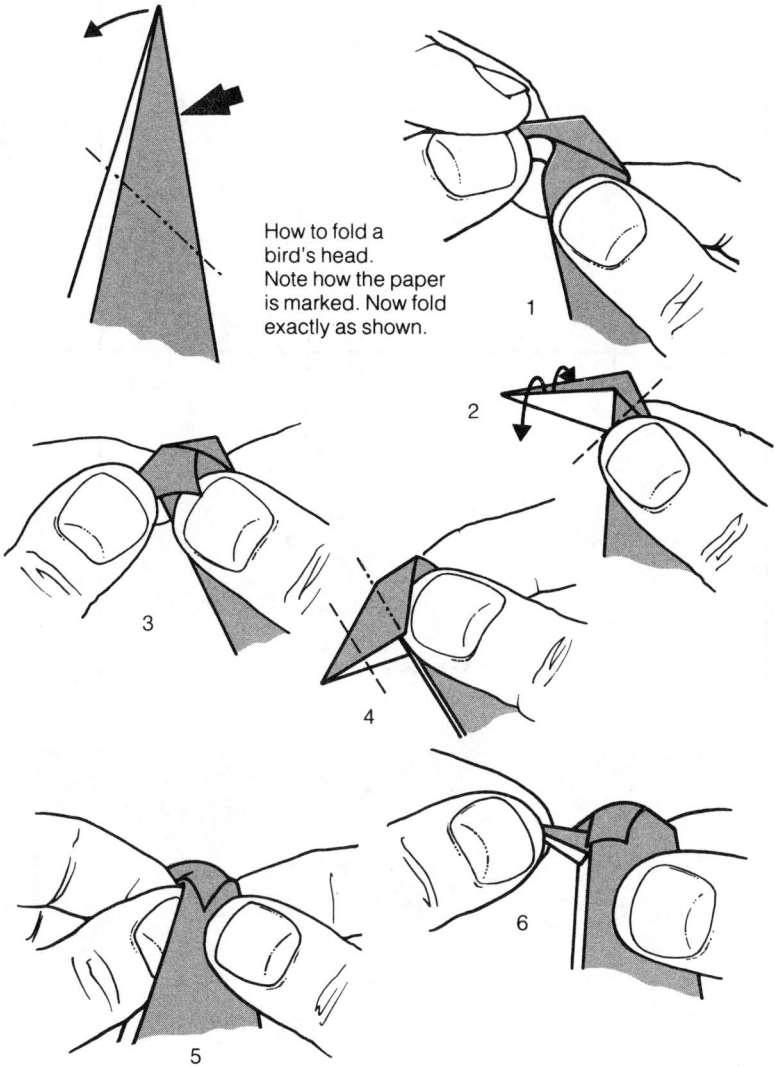

How to fold a bird's head. Note how the paper is marked. Now fold exactly as shown.

Start with the white side of the paper facing you.

1

Fold this side down

to here.

2

Fold over

here.

3

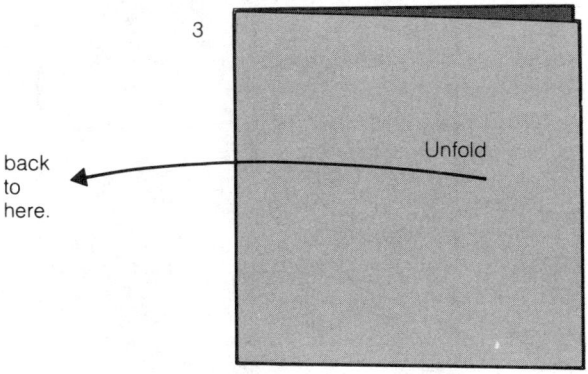

4

Fold sides to middle.

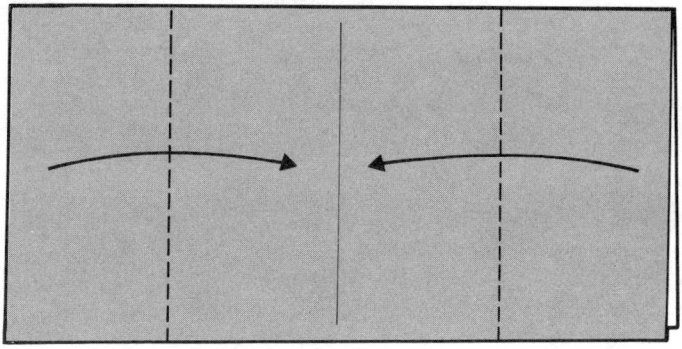

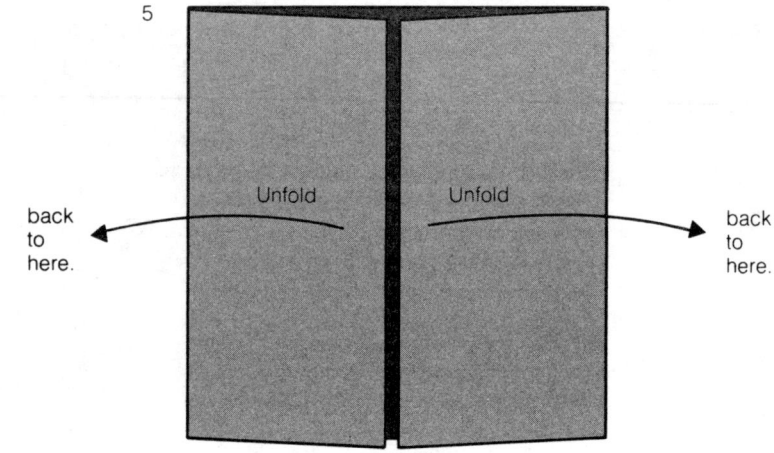
5
Unfold
Unfold
back
to
here.
back
to
here.

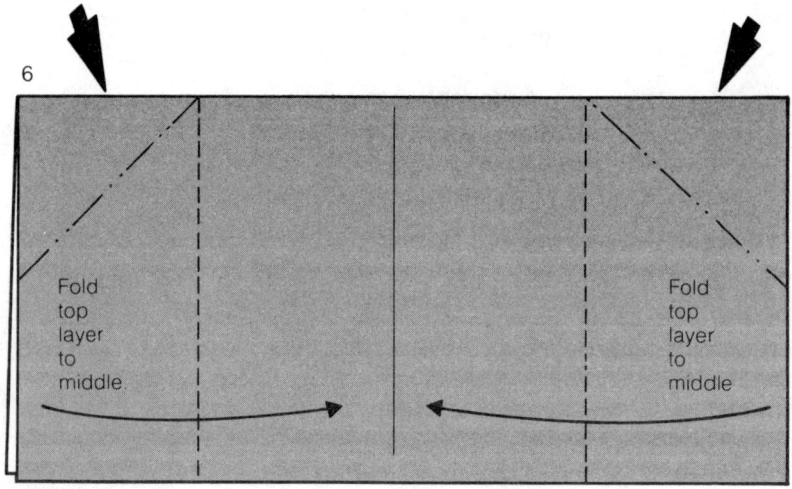
6
Fold
top
layer
to
middle.
Fold
top
layer
to
middle

7

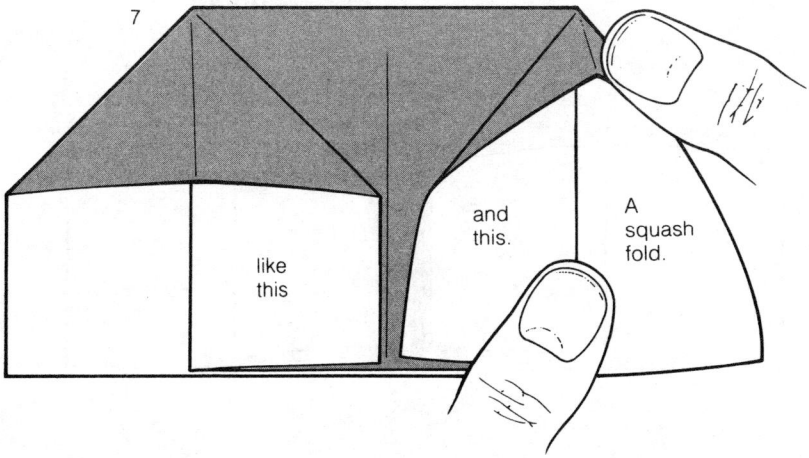

Now draw doors and windows.

8

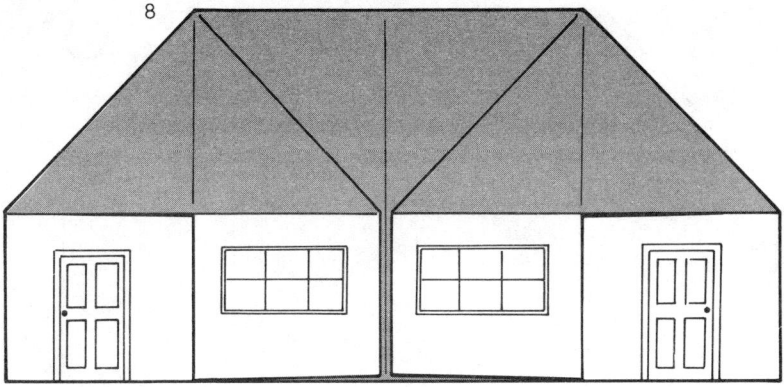

G.I. CAP *Start with House Fold*

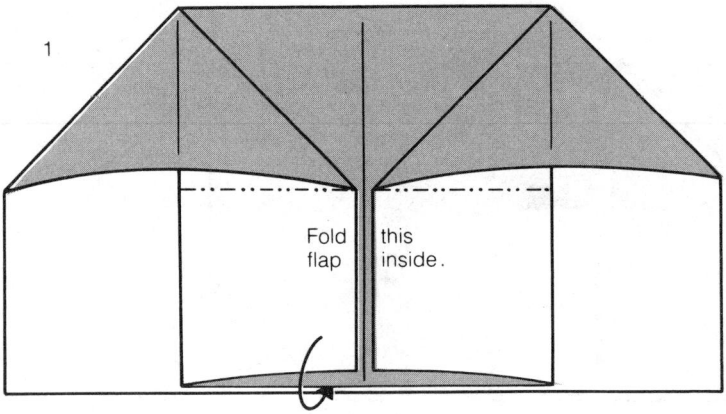

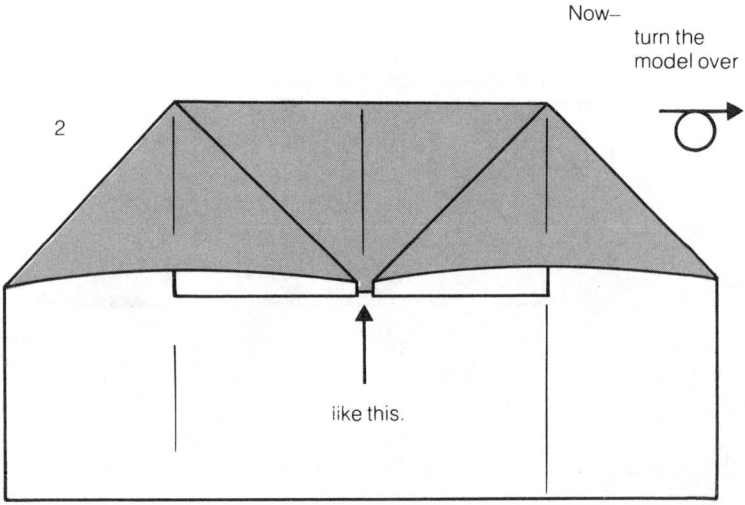

3

Fold here. Fold.

4

Fold flap this inside

like this.

5

BOAT *Use a square of paper*

1

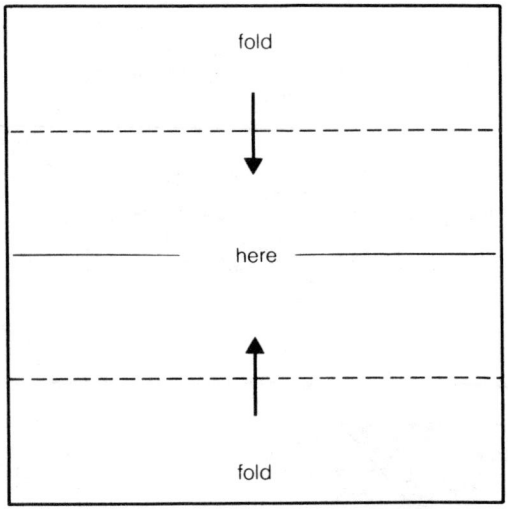

First crease along the middle.

2

Fold in half.

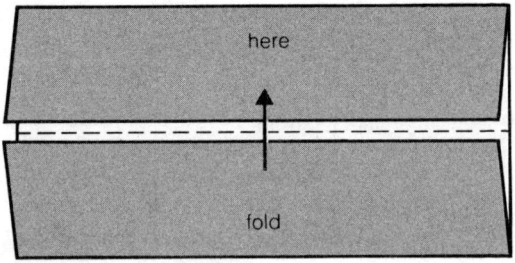

like this.

3

Now fold the two corners up

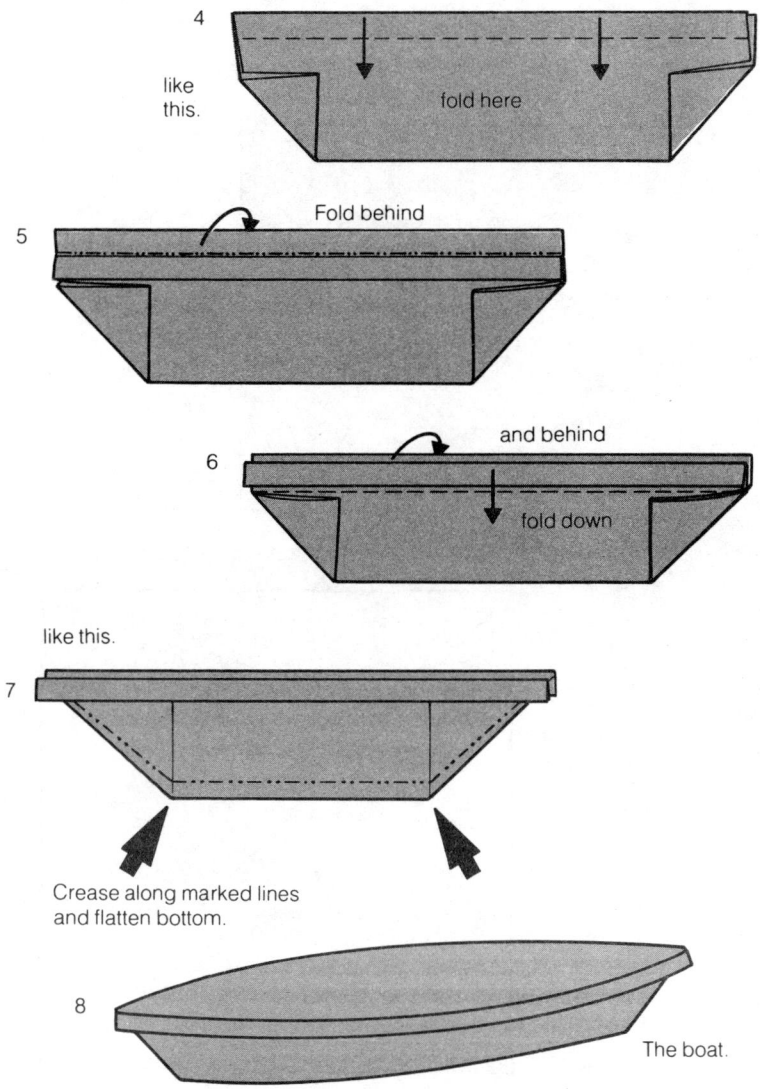
4
like
this.
fold here
5
Fold behind
6
and behind
fold down
like this.
7
Crease along marked lines
and flatten bottom.
8
The boat.

SALT CELLAR AND COLOUR CHANGER *Traditional*

1

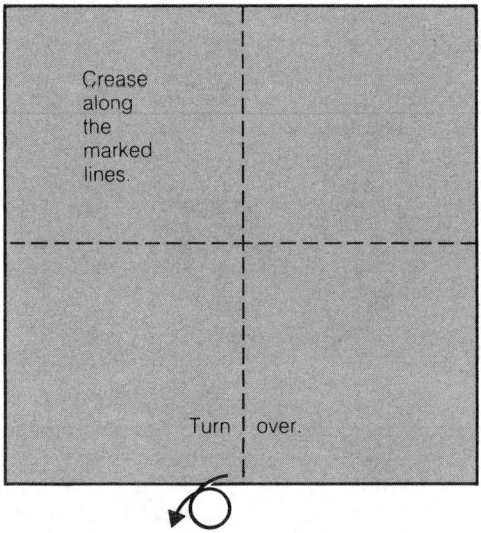

2

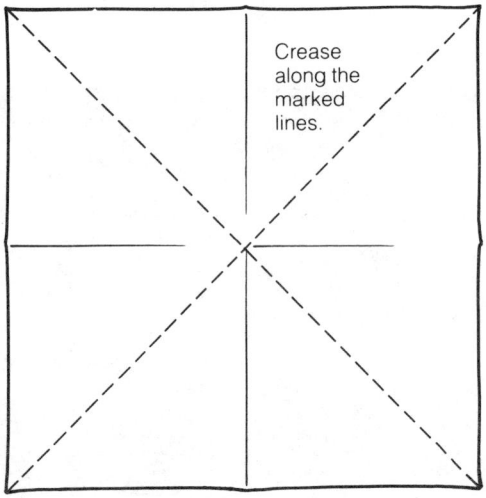

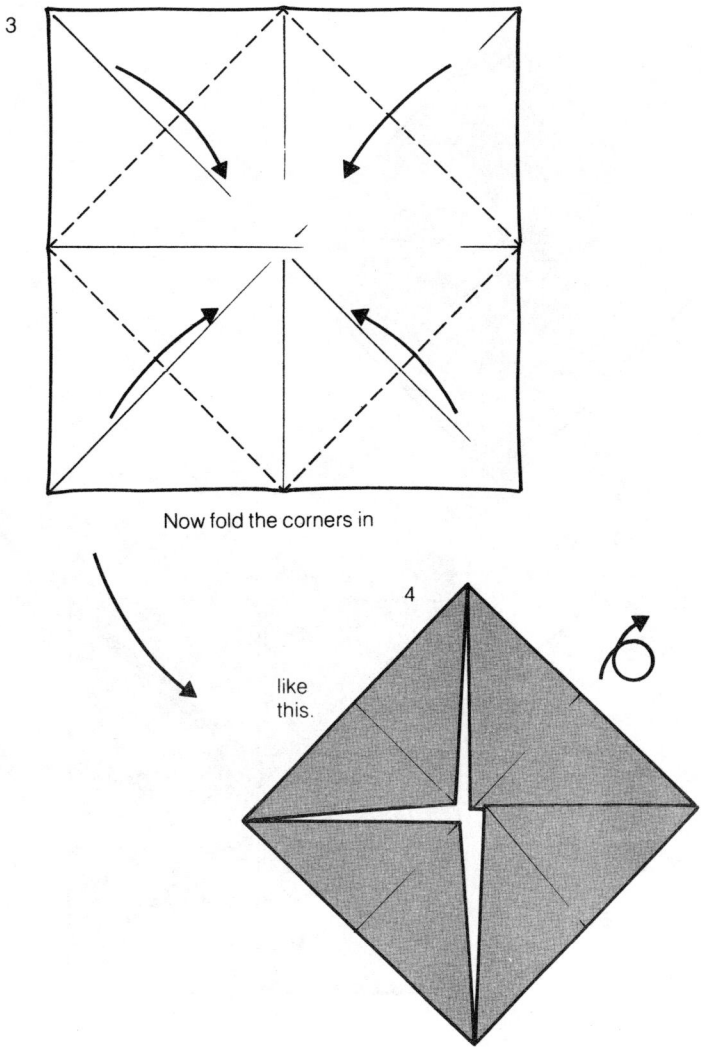
3
Now fold the corners in
like
this.
4

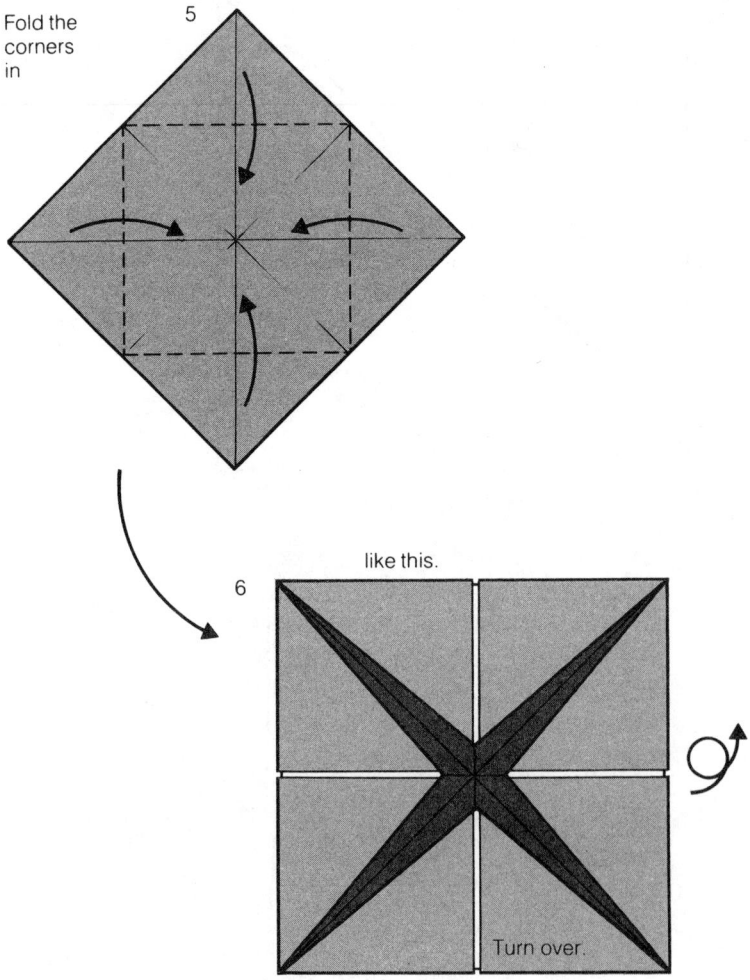
5
Fold the corners in
6
like this.
Turn over.

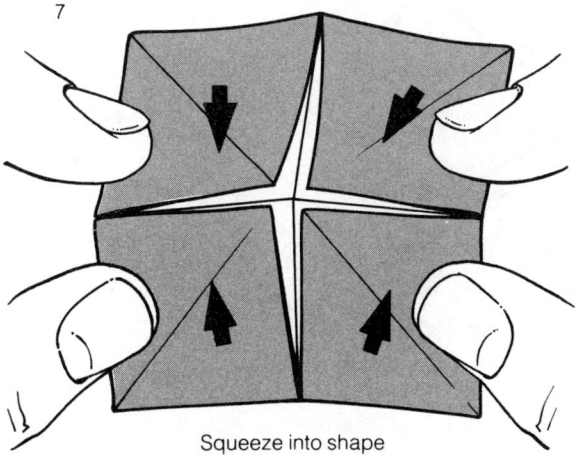

like this.

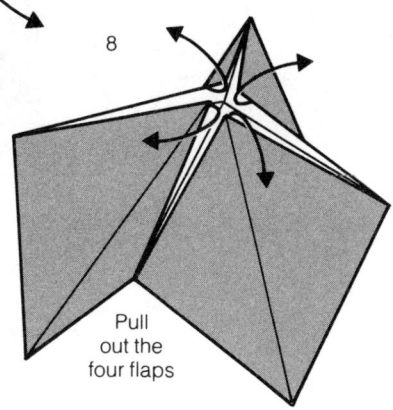

9 like this.

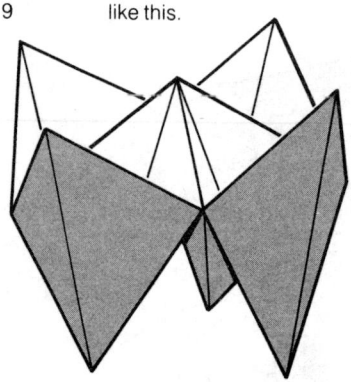

The salt cellar.

10

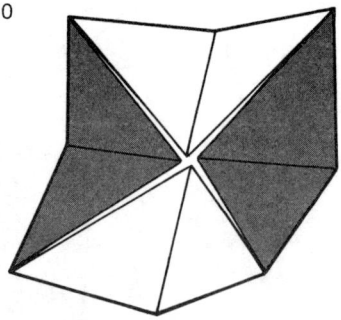

This is the salt cellar upside down. Colour the areas shown

11

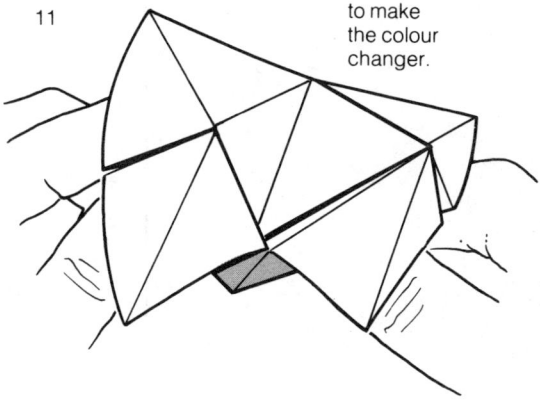

to make
the colour
changer.

And this
shows how you
make it work.

12

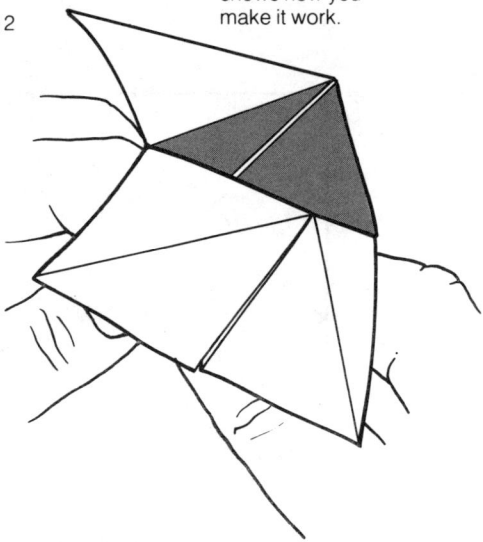

SPANISH BOX *Spanish, originally Japanese*

1

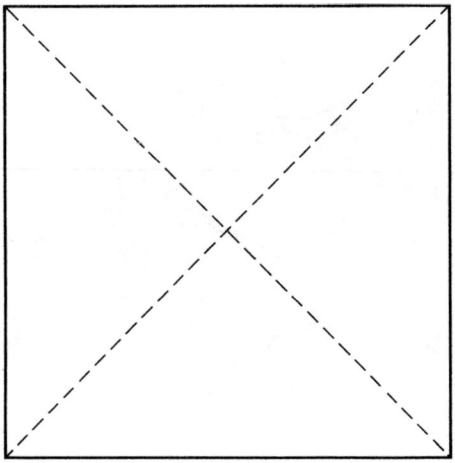

Crease along the marked lines.

2

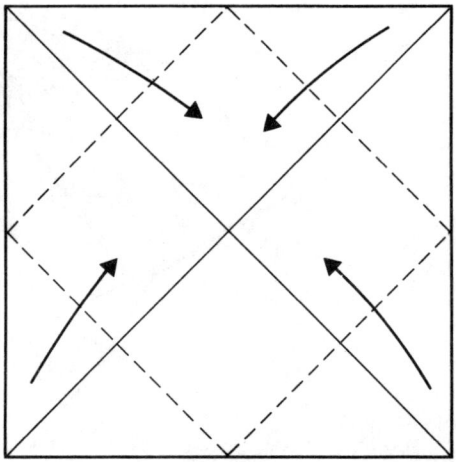

Fold the four corners to the centre.

3

so.

Turn over.

4

Fold four corners to the centre

enlarged view

5

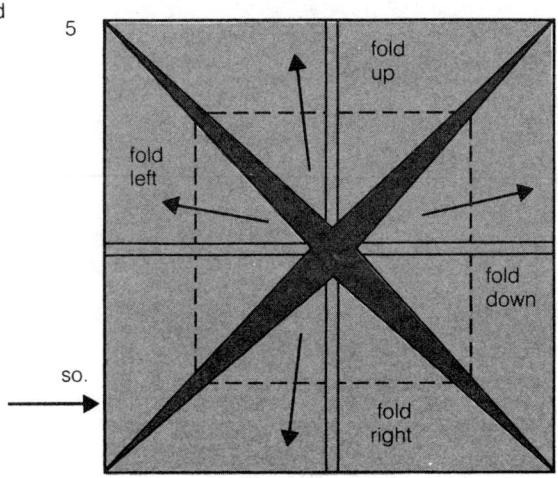

6

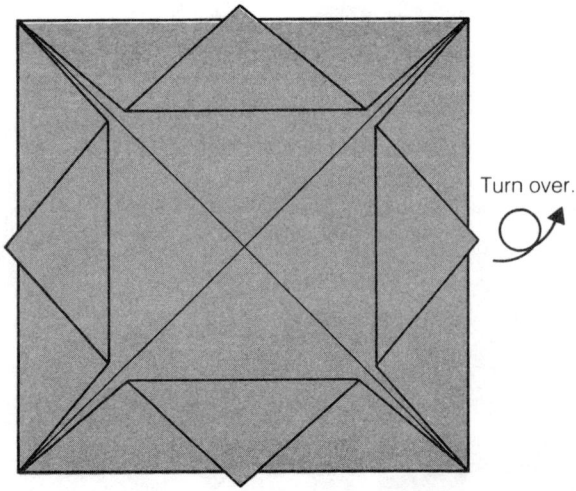

7

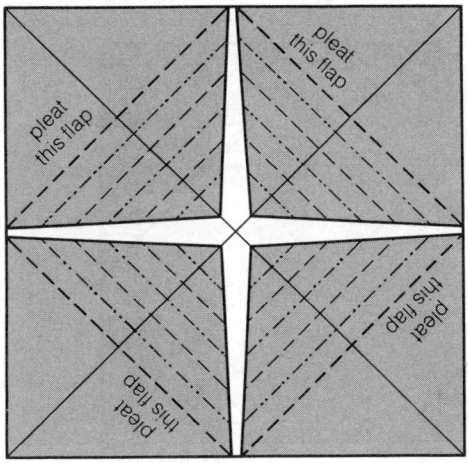
pleat
this flap
pleat
this flap
pleat
this flap
pleat
this flap

8

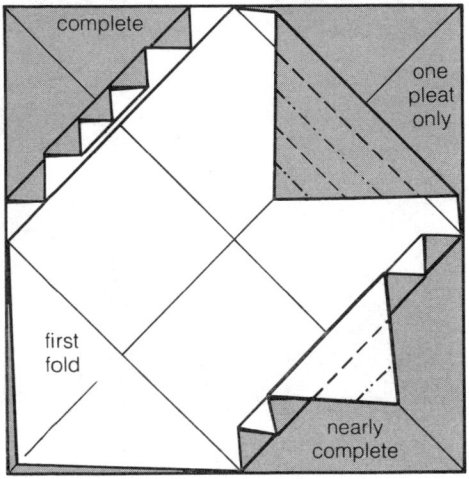
complete
one
pleat
only
first
fold
nearly
complete

9

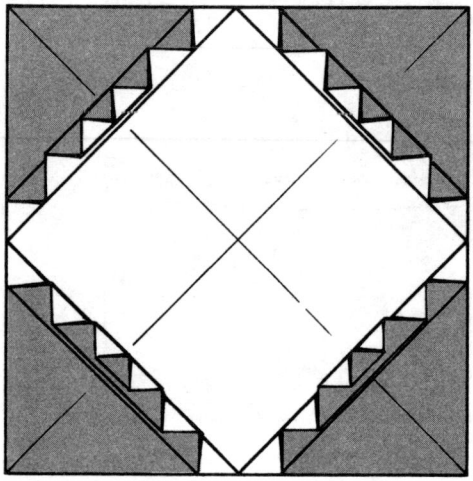

Completed pleats.

10

A KETCHUP BOTTLE SHOULD FIT THIS

Push left thumb into each corner and press together on the outside until the fancy box is completed.

SO.

11

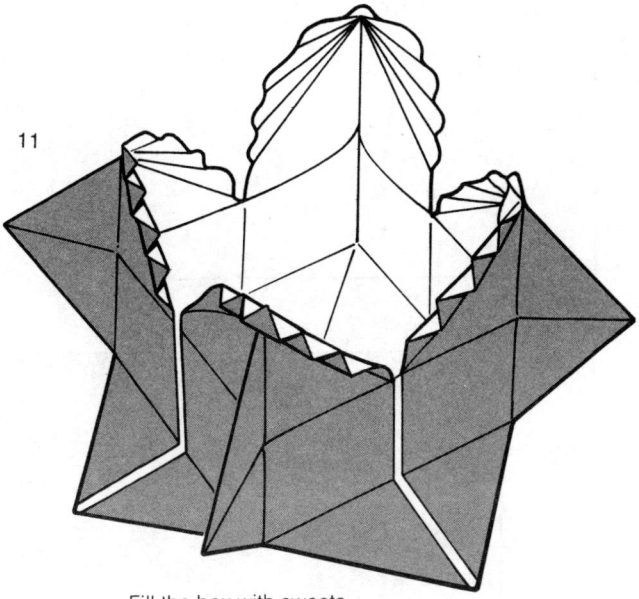

Fill the box with sweets.

1

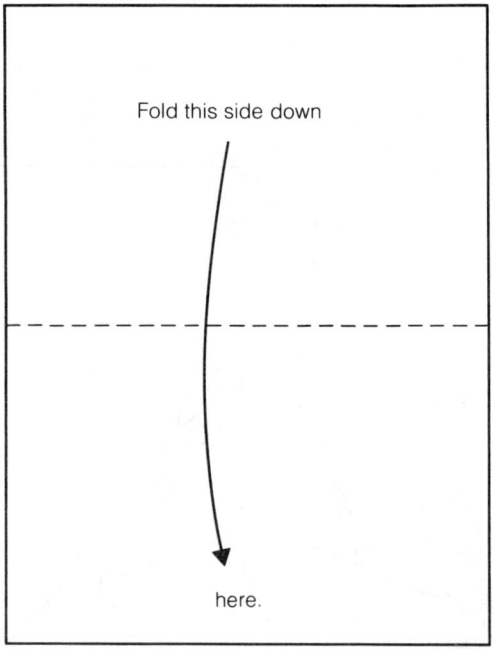

2

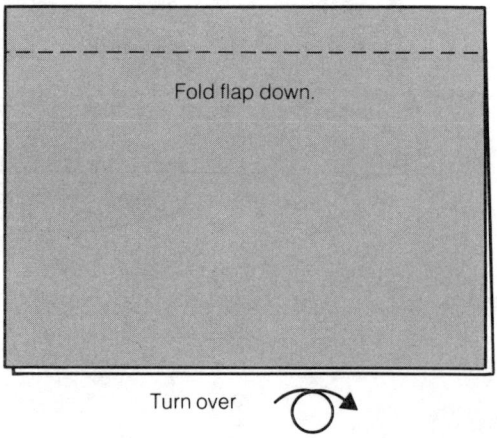

3

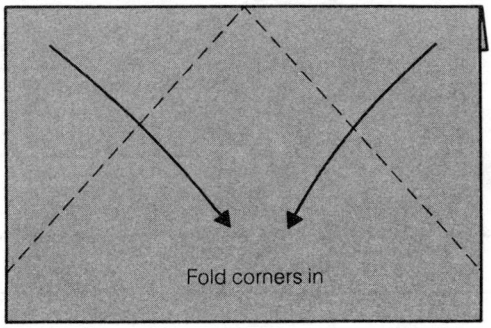

like this.

4

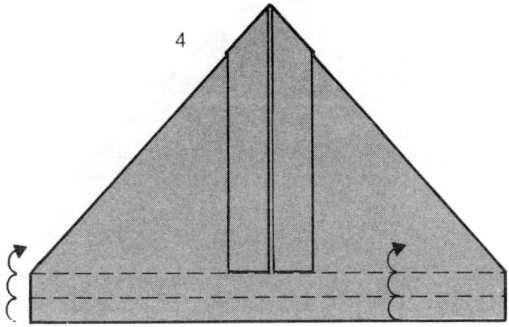

Fold this flap over twice.

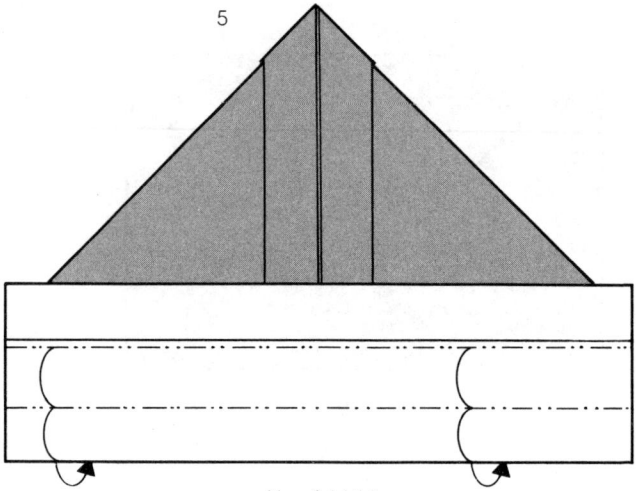

Now fold this
flap under twice.

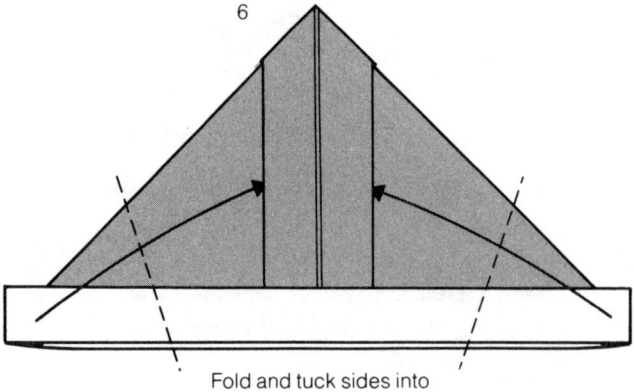

Fold and tuck sides into
pockets

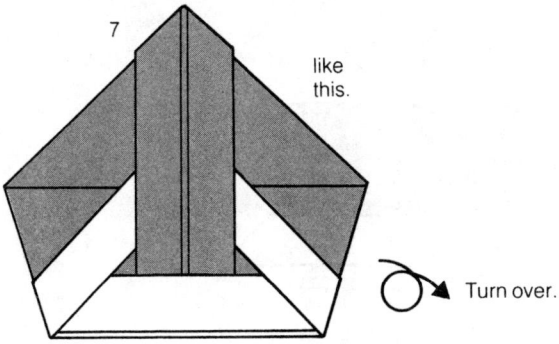
7
like
this.
Turn over.

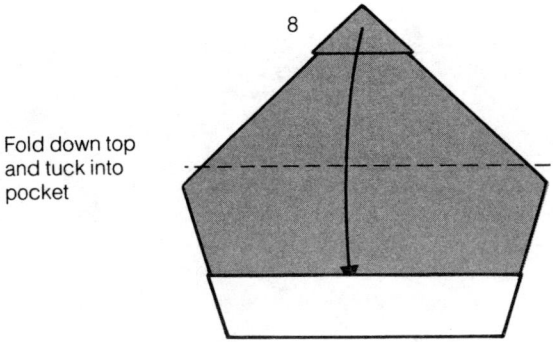
8
Fold down top
and tuck into
pocket

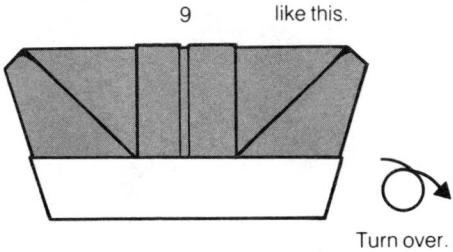
9
like this.
Turn over.

10

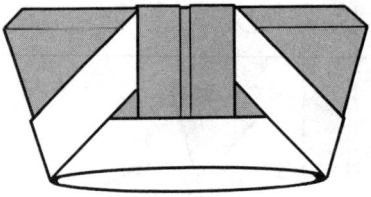

The turban complete.

Try this with
a sheet of
newspaper.

SAMURAI HAT *Traditional Japanese*

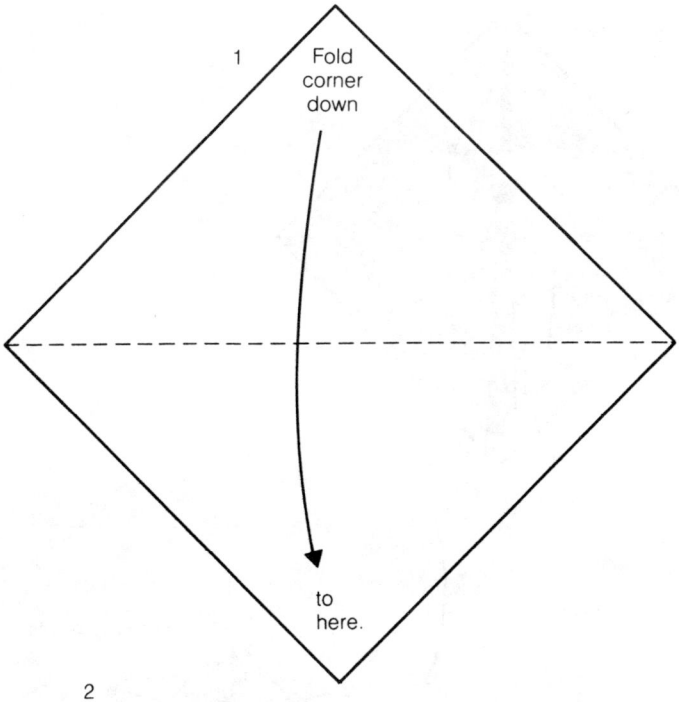

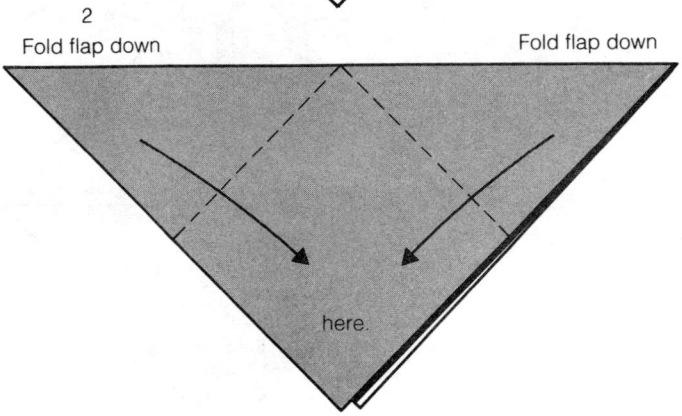

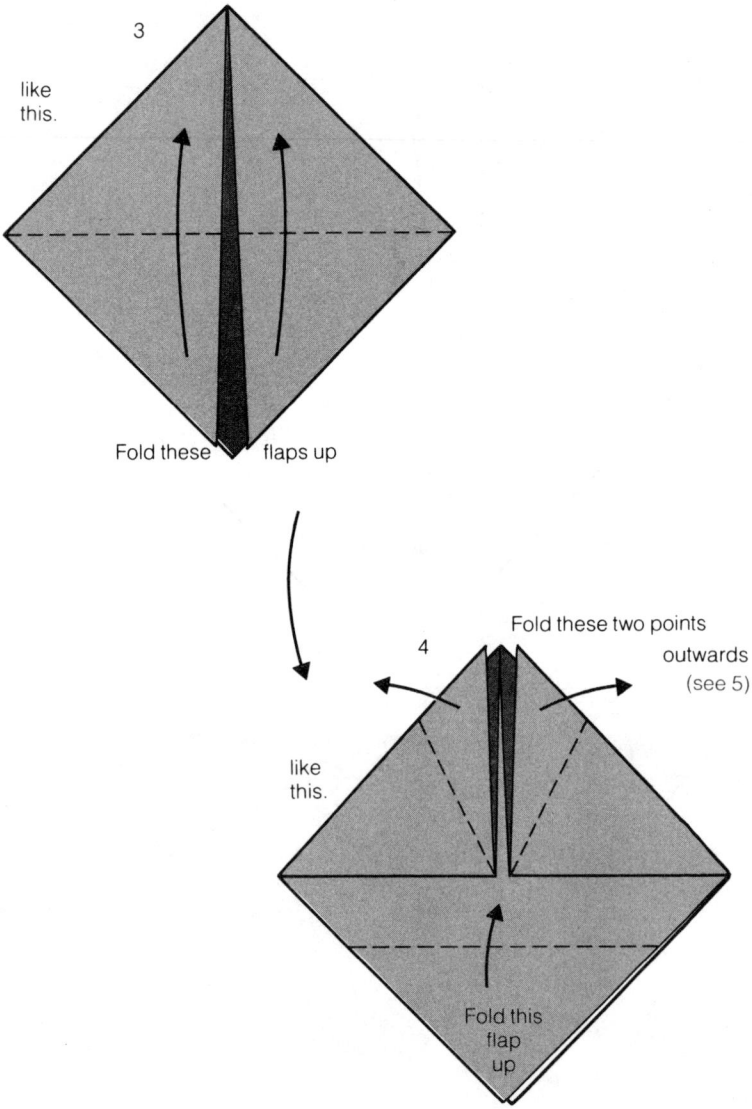
3
like
this.
Fold these
flaps up
4
Fold these two points
outwards
(see 5)
like
this.
Fold this
flap
up

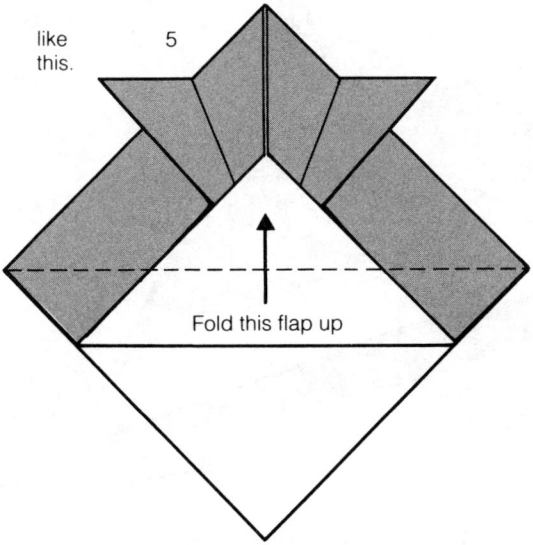
like
this.
5
Fold this flap up

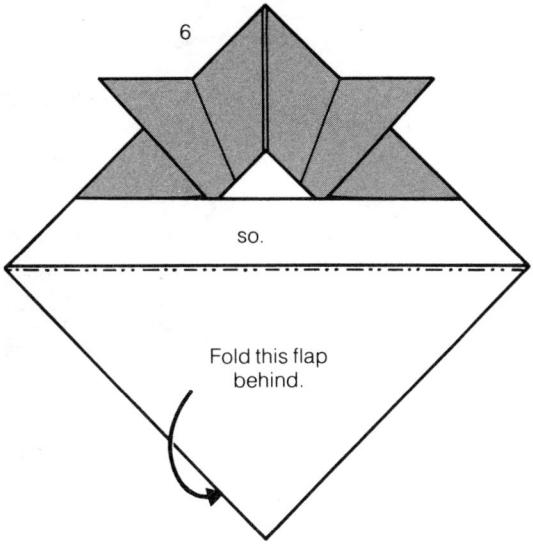
6
so.
Fold this flap
behind.

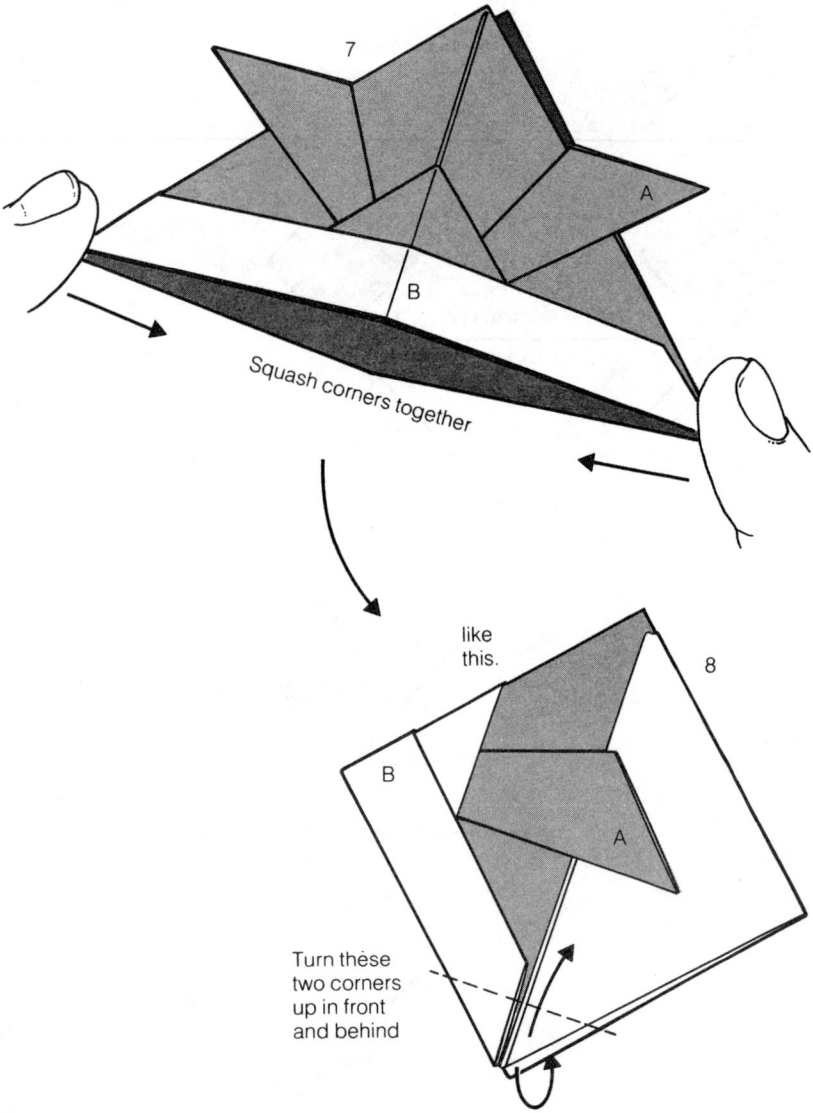
7
A
B
Squash corners together
like
this.
8
B
A
Turn these
two corners
up in front
and behind

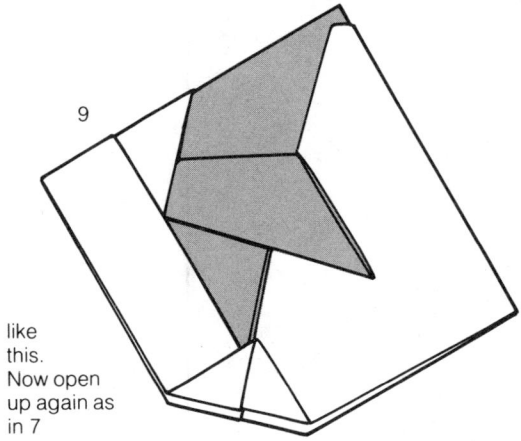

A piece of paper
20 inches square
will make a hat
to fit your head

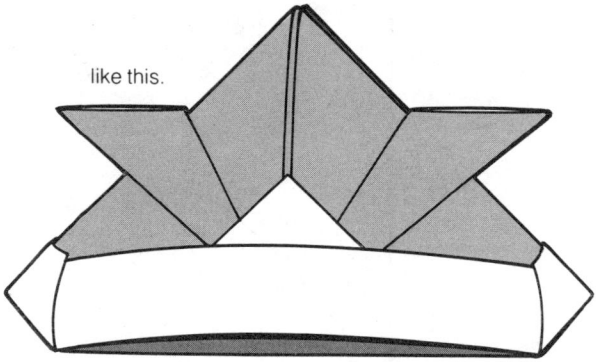

1

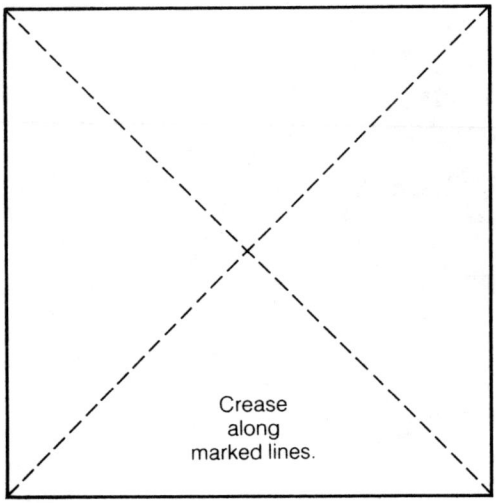

2

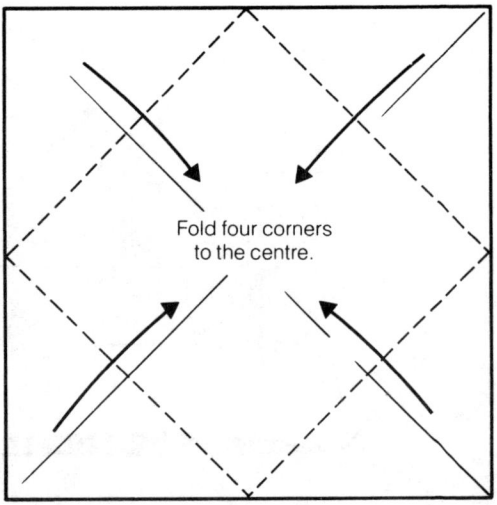

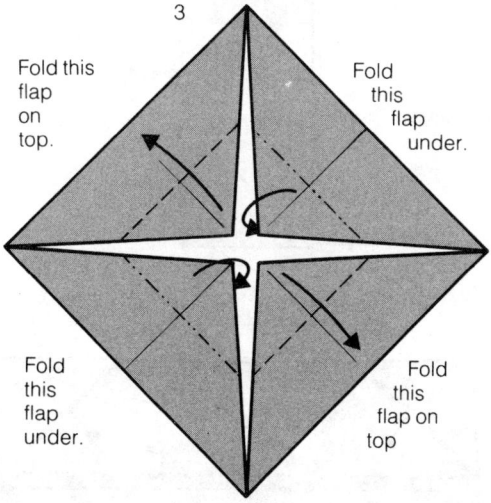
3
Fold this flap on top.
Fold this flap under.
Fold this flap under.
Fold this flap on top

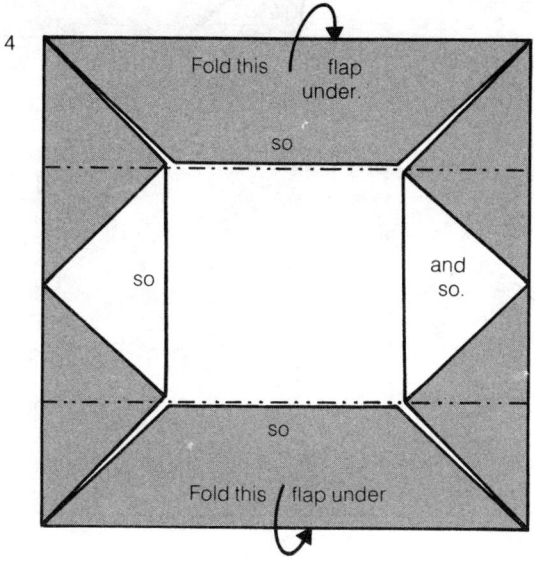
4
Fold this flap under.
so
so
and so.
so
Fold this flap under

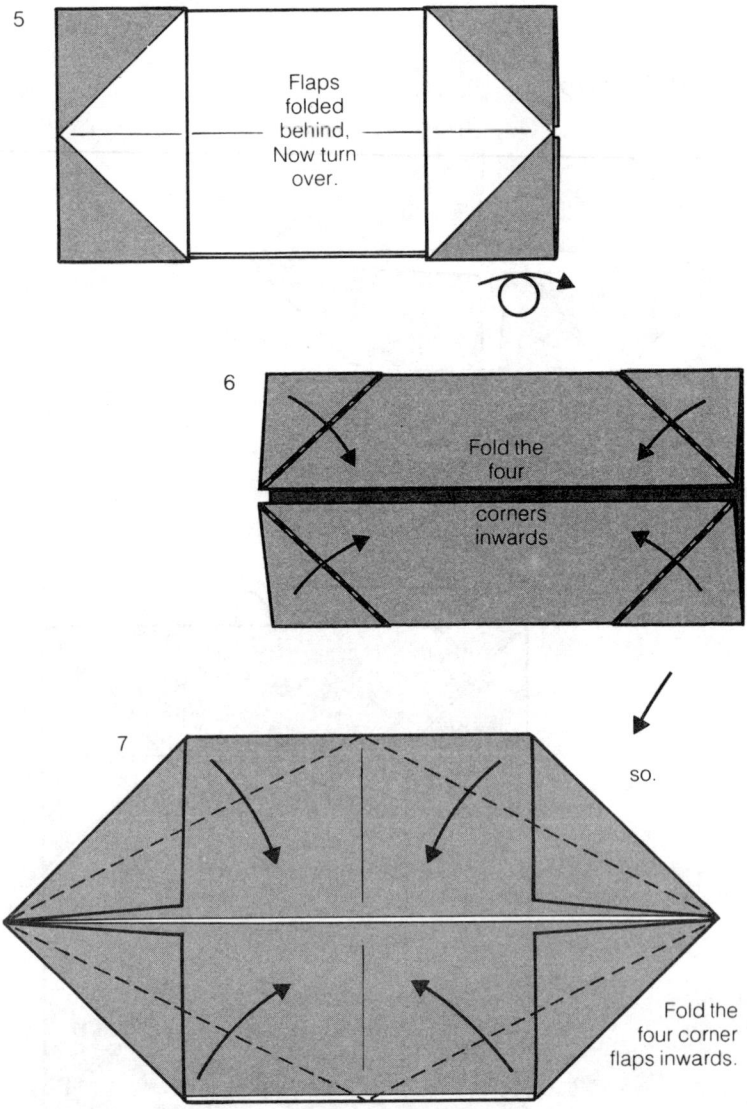
5
Flaps folded behind, Now turn over.
6
Fold the four
corners inwards
so.
7
Fold the four corner flaps inwards.

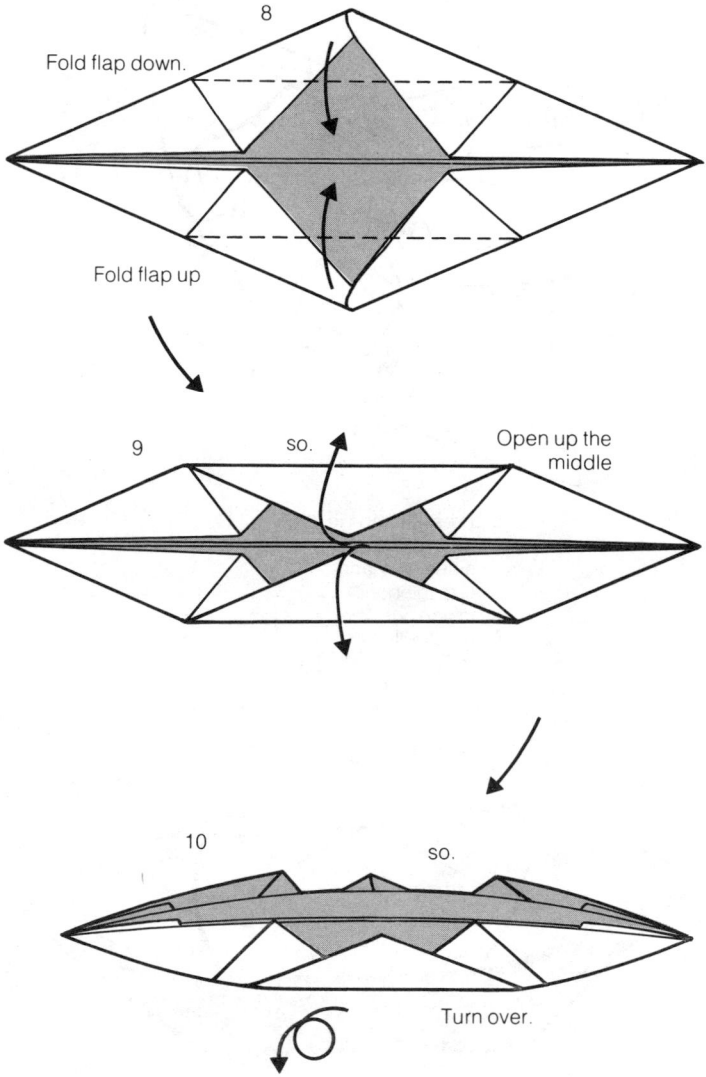
8
Fold flap down.
Fold flap up
9
so.
Open up the middle
10
so.
Turn over.

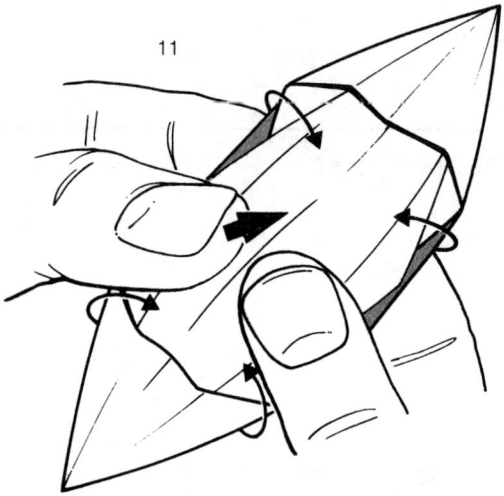

Press thumbs in, then with fingers pull sides up – and so turn the boat inside out. The result will be this.

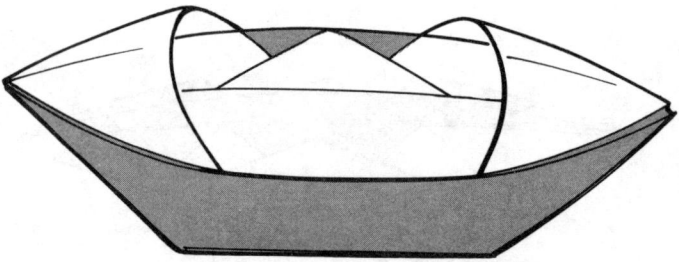

WATER BOMB OR JAPANESE PLAYBALL

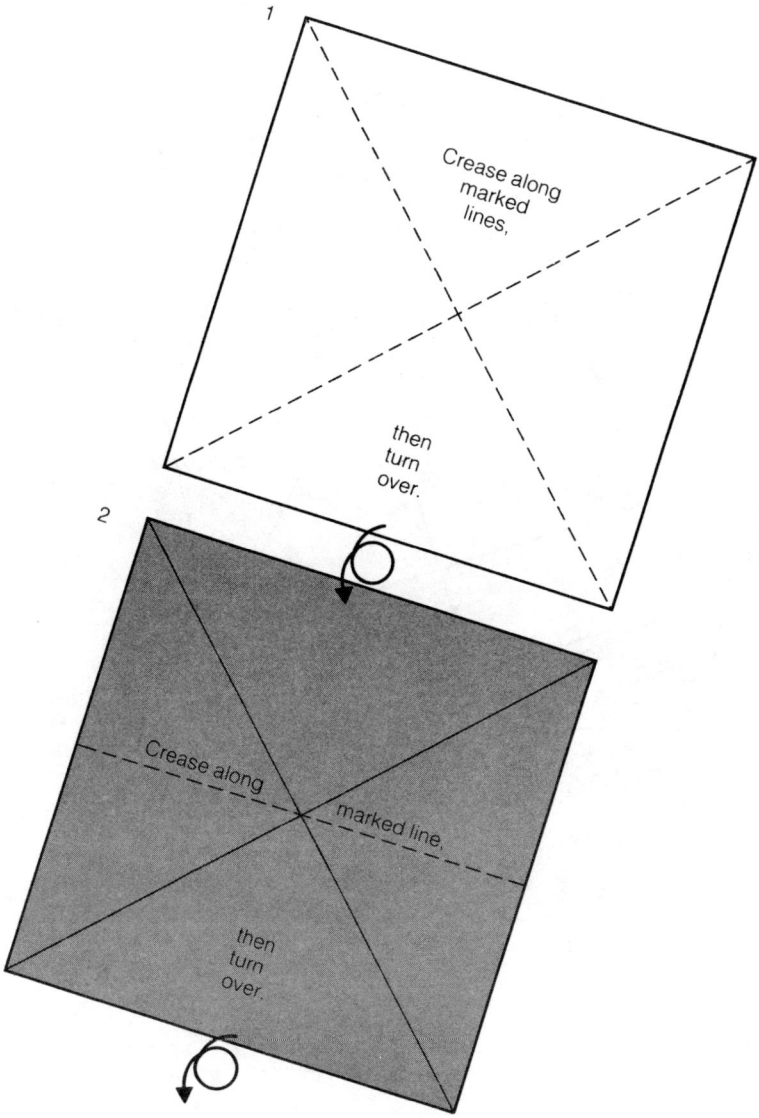

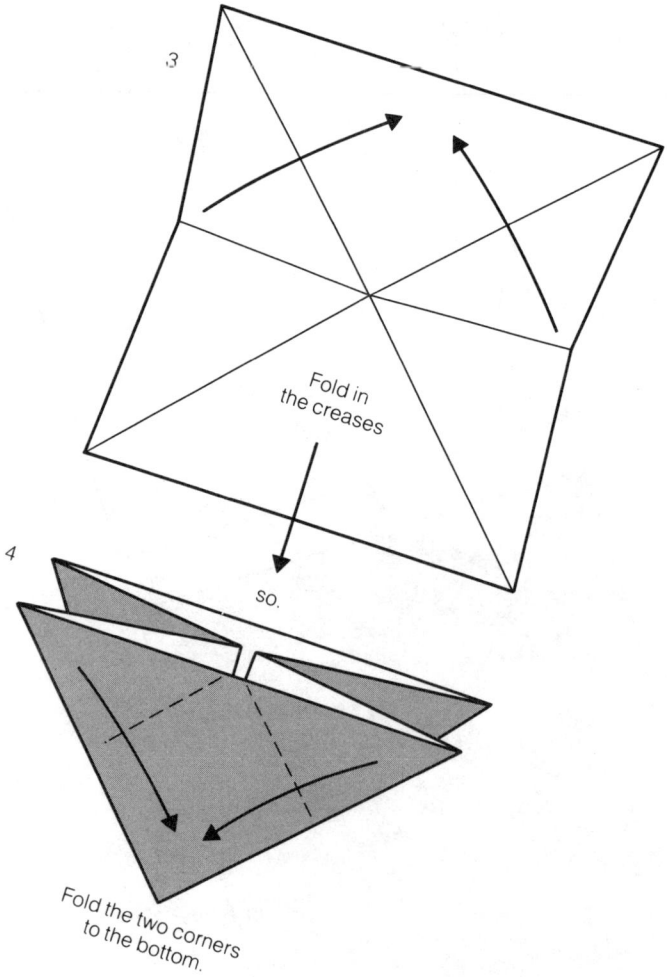
3
Fold in
the creases
4
so.
Fold the two corners
to the bottom.

5

Fold the two corners behind.

6

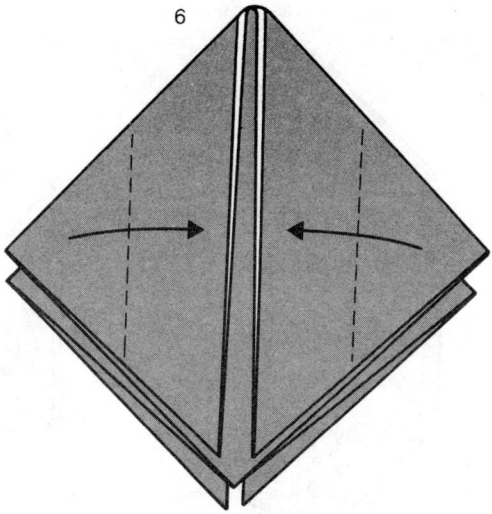

Fold the two flaps
to the centre.

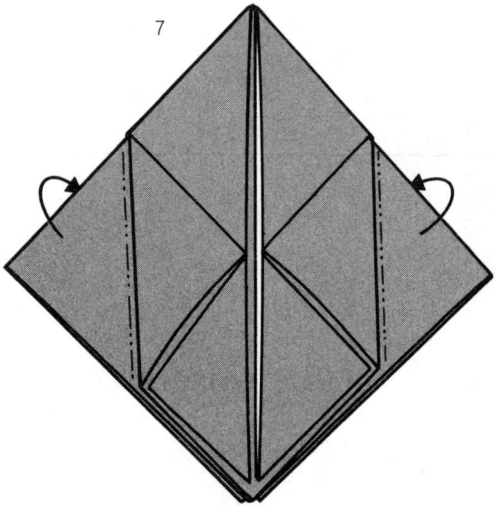

Fold the two flaps behind.

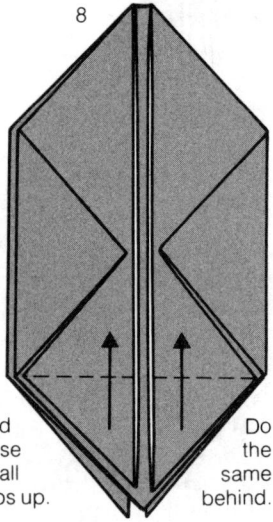

Fold these small flaps up.

Do the same behind.

Tuck these flaps into pockets.

Do the same behind

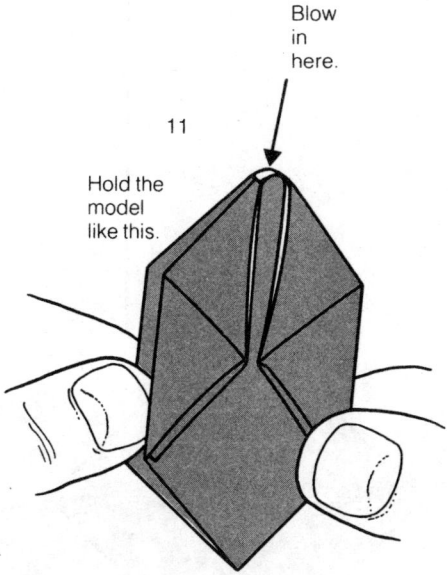

The water
bomb
completed.

12

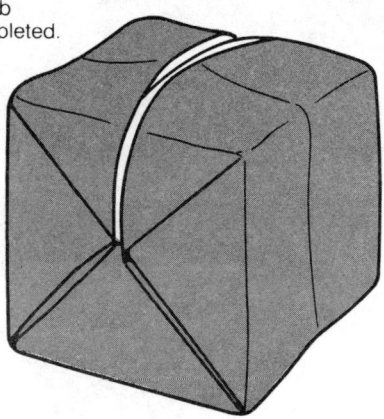

SANBOW 1 *Japanese Offering Tray*

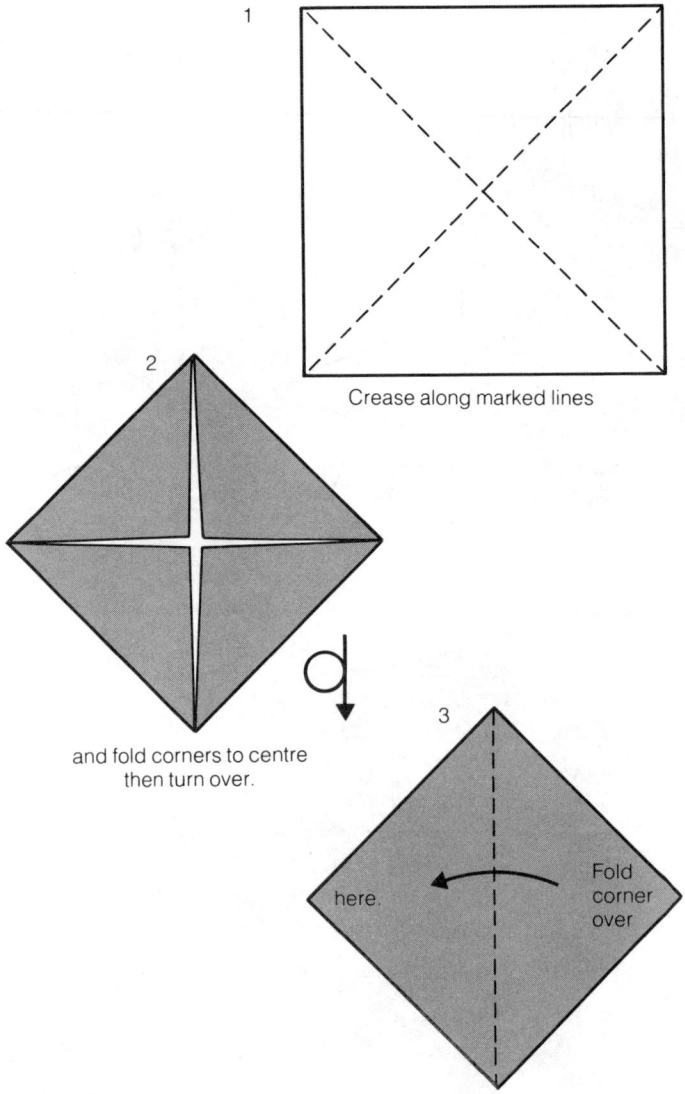

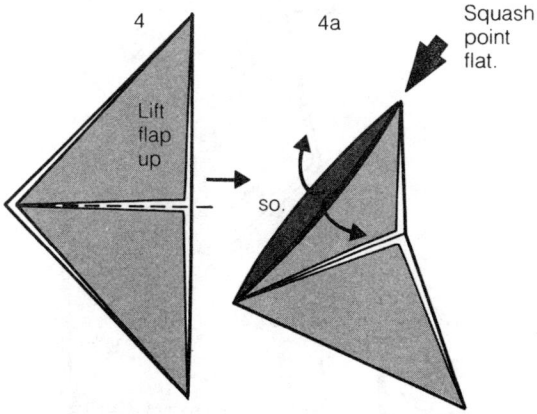
4
Lift
flap
up
4a
Squash
point
flat.
so.

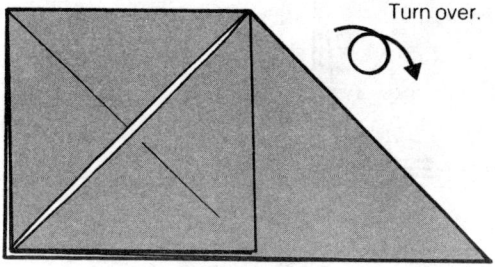
Turn over.

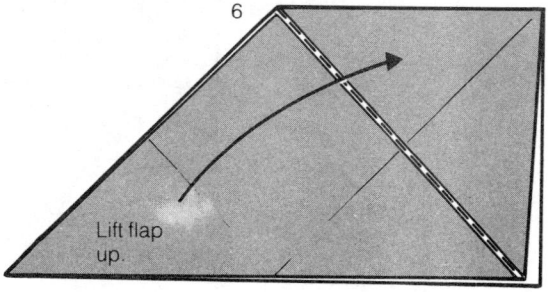
6
Lift flap
up.

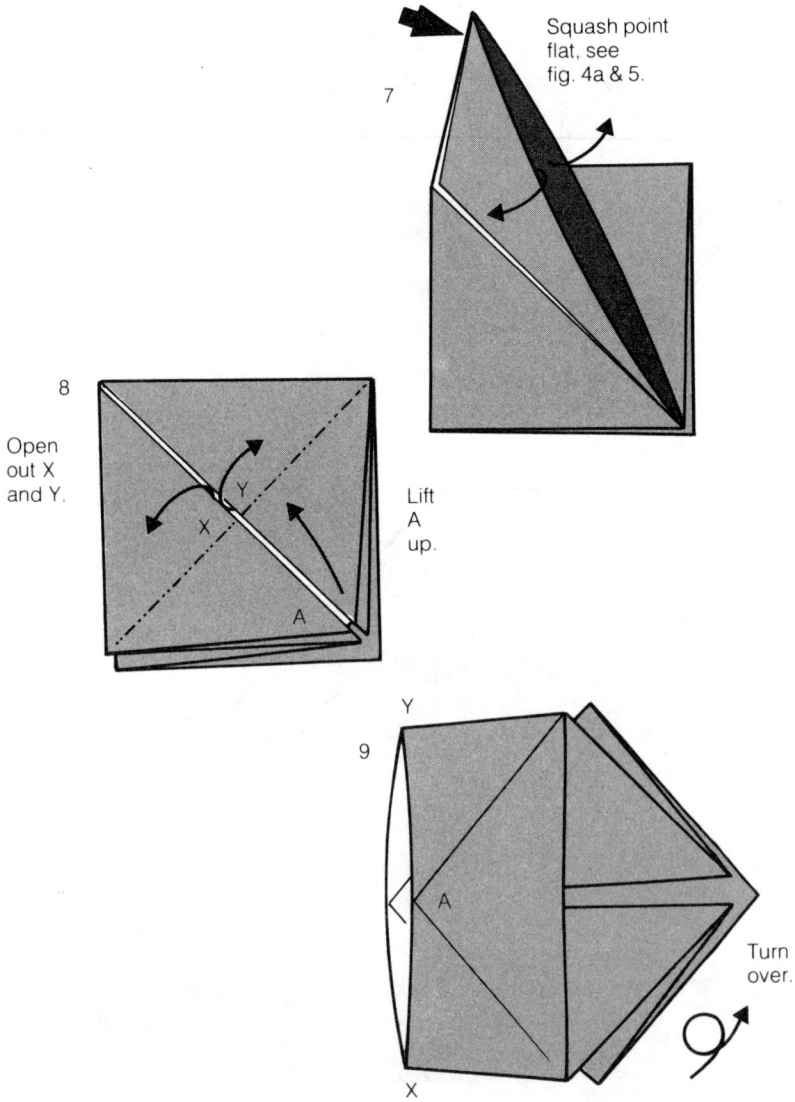
7
Squash point flat, see fig. 4a & 5.
8
Open out X and Y.
Y
X
A
Lift A up.
9
Y
A
X
Turn over.

Open out X and Y.

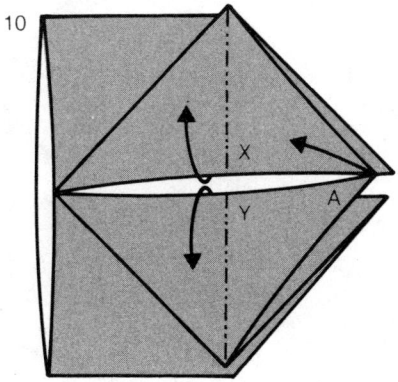

Lift A up as in fig. 8 and 9

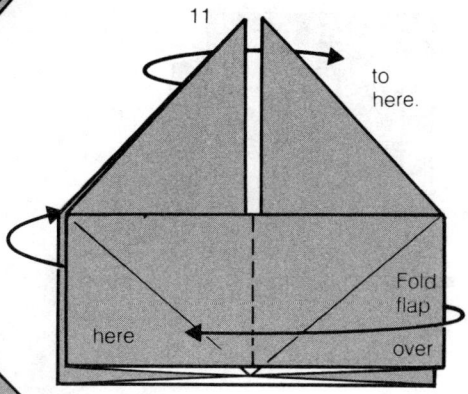

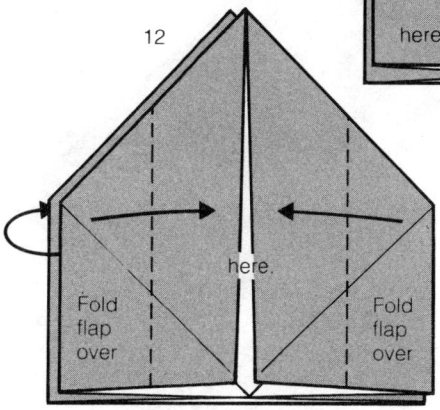

Do the same behind.

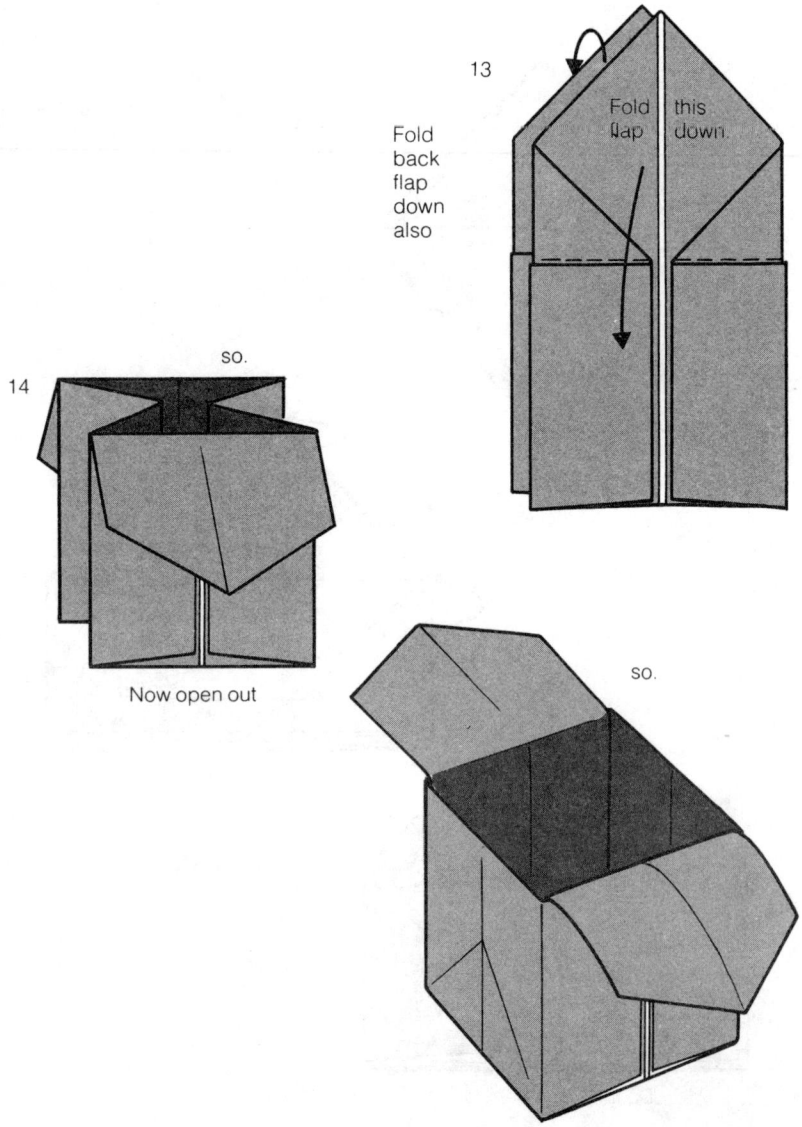
13
Fold back flap down also
Fold flap
this down.
so.
14
Now open out
so.

SANBOW 2 *Begin with corners folded to the centre*

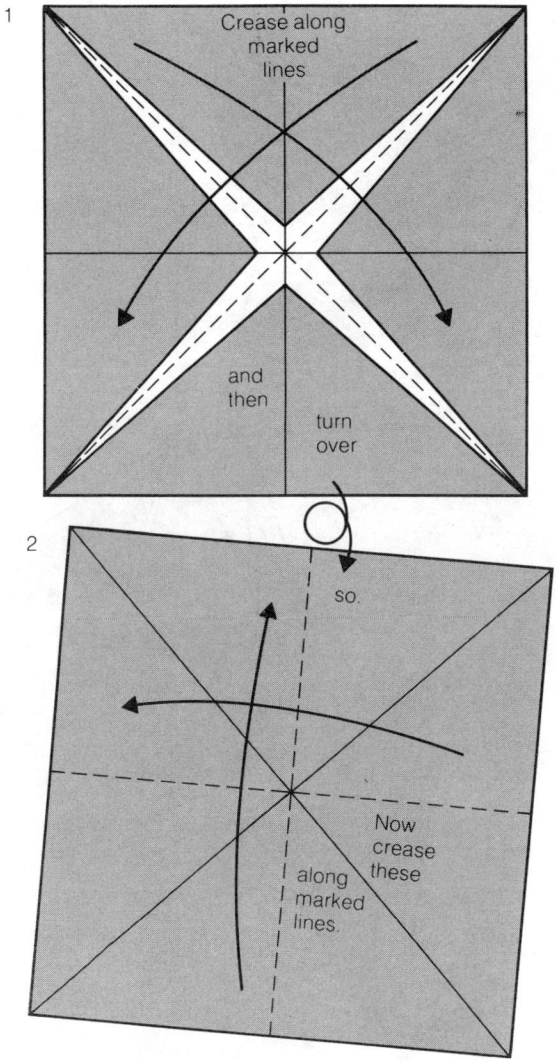

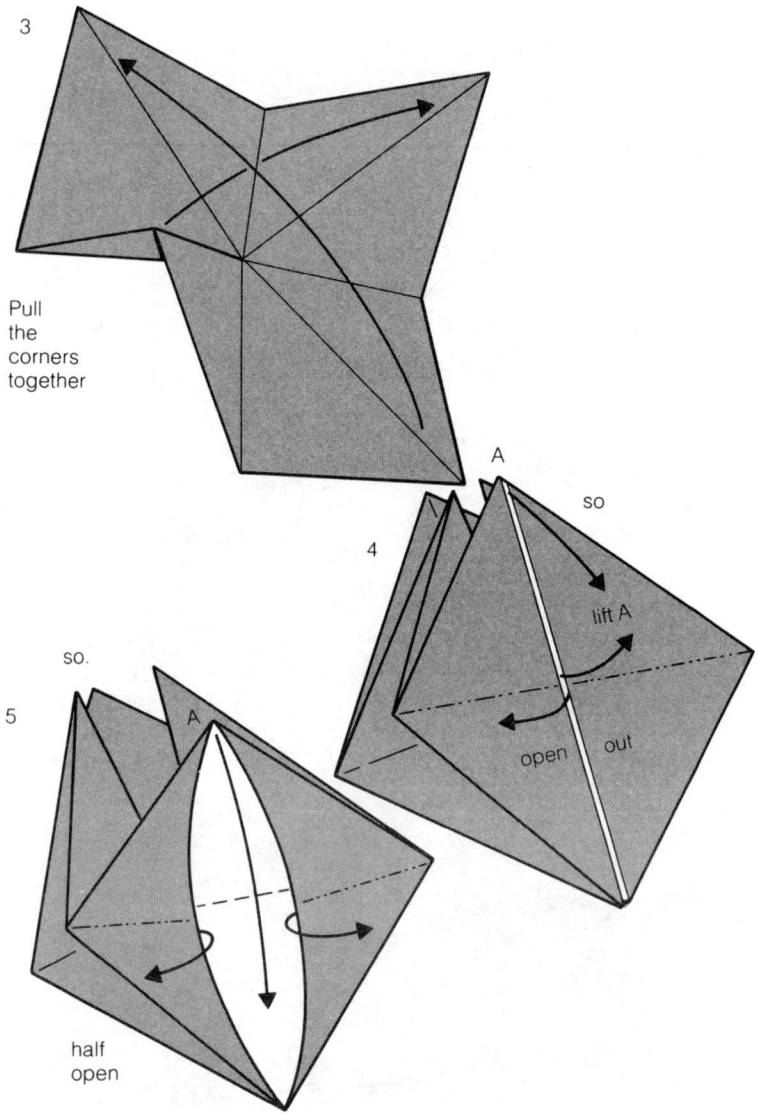
3
Pull
the
corners
together
A
so
4
lift A
open
out
so.
5
A
half
open

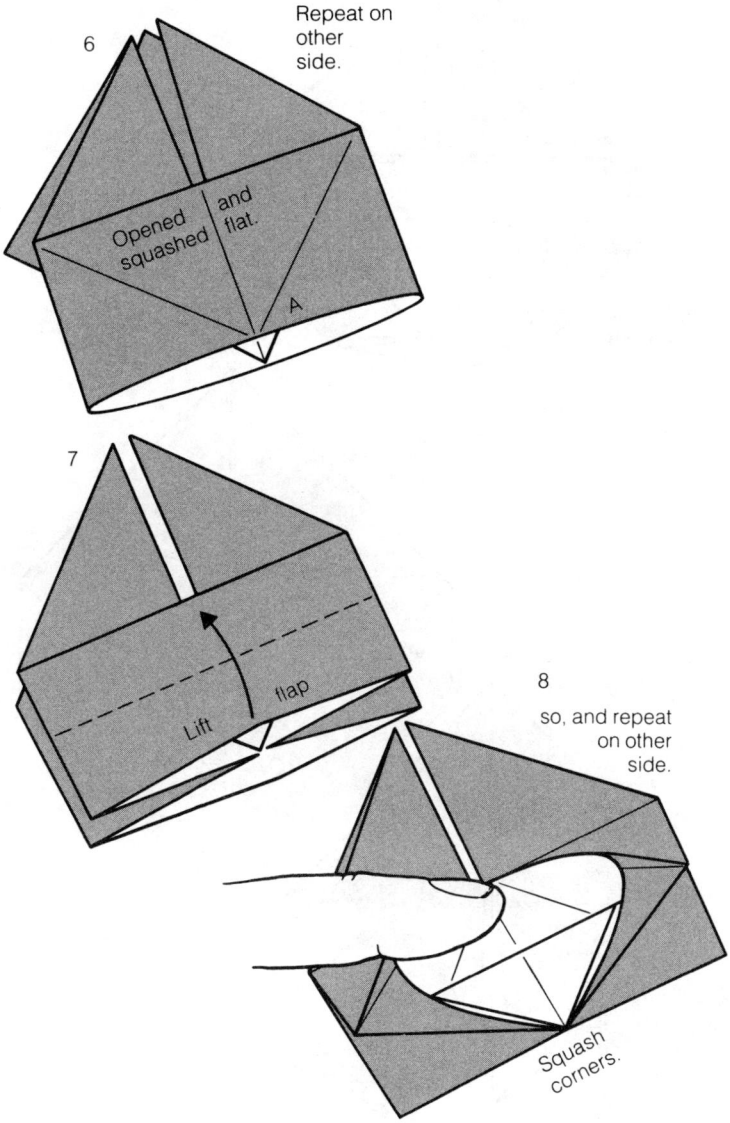
6
Repeat on other side.
Opened squashed
and flat.
A
7
Lift
flap
8
so, and repeat on other side.
Squash corners.

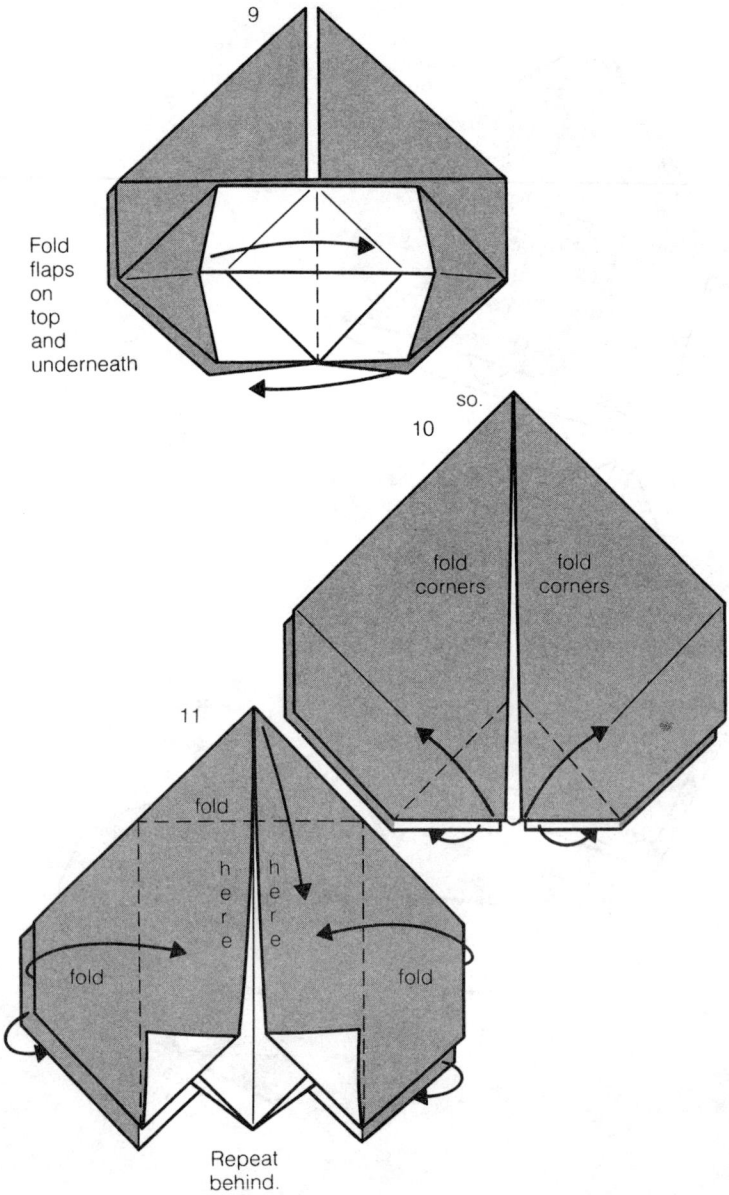
9
Fold flaps on top and underneath
so.
10
fold corners
fold corners
11
fold
here
here
fold
fold
Repeat behind.

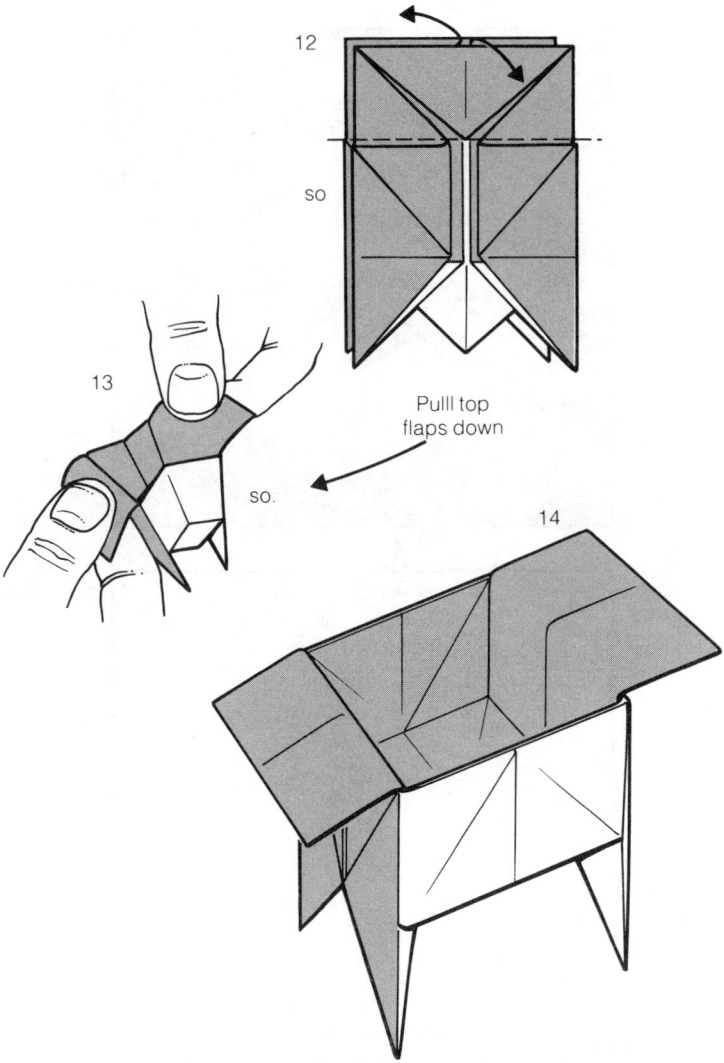
12
so
13
Pulll top
flaps down
so.
14

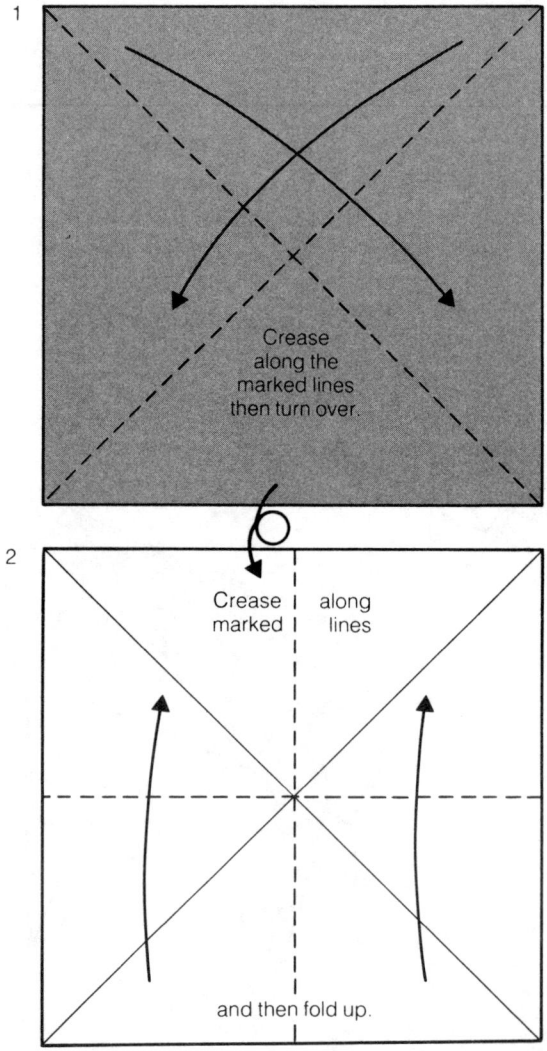
1
Crease
along the
marked lines
then turn over.
2
Crease along
marked lines
and then fold up.

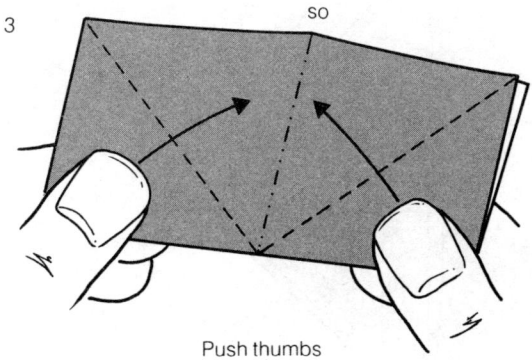

Push thumbs
together
until
they meet

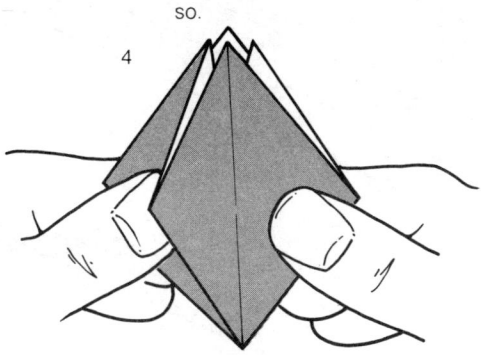

Now look at
fig. 5.

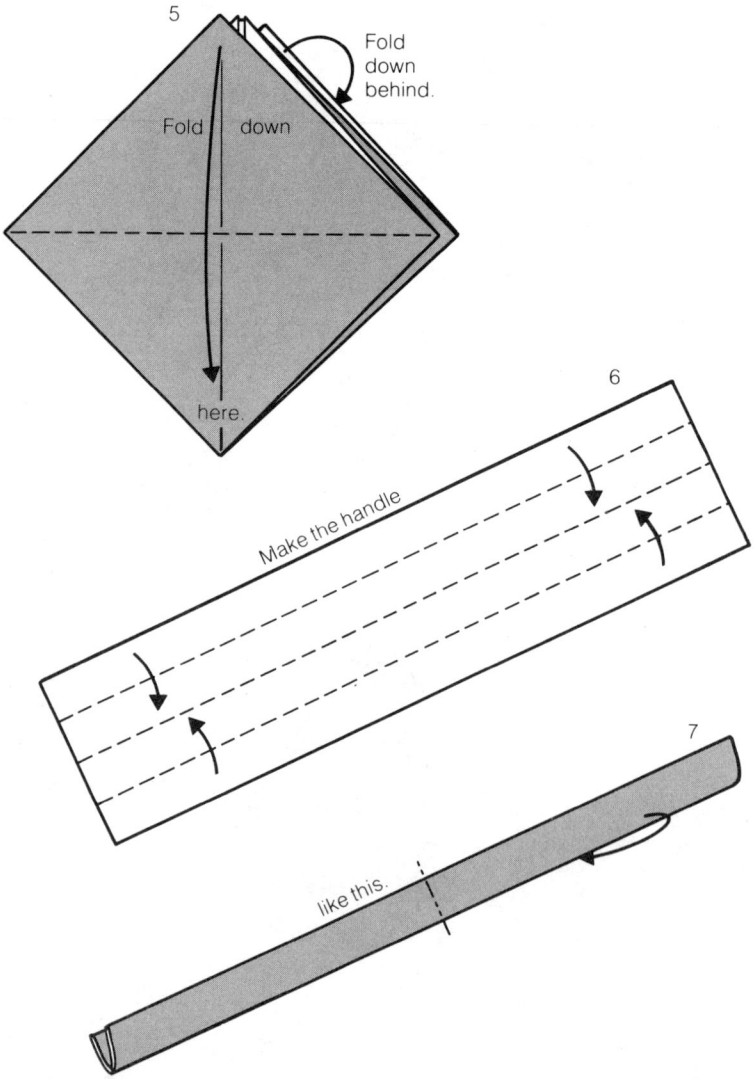
5
Fold down behind.
Fold down
here.
6
Make the handle
7
like this.

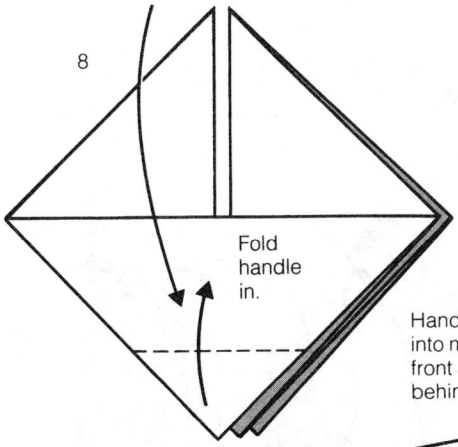
8
Fold
handle
in.

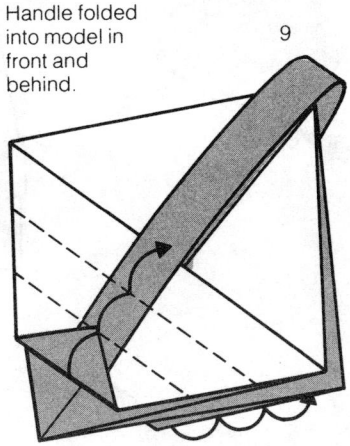
Handle folded
into model in
front and
behind.
9

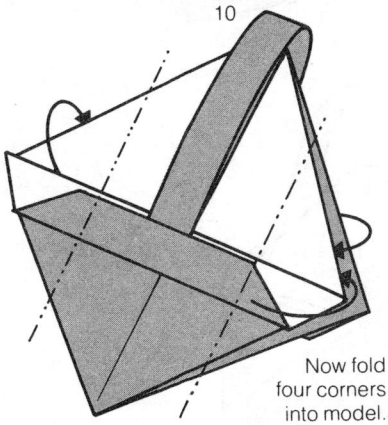
10
Now fold
four corners
into model.

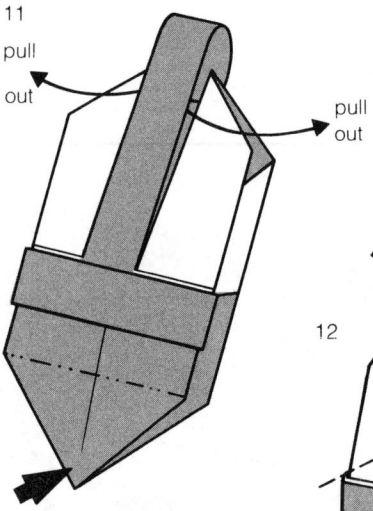
11
pull
out
pull
out

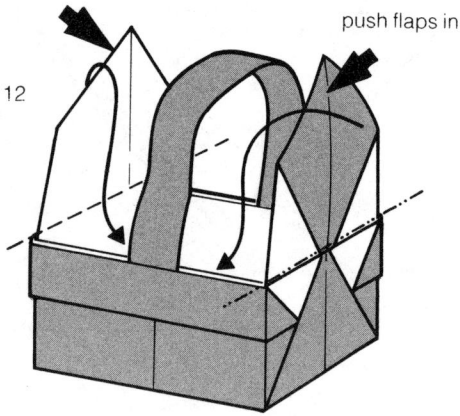
push flaps in
12

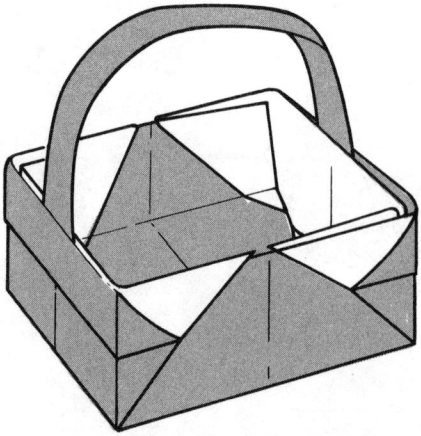

1

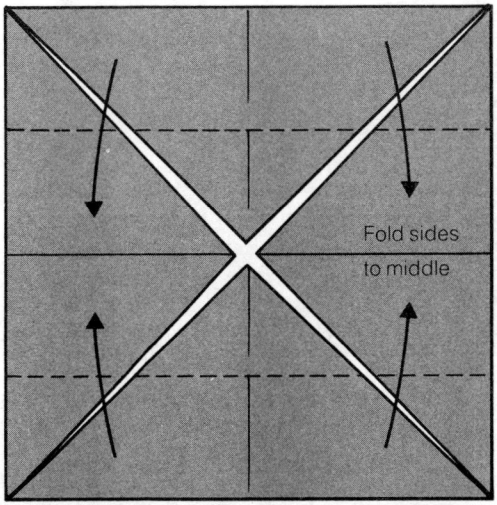

2

like this.

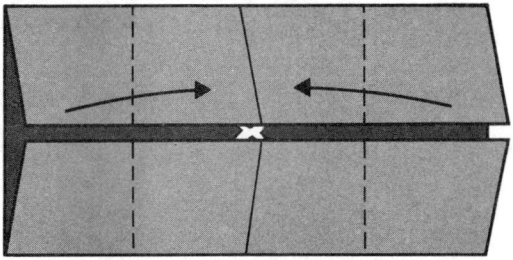

Fold sides to the middle.

3

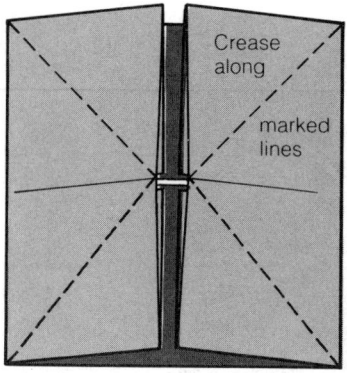

4

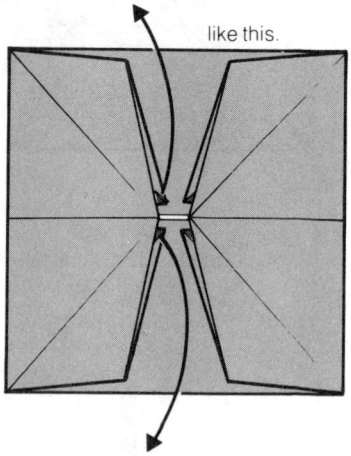

Now pull out the two arrowed points. The creases will guide you and they will fall into place as in fig. 5

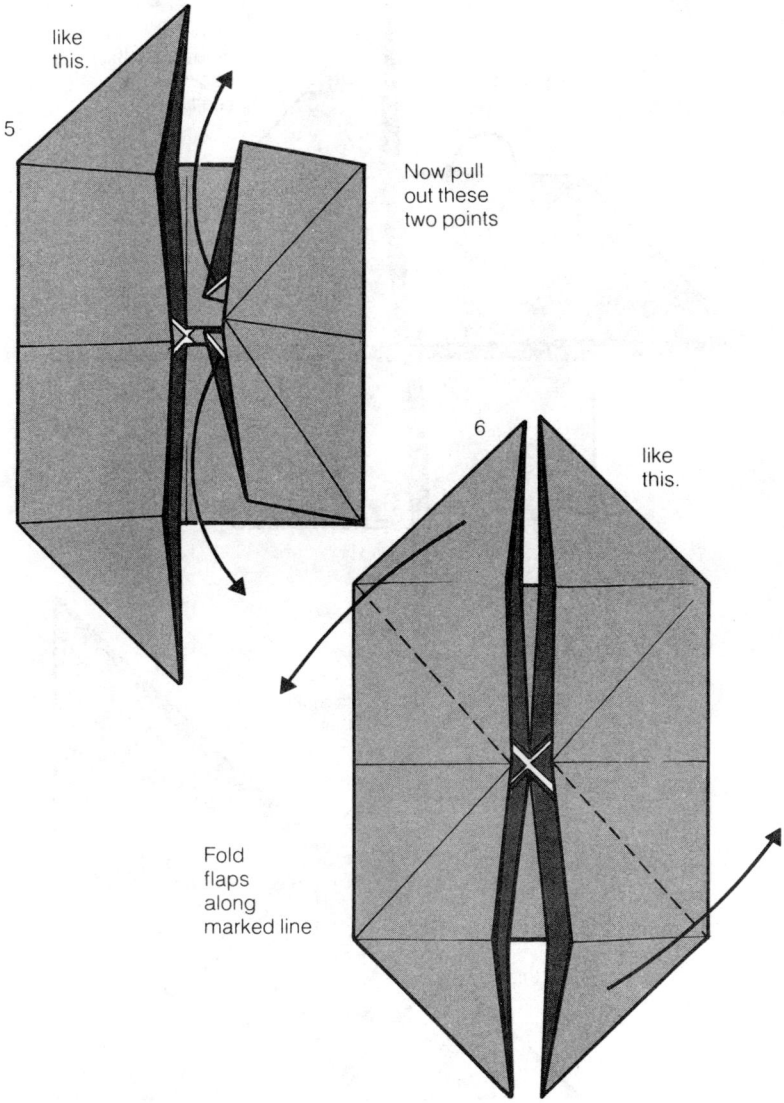
like
this.
5
Now pull
out these
two points
6
like
this.
Fold
flaps
along
marked line

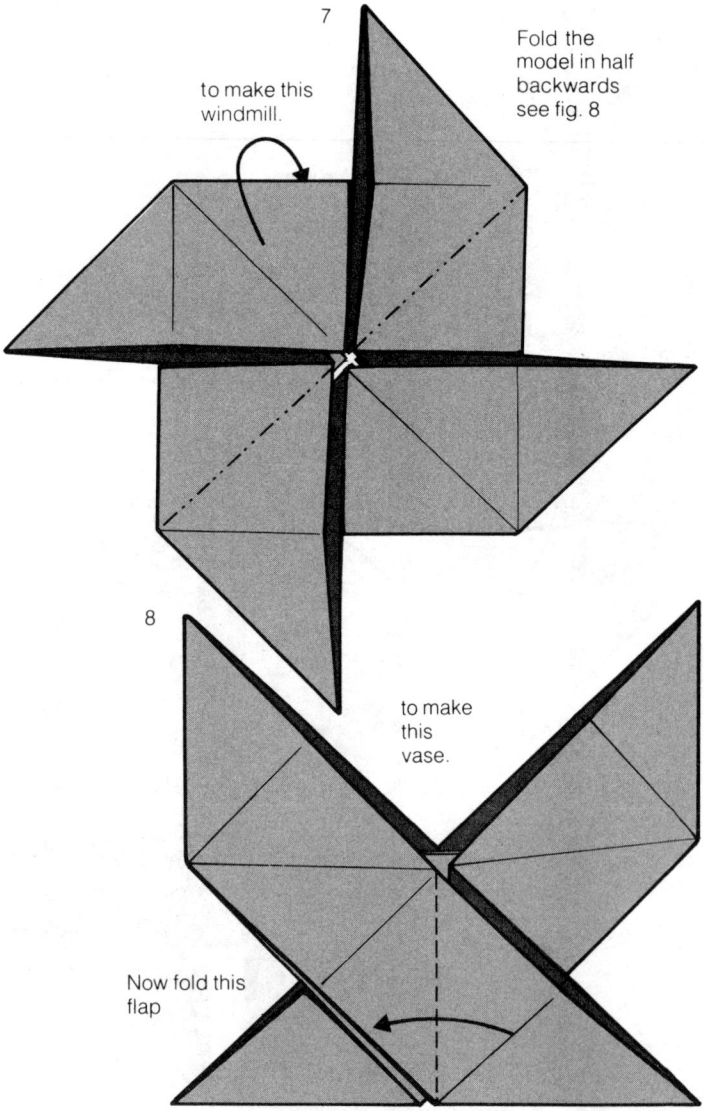
7
to make this windmill.
Fold the model in half backwards see fig. 8
8
to make this vase.
Now fold this flap

9

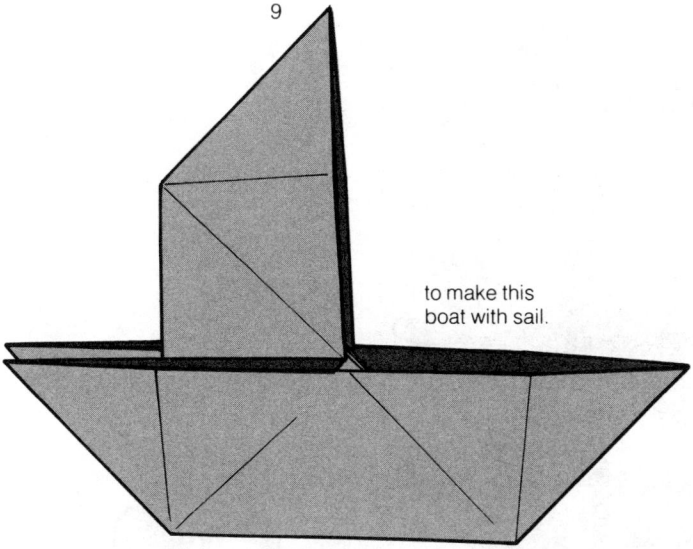

to make this
boat with sail.

Now start at fig. 6
and fold the model
in half to
make this
catamaran.

10

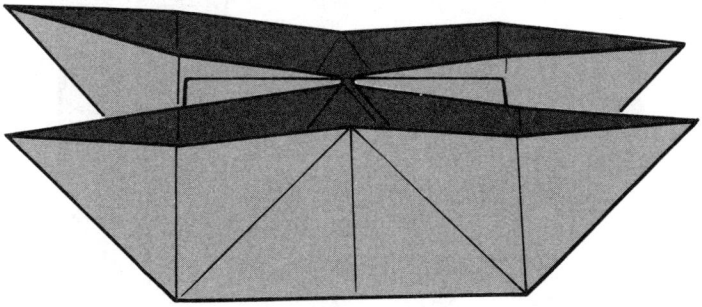

GONDOLA *Begin with Multiform fold 6*

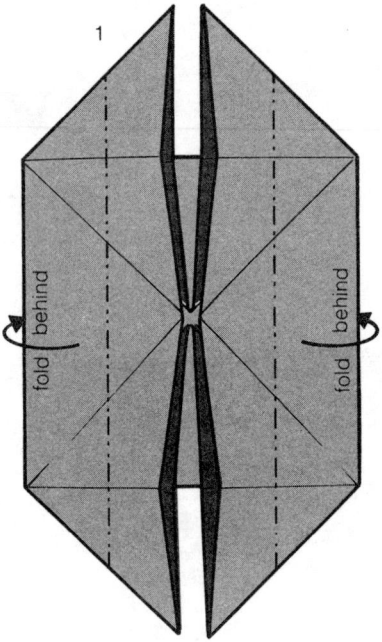

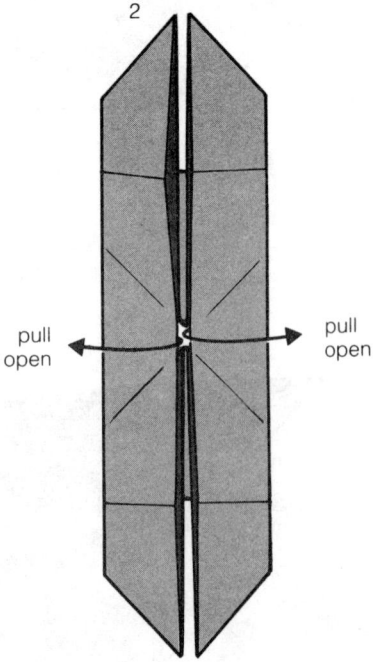

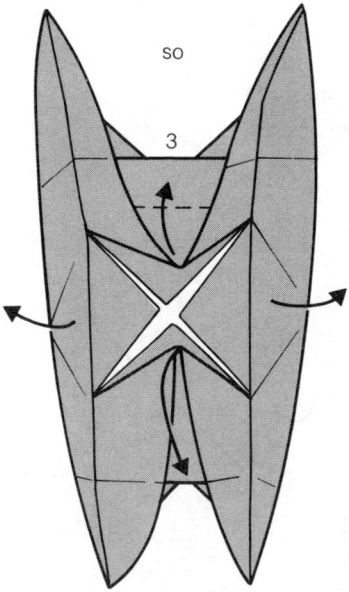

squash flat

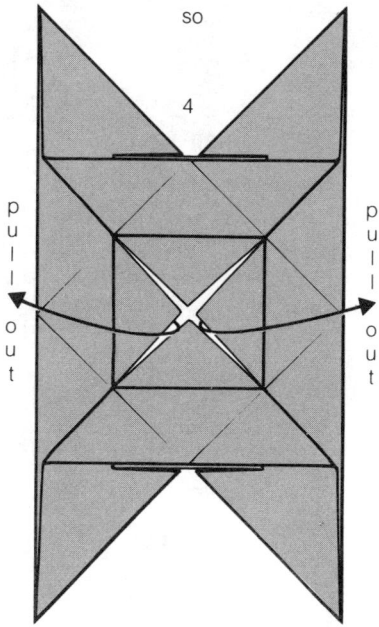

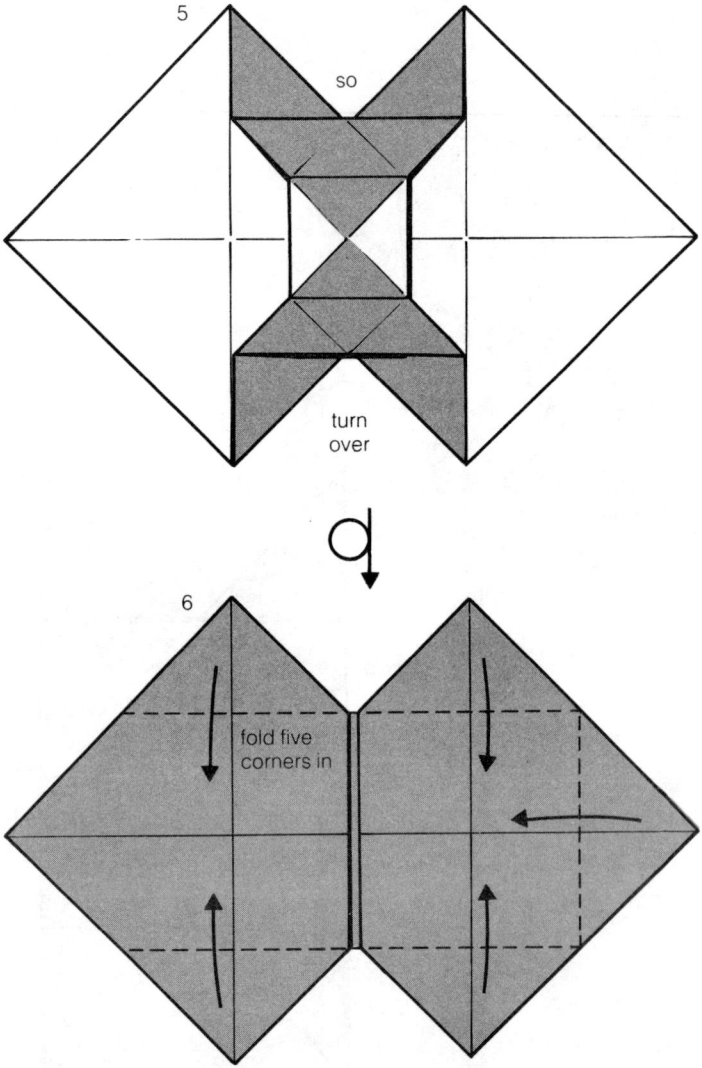
5
so
turn
over
6
fold five
corners in

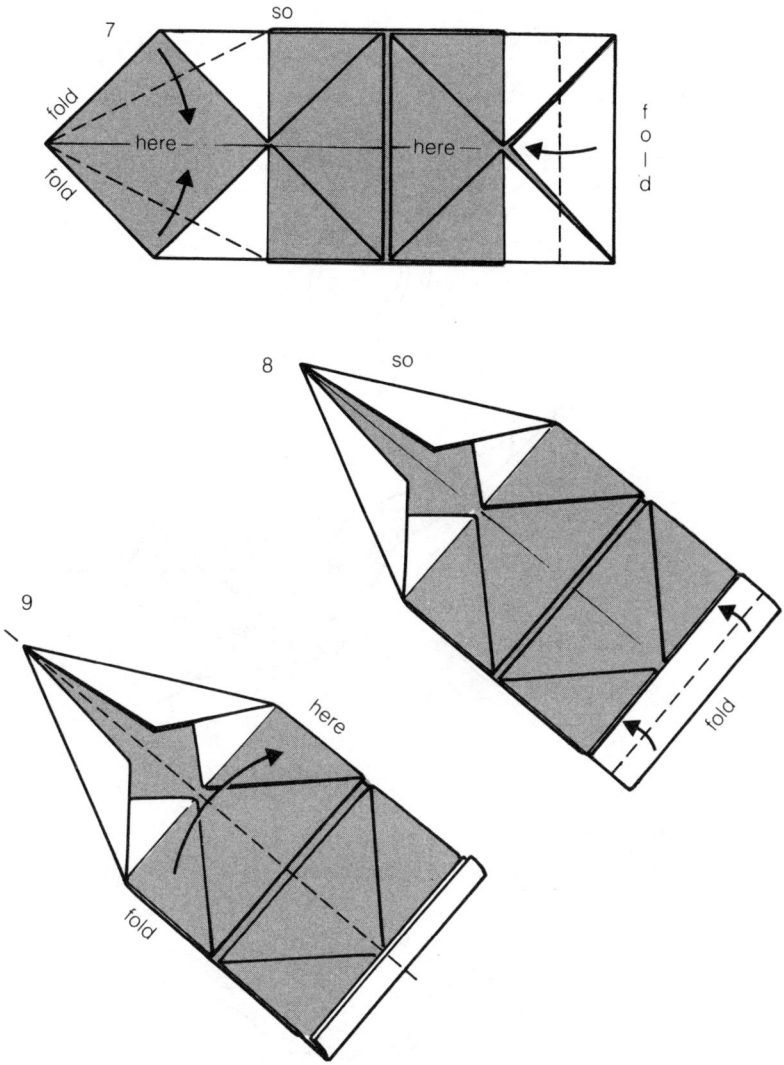
7
so
fold
here
here
fold
fold
8
so
fold
9
here
fold

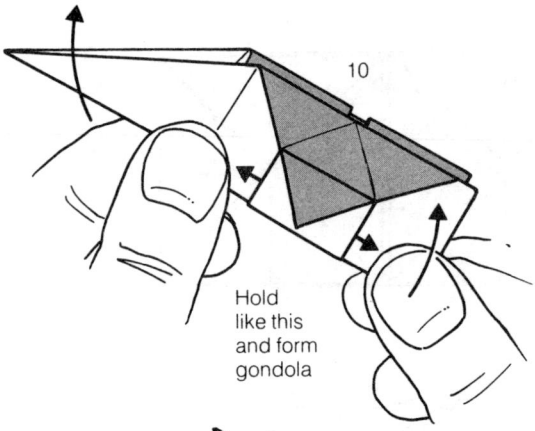
10
Hold
like this
and form
gondola

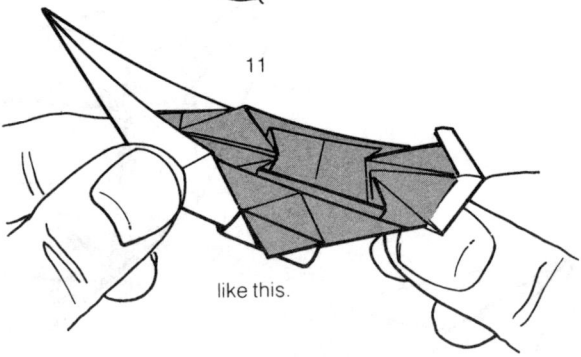
11
like this.

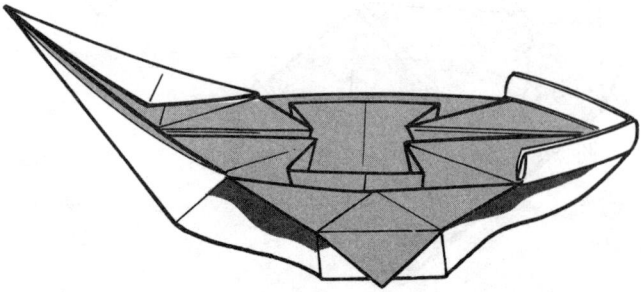

BIRD BASE *The most important base in Origami*

1

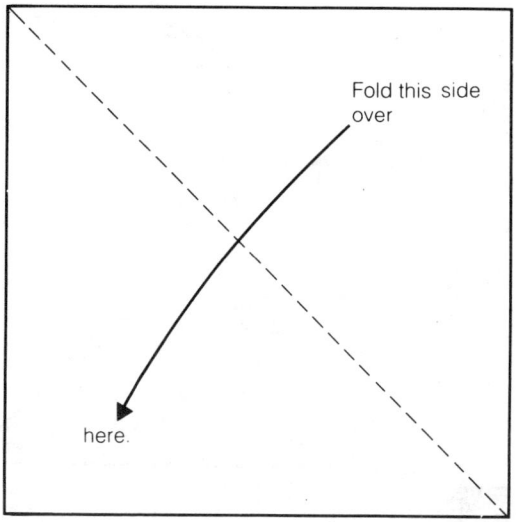

2

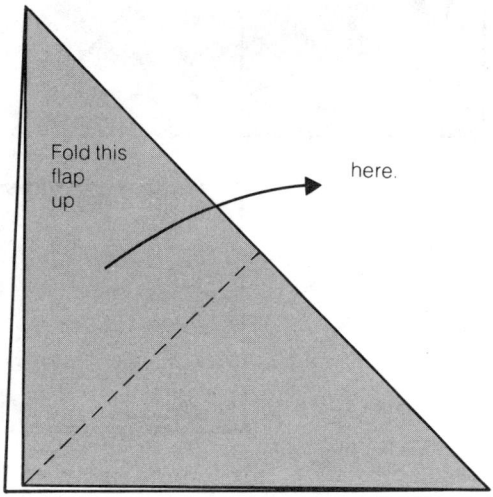

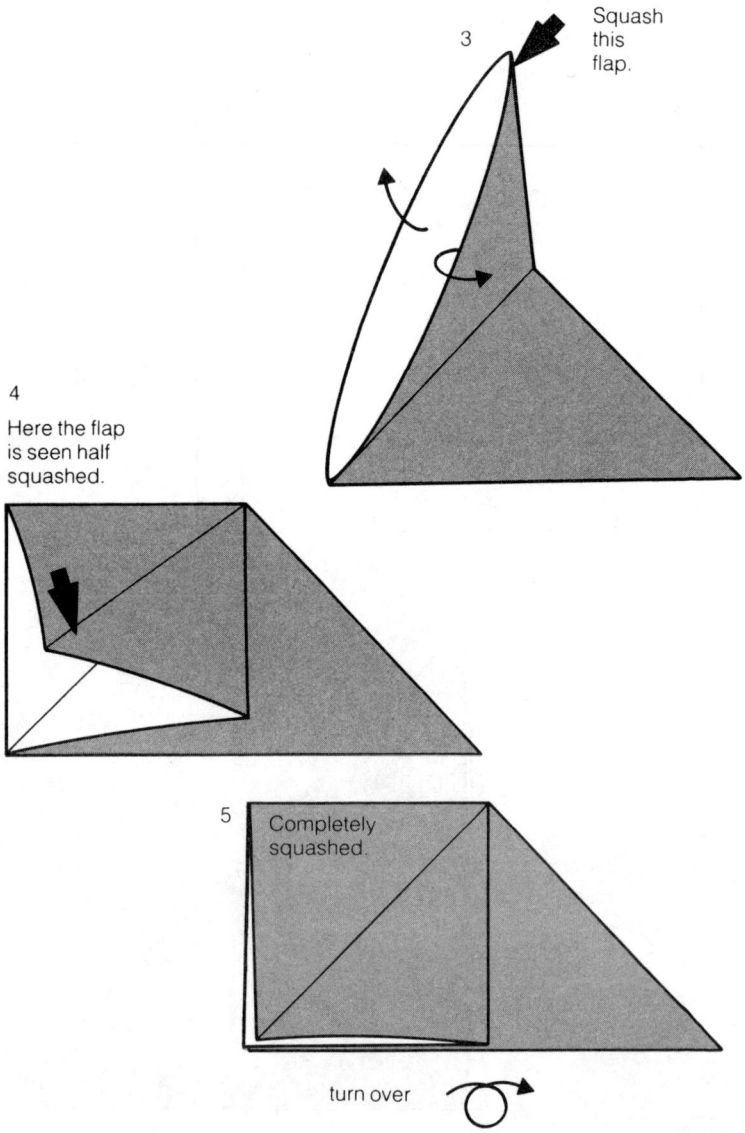
3
Squash this flap.
4
Here the flap is seen half squashed.
5
Completely squashed.
turn over

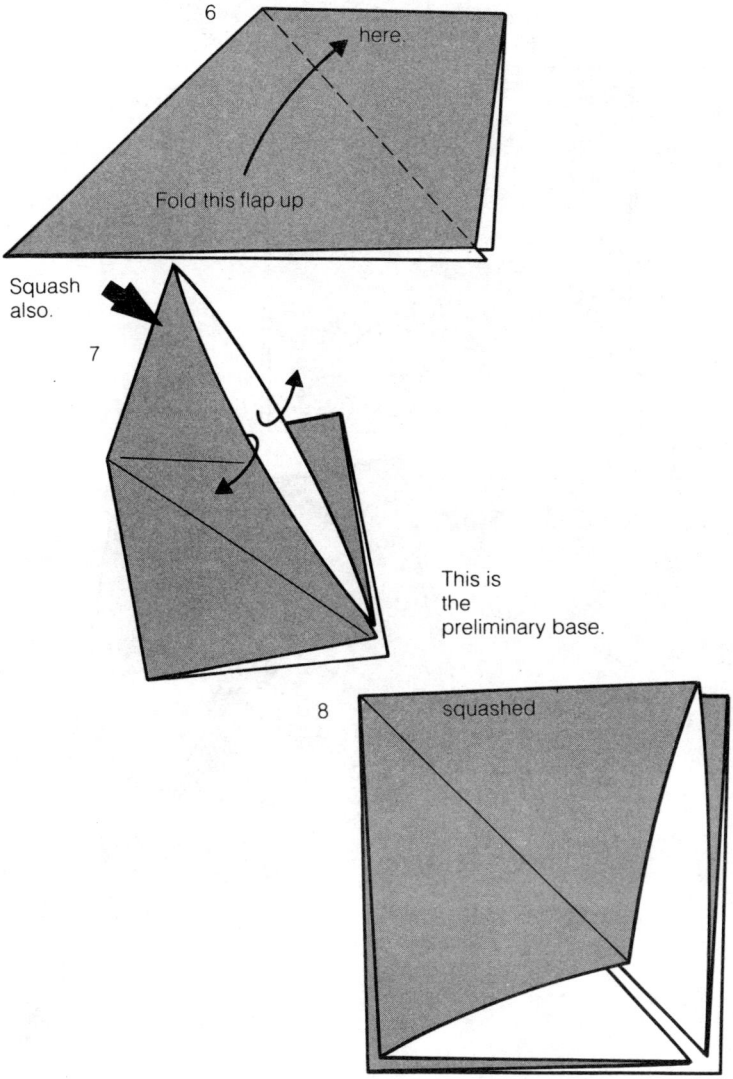
6
here.
Fold this flap up
Squash
also.
7
This is
the
preliminary base.
8
squashed

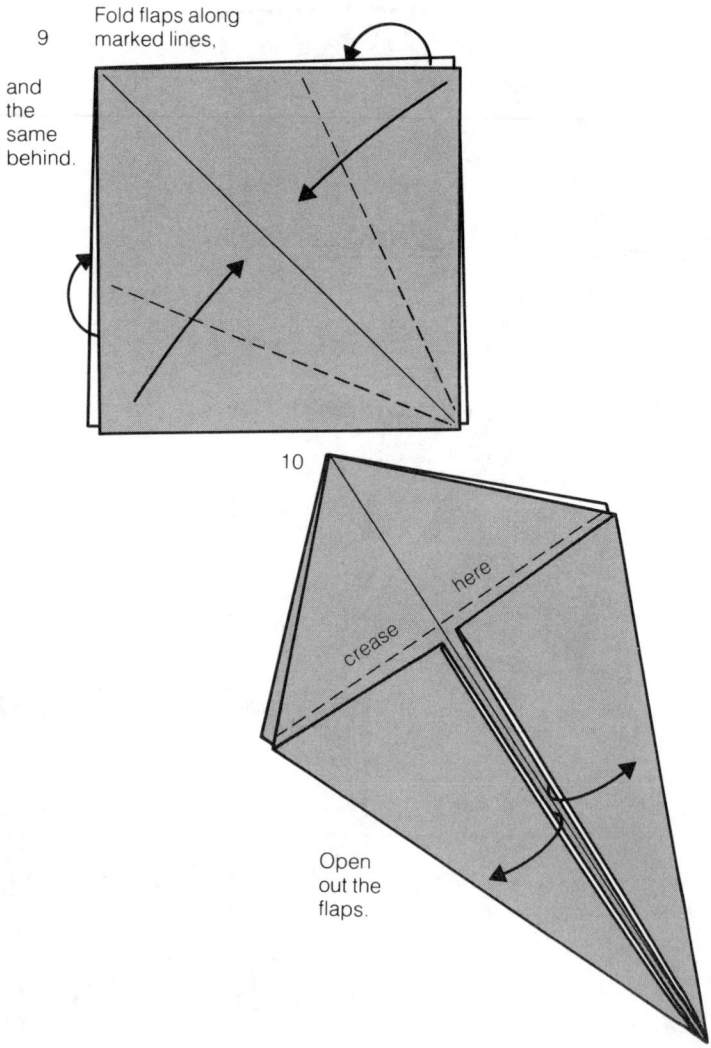
9
Fold flaps along marked lines,
and the same behind.
10
here
crease
Open out the flaps.

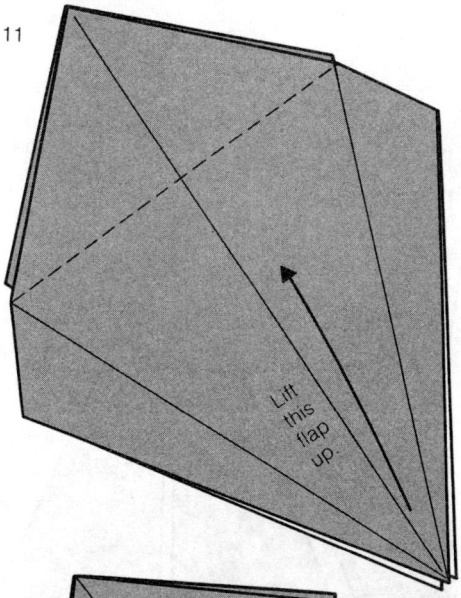
11
Lift this flap up.

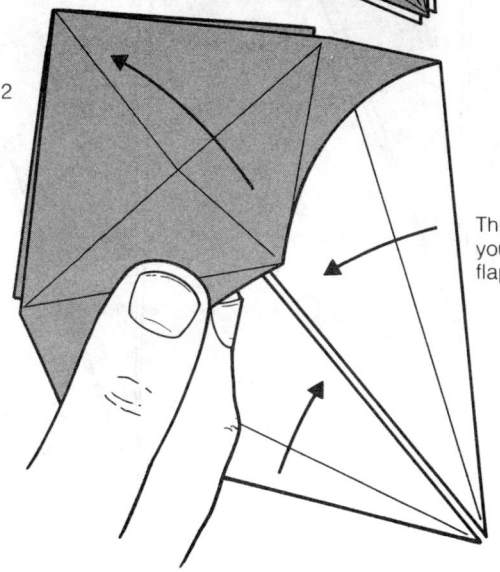
12
This is how you hold the flap.

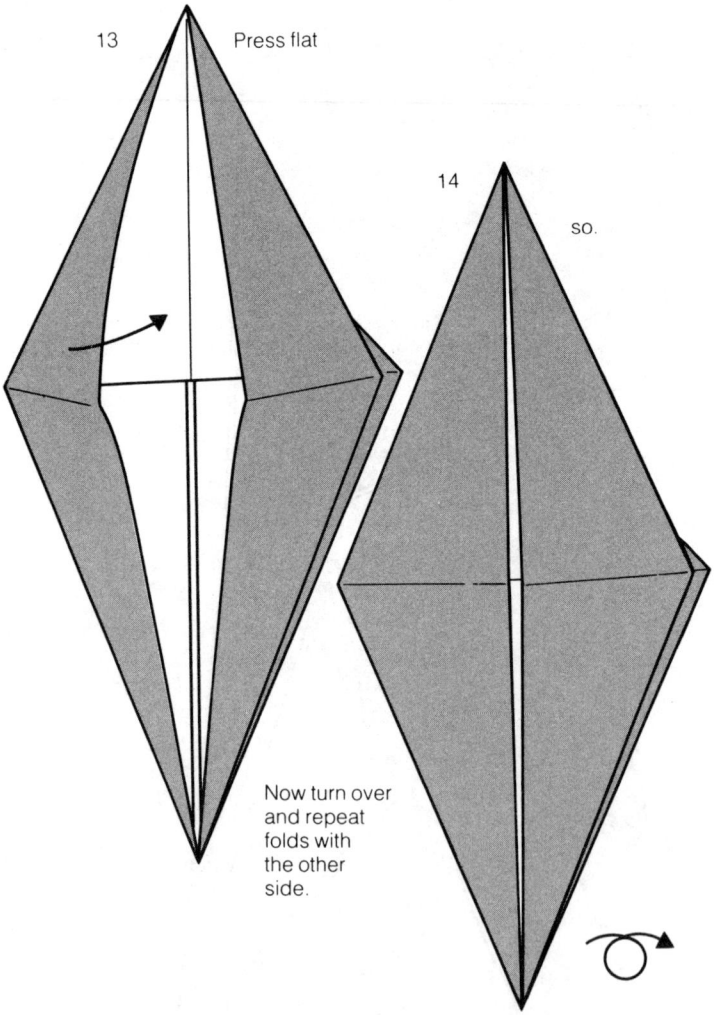
13
Press flat
14
so.
Now turn over
and repeat
folds with
the other
side.

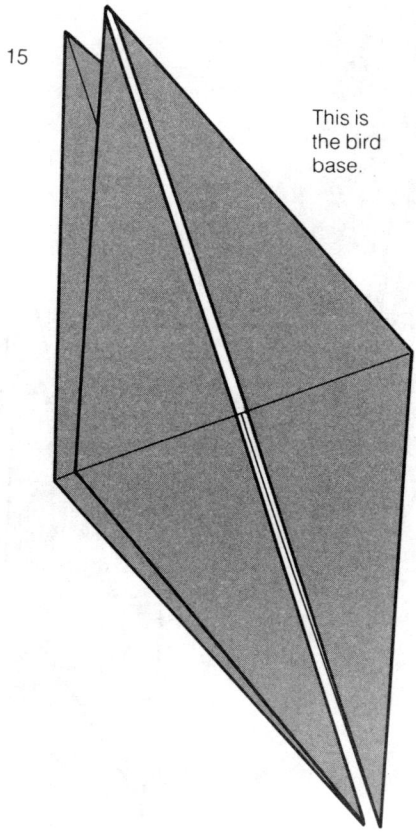
15
This is
the bird
base.

FLAPPING BIRD *Ancient Japanese*

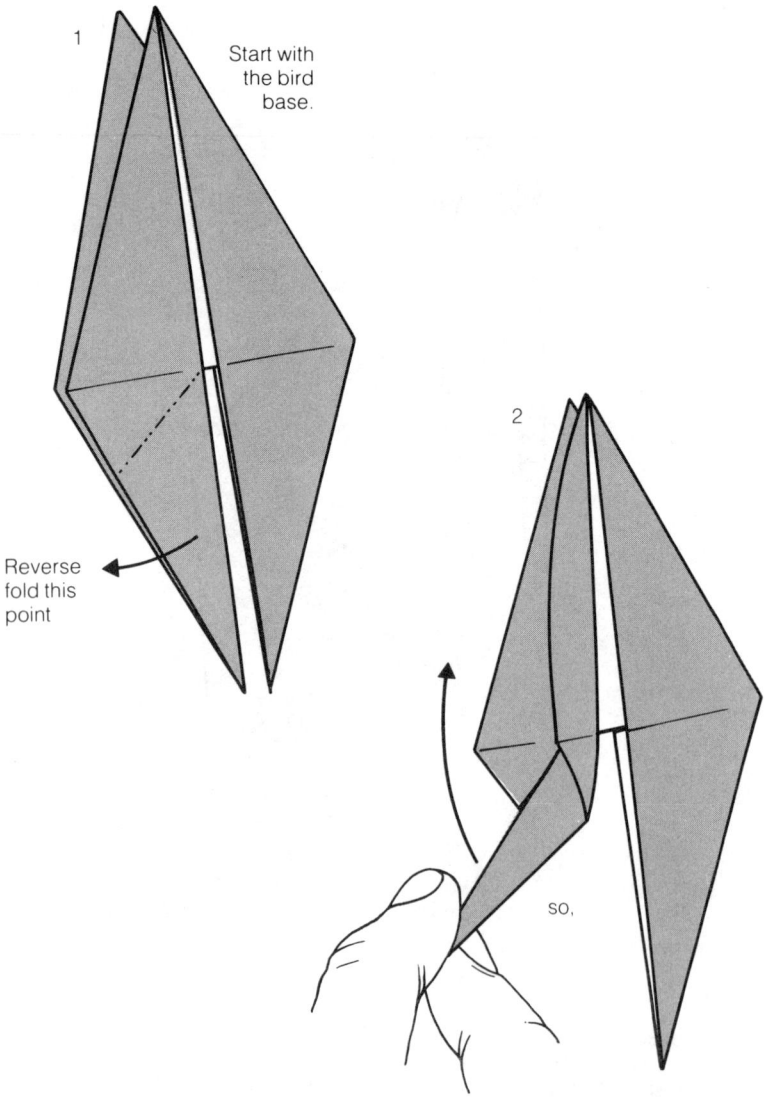

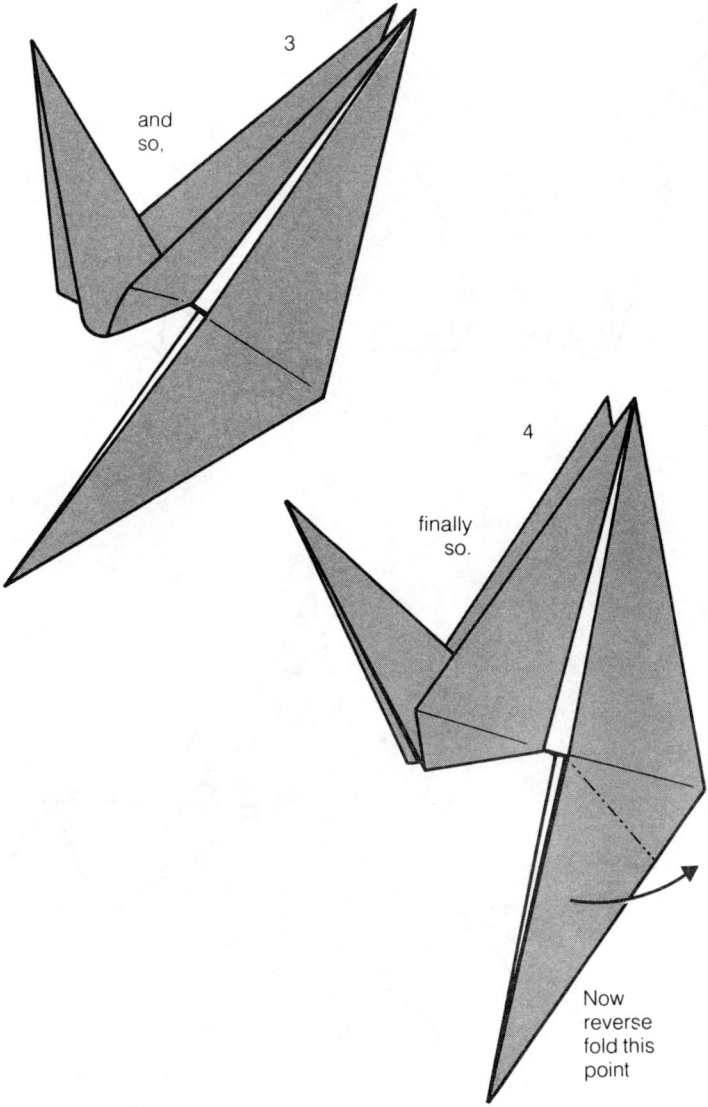
3
and
so,
4
finally
so.
Now
reverse
fold this
point

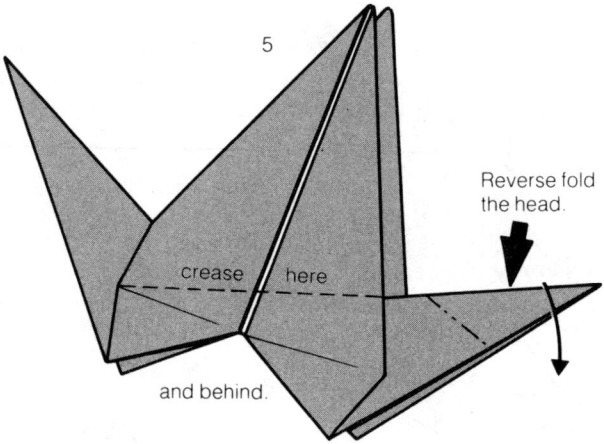
5
Reverse fold
the head.
crease
here
and behind.

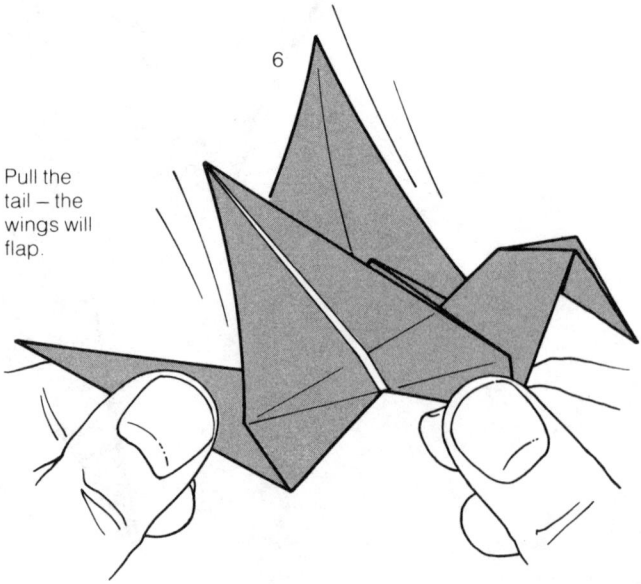
6
Pull the
tail – the
wings will
flap.

PIGEON *Akira Yoshizawa, Tokio, Japan*

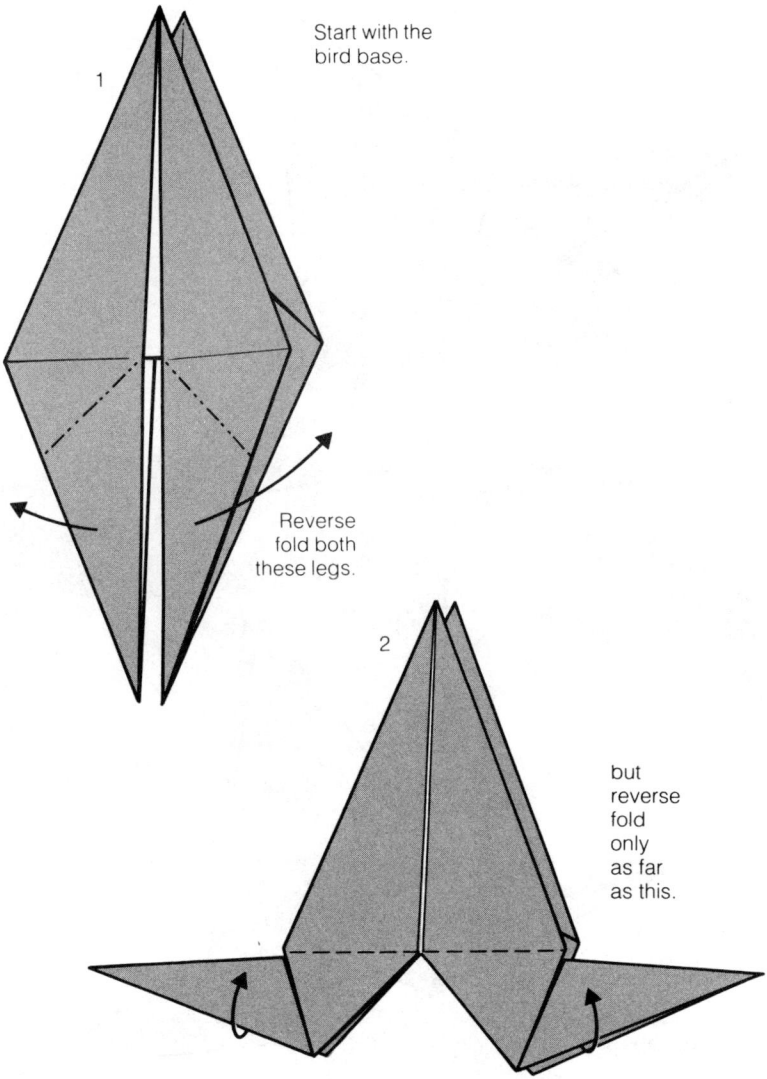

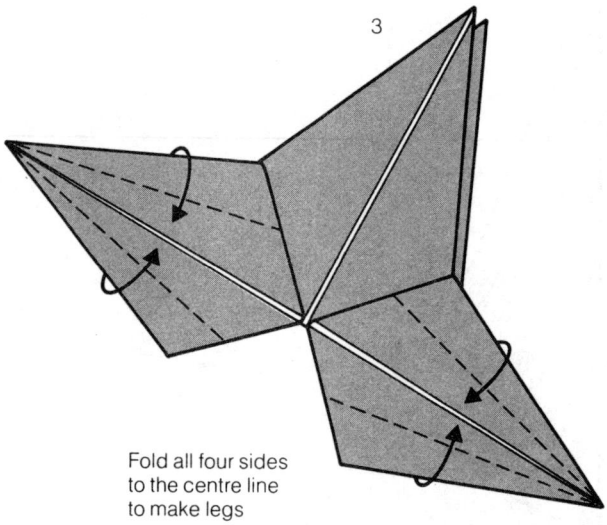
3
Fold all four sides
to the centre line
to make legs

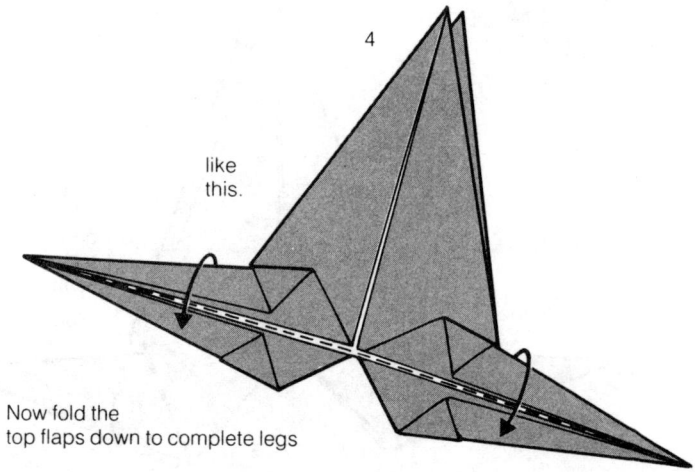
4
like
this.
Now fold the
top flaps down to complete legs

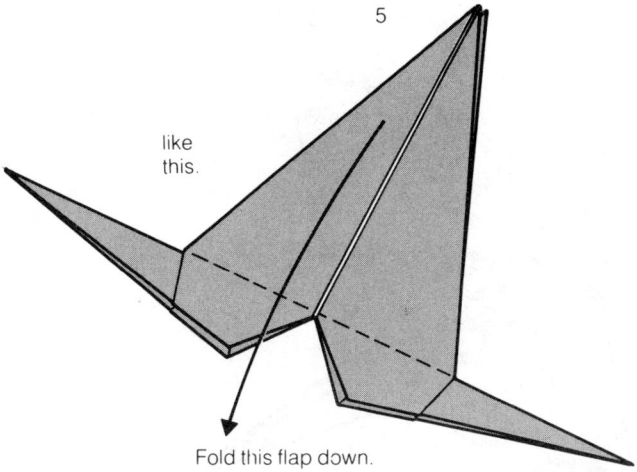
5
like
this.
Fold this flap down.

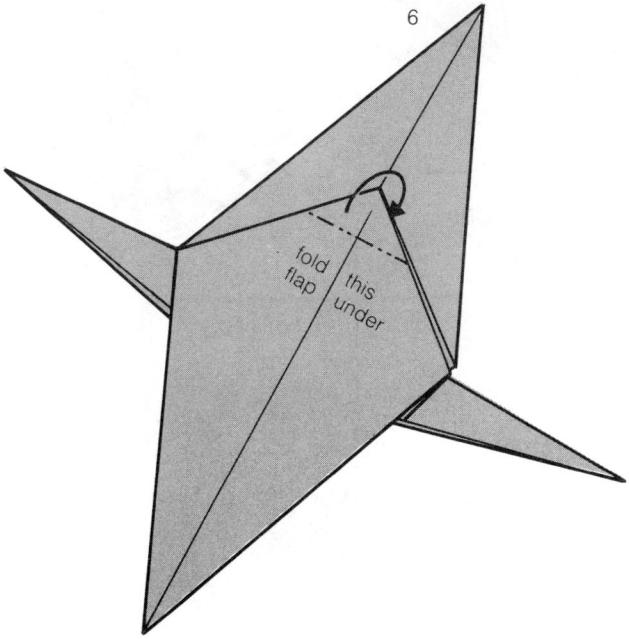
6
fold
flap
this
under

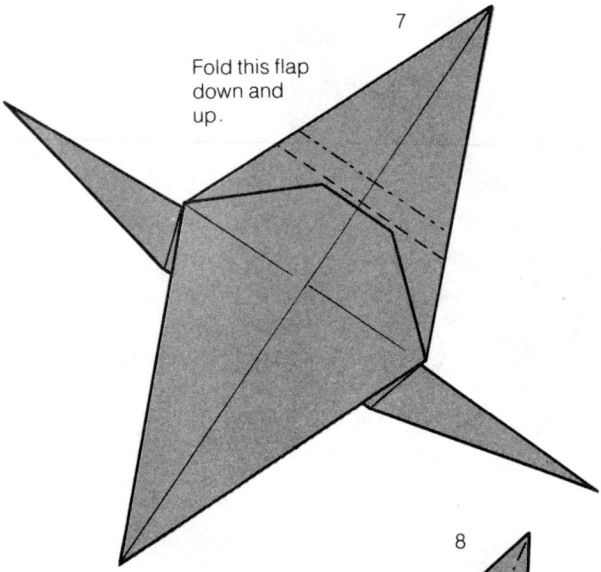
7
Fold this flap
down and
up.

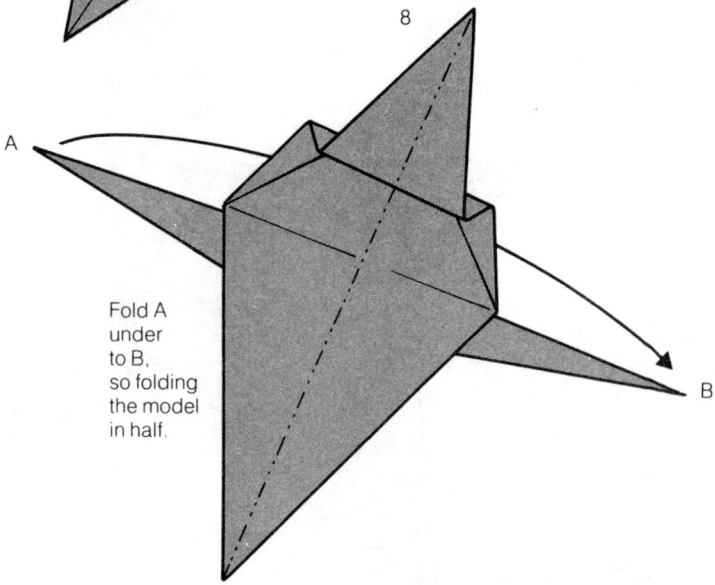
8
A
Fold A
under
to B,
so folding
the model
in half.
B

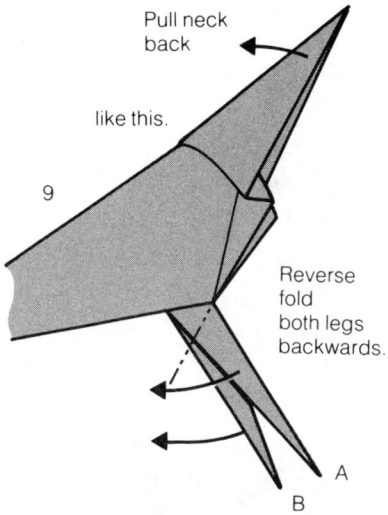
Pull neck
back
like this.
9
Reverse
fold
both legs
backwards.
A
B

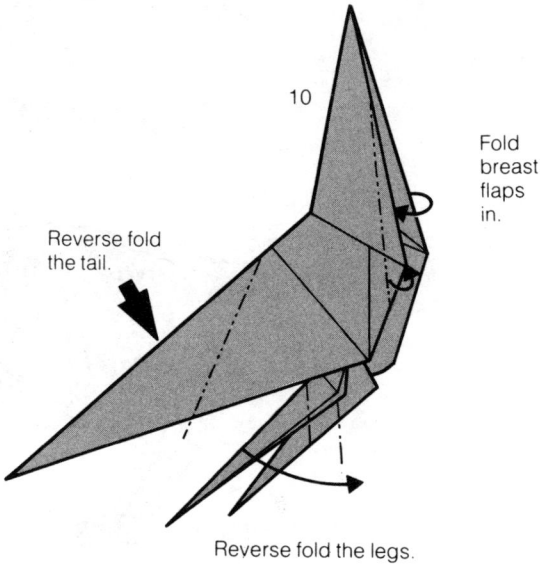
10
Fold
breast
flaps
in.
Reverse fold
the tail.
Reverse fold the legs.

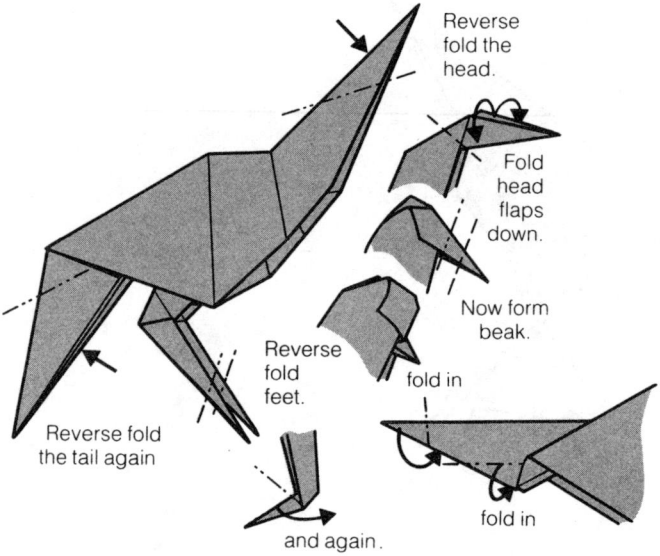
Reverse fold the head.
Fold head flaps down.
Now form beak.
Reverse fold feet.
fold in
Reverse fold the tail again
fold in
and again.

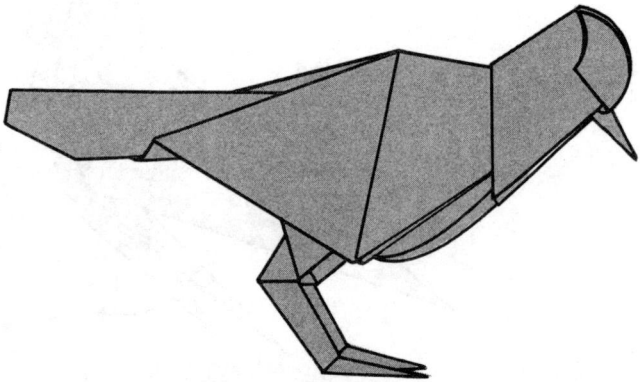

PRAYING MOOR *Spanish Origin. Start with Bird Base*

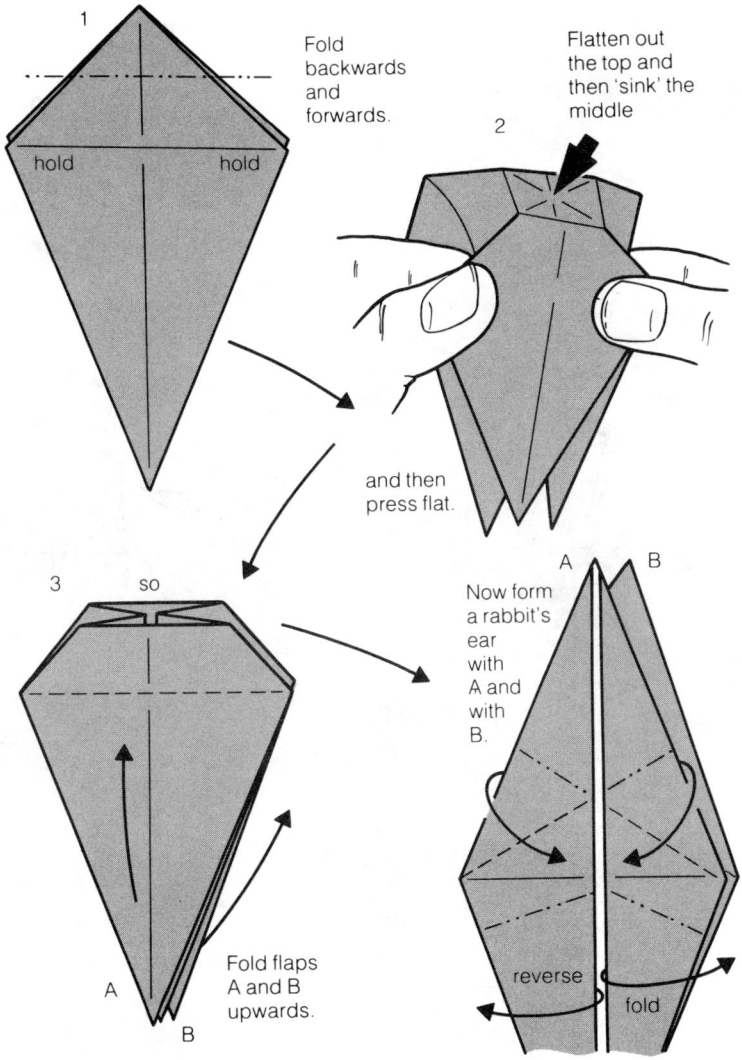

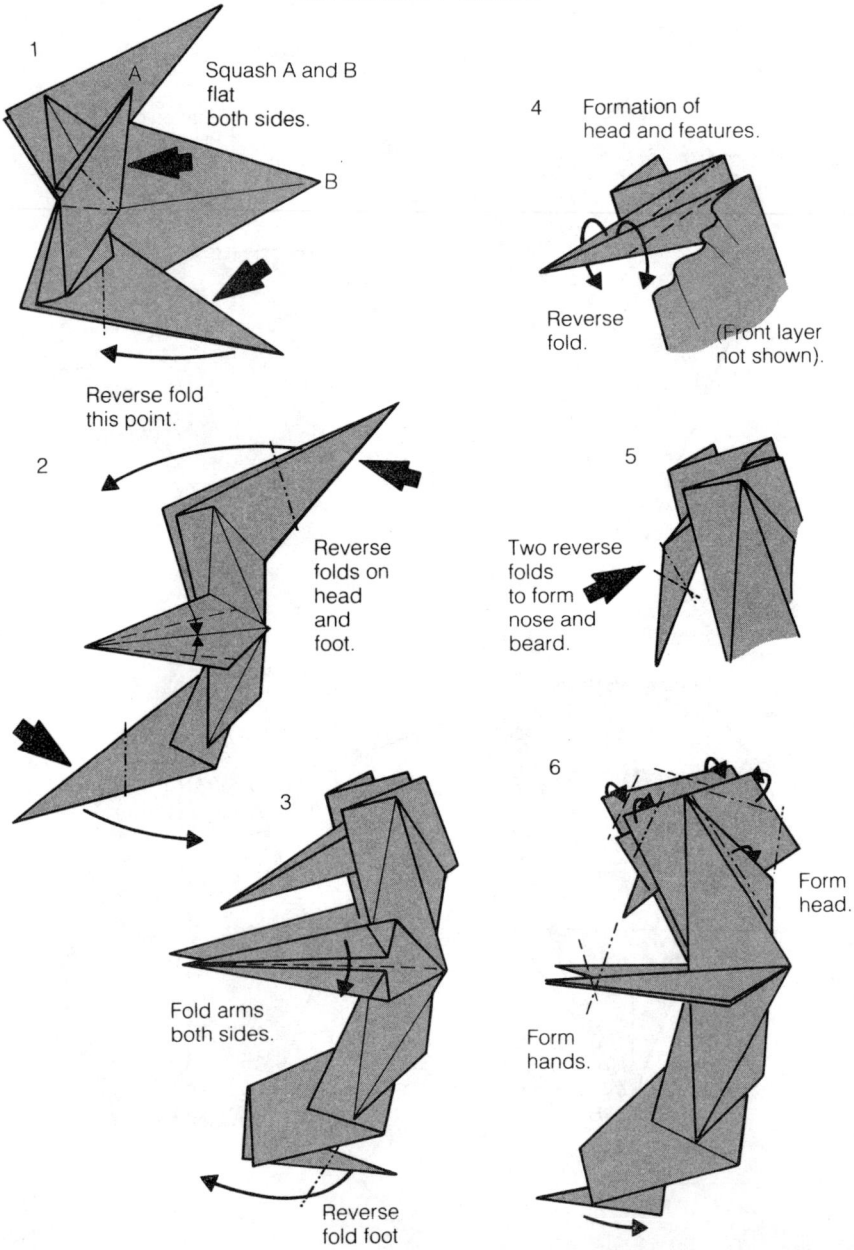
1
A
Squash A and B
flat
both sides.
B
Reverse fold
this point.
2
Reverse
folds on
head
and
foot.
3
Fold arms
both sides.
Reverse
fold foot
4
Formation of
head and features.
Reverse
fold.
(Front layer
not shown).
5
Two reverse
folds
to form
nose and
beard.
6
Form
head.
Form
hands.

The praying moor completed

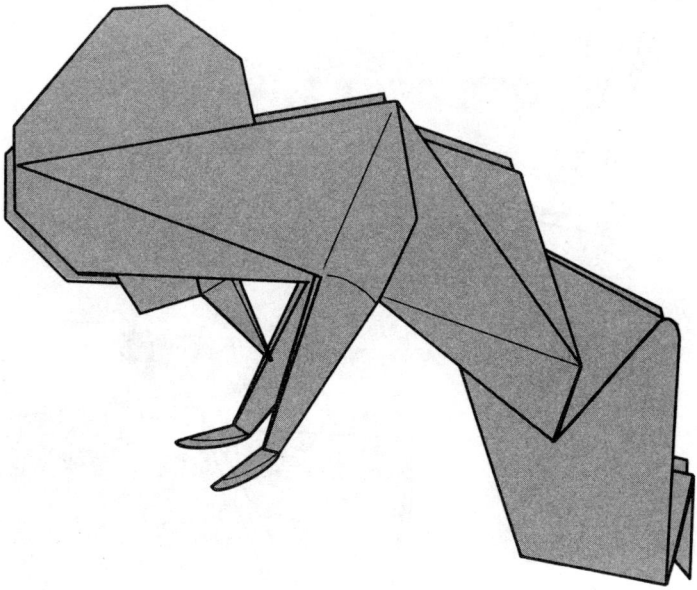

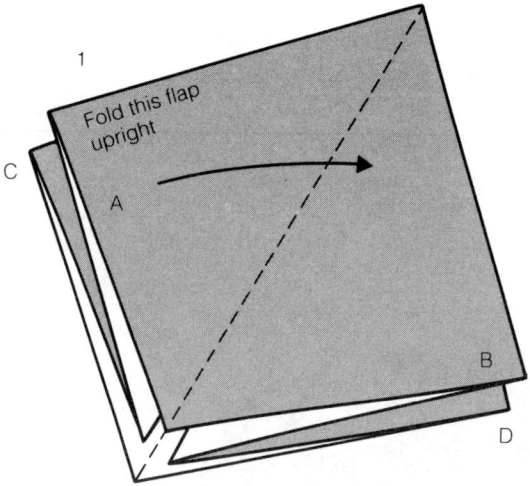
1
Fold this flap upright
C
A
B
D

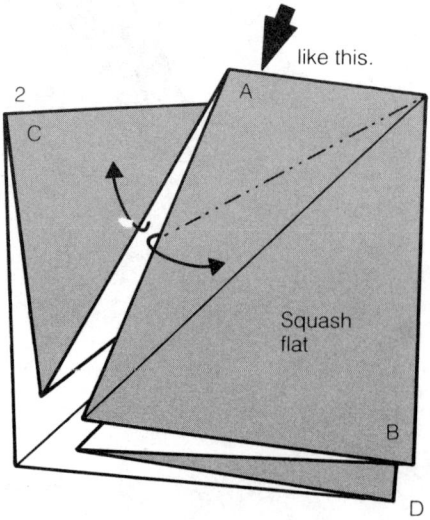
like this.
2
A
C
Squash flat
B
D

3

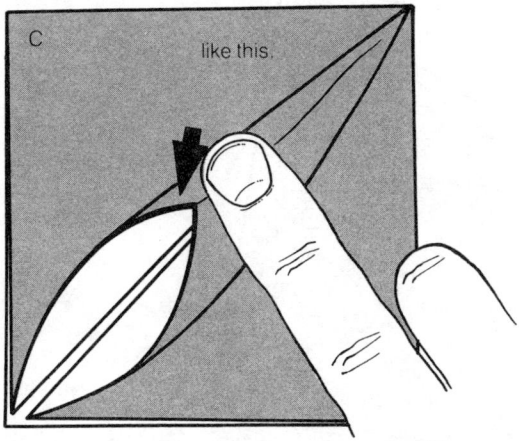

4

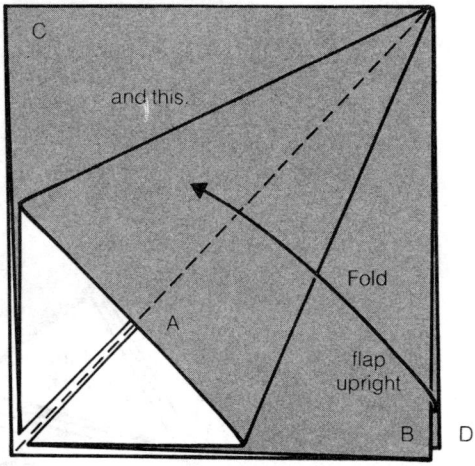

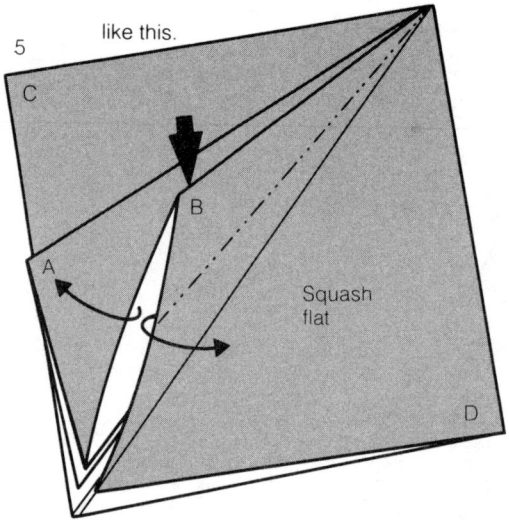
5
like this.
C
B
A
Squash
flat
D

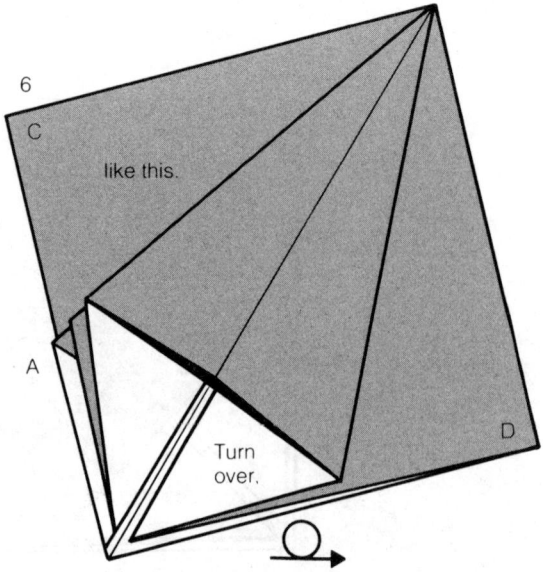
6
C
like this.
A
Turn
over.
D

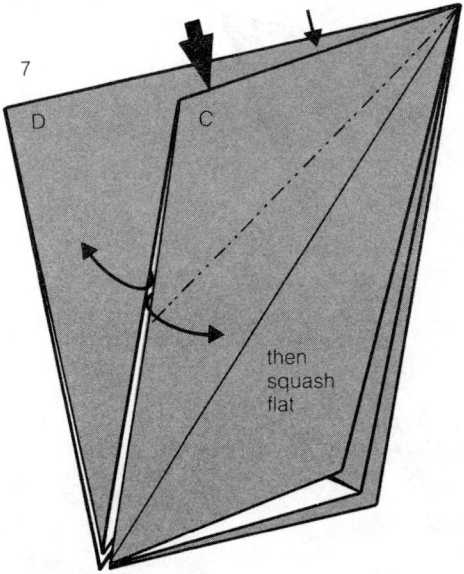
7
D
C
then
squash
flat

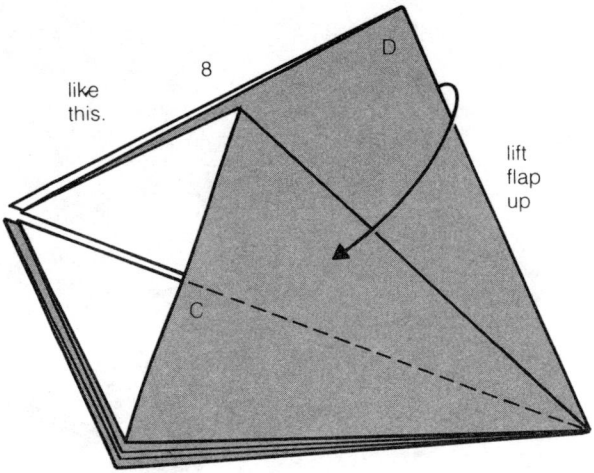
8
like
this.
D
lift
flap
up
C

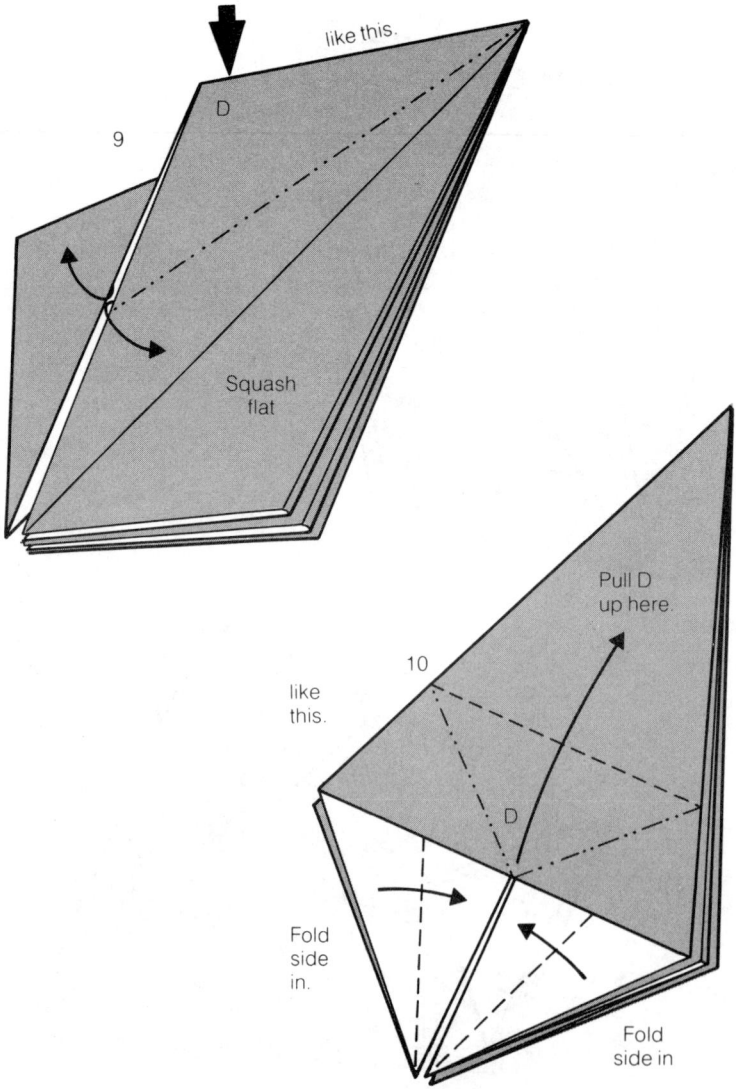
like this.
D
9
Squash
flat
Pull D
up here.
10
like
this.
D
Fold
side
in.
Fold
side in

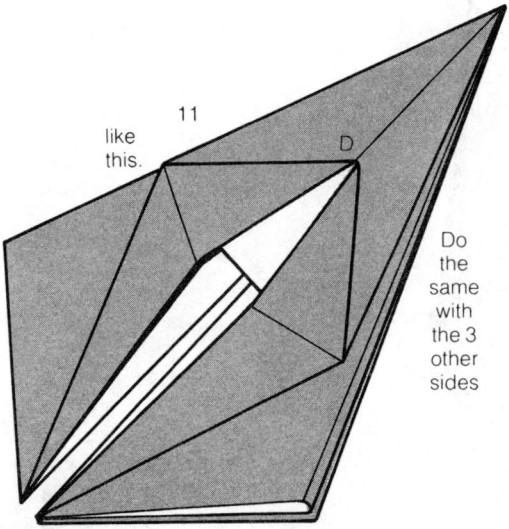
11
like
this.
D
Do
the
same
with
the 3
other
sides

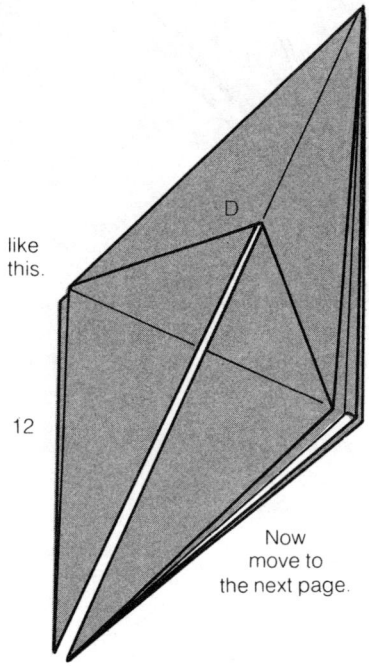
D
like
this.
12
Now
move to
the next page.

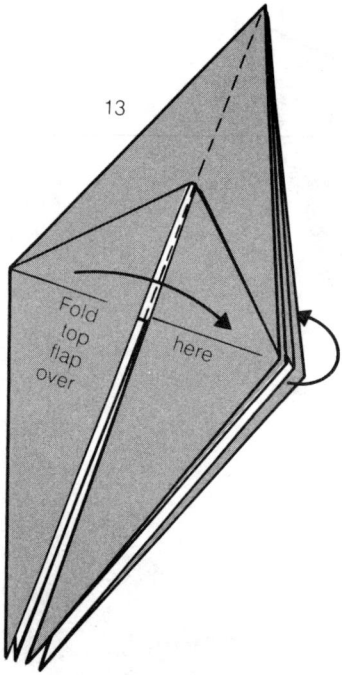
13
Fold
top
flap
over
here

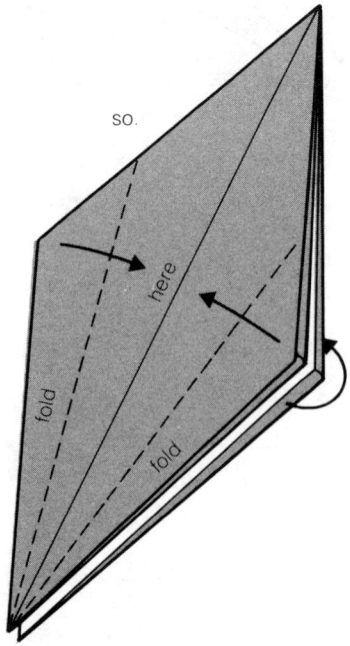
so.
here
fold
fold

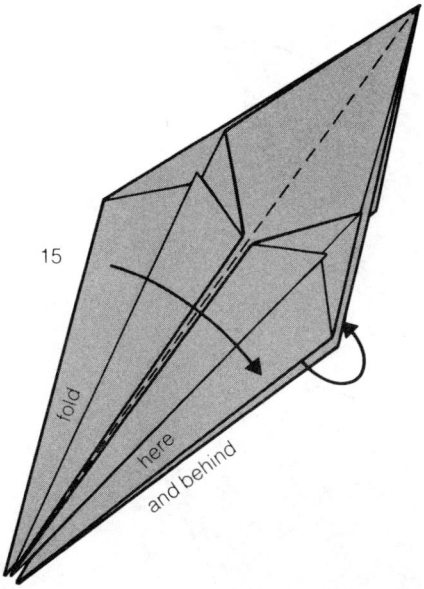
15
fold
here
and behind

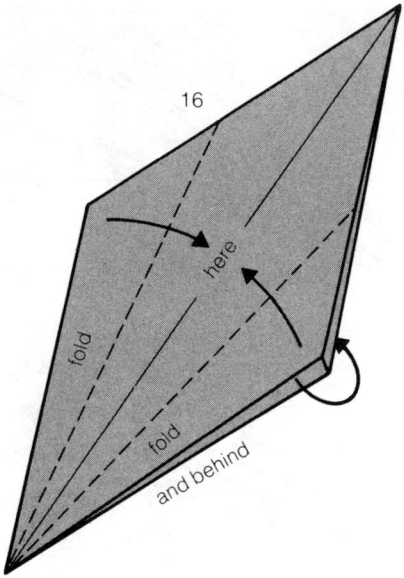
16
here
fold
fold
and behind

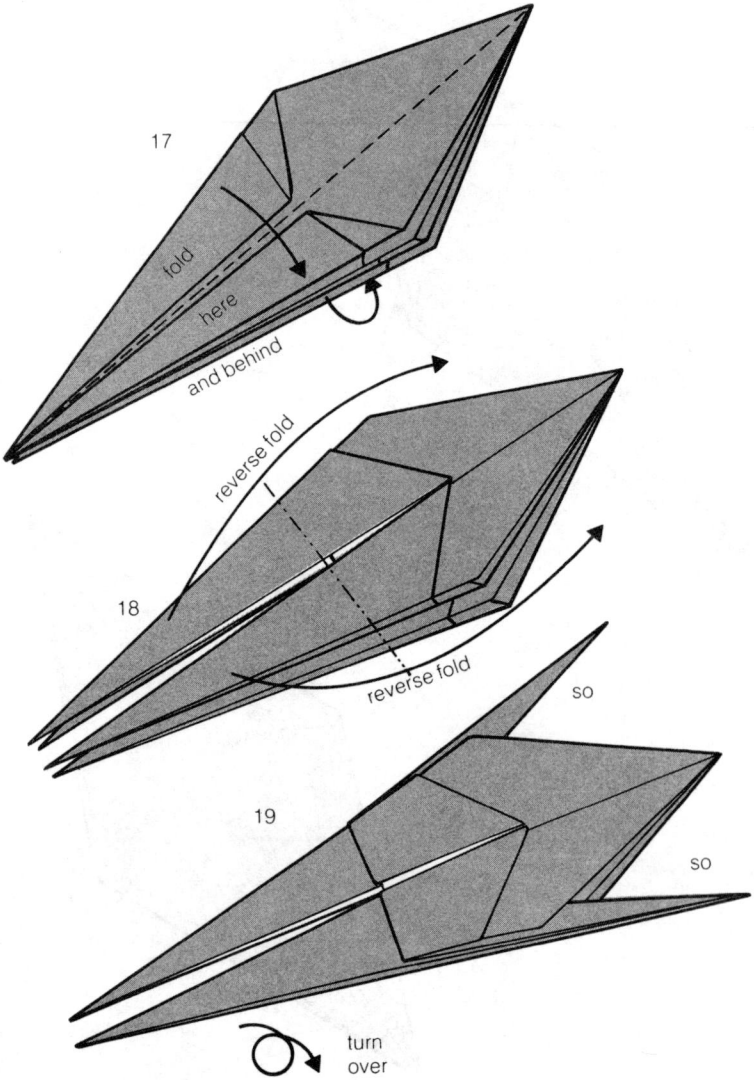
17
fold
here
and behind
reverse fold
18
reverse fold
so
19
so
turn
over

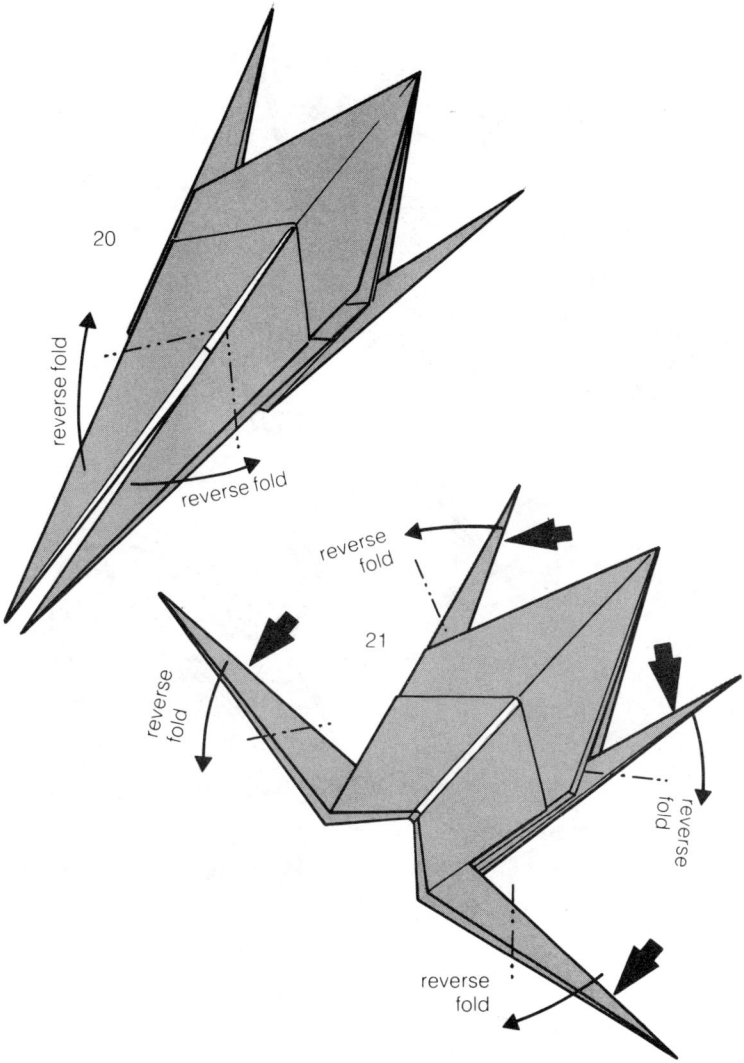
20
reverse fold
reverse fold
21
reverse fold
reverse fold
reverse fold
reverse fold

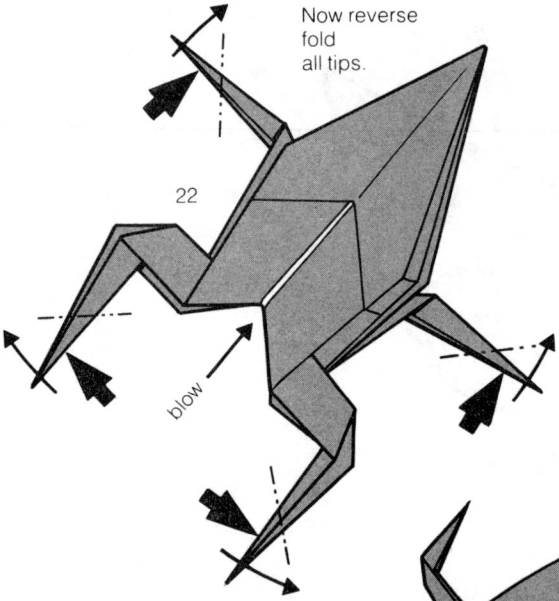
Now reverse
fold
all tips.
22
blow

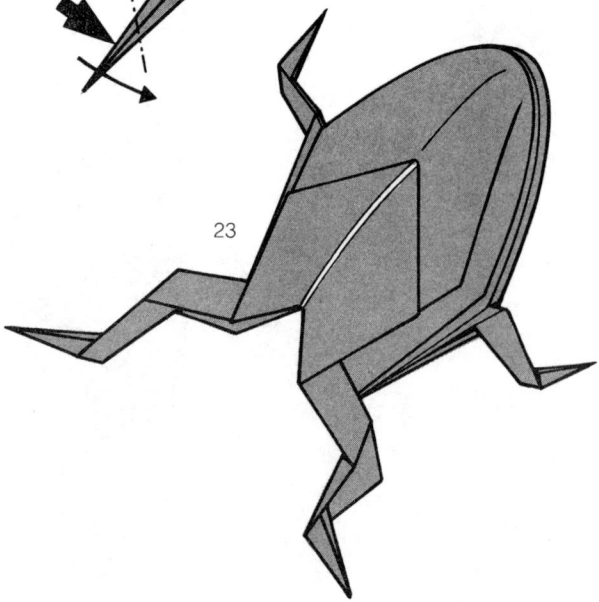
23

BAT MASK *Peter Van Note, New York*

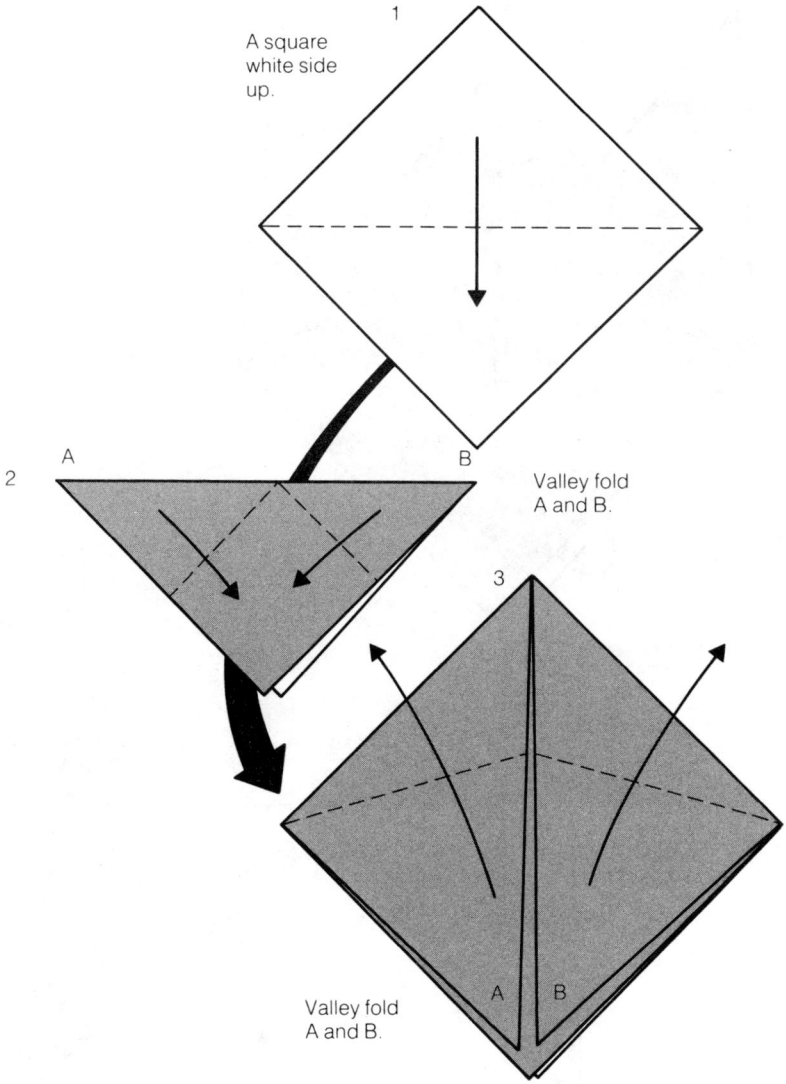

4

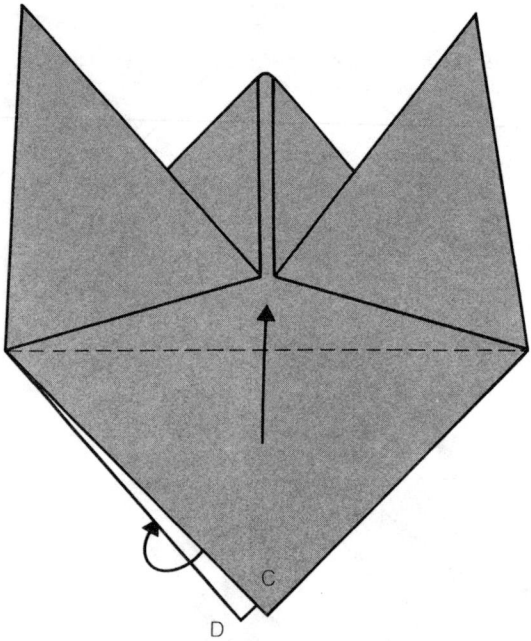

Fold
C in front
B behind.

5

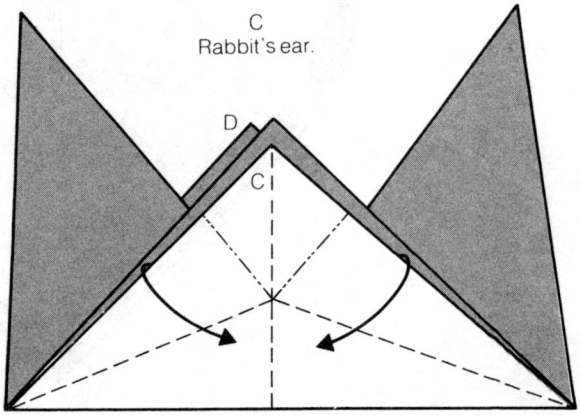

C
Rabbit's ear.

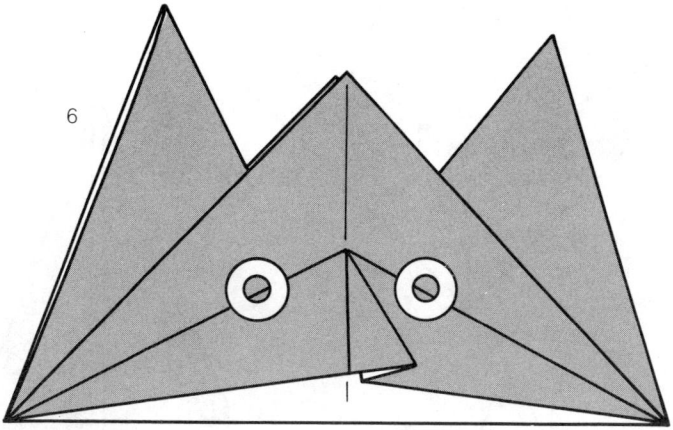

Make eyes with gummed eyelets.

PENGUINS *Robert Harbin, London*

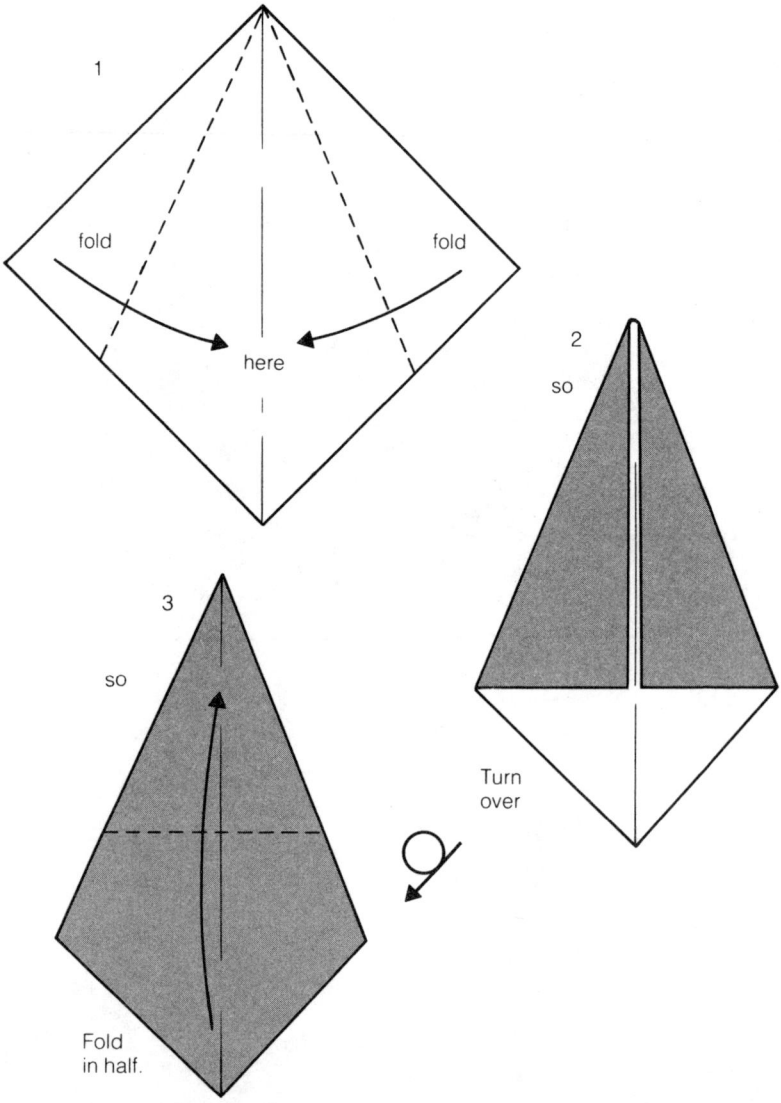

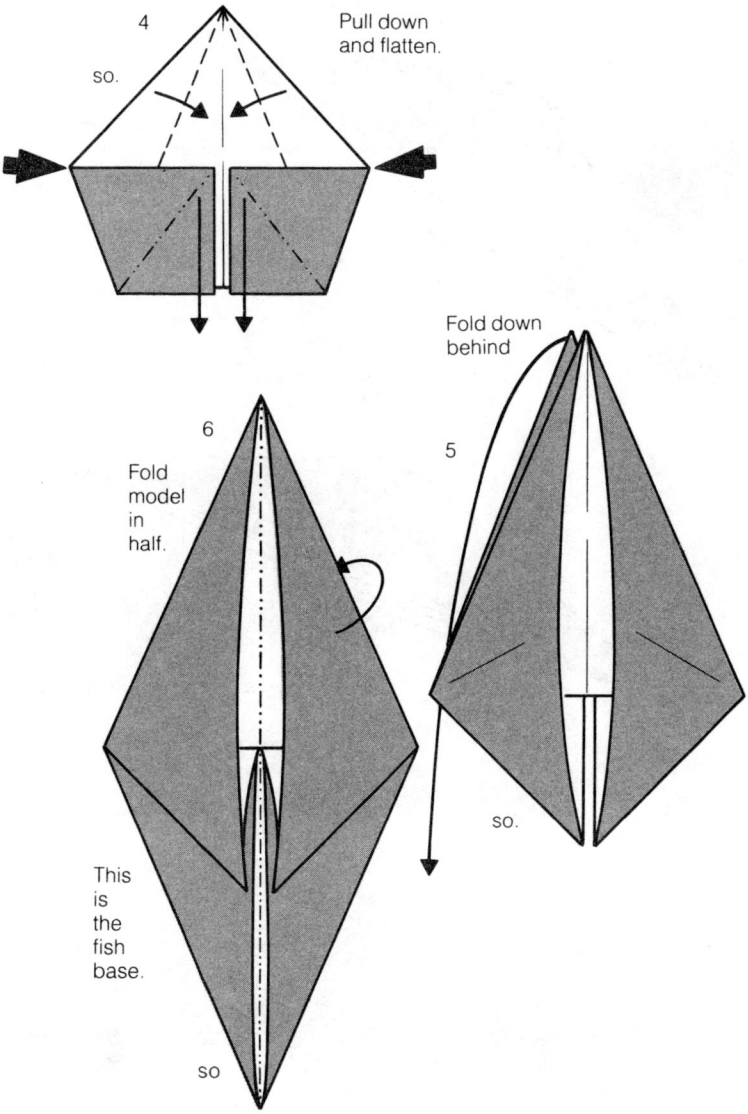
4
Pull down
and flatten.
so.
Fold down
behind
5
so.
6
Fold
model
in
half.
This
is
the
fish
base.
so

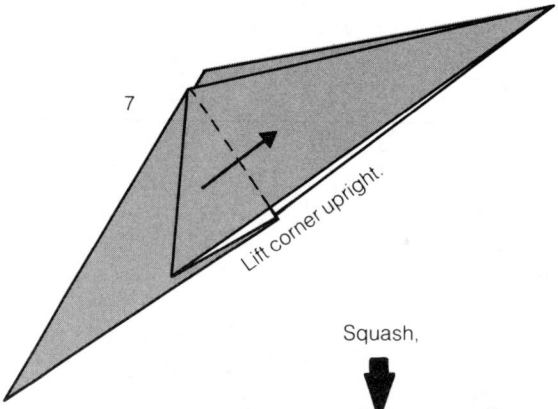
7
Lift corner upright.

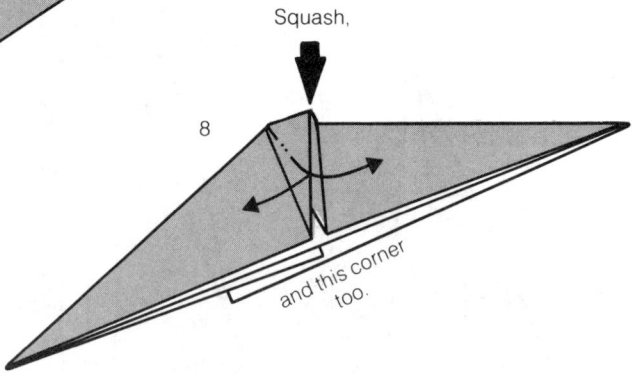
Squash,
8
and this corner
too.

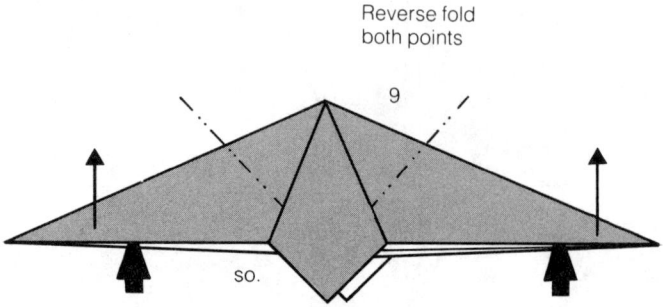
Reverse fold
both points
9
so.

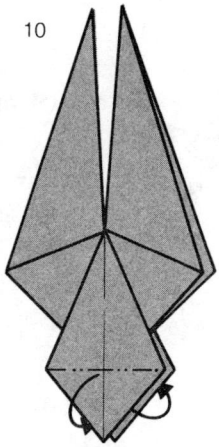
10
Tuck flaps
under and
in

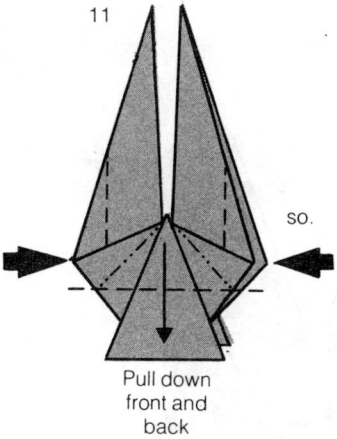
11
so.
Pull down
front and
back

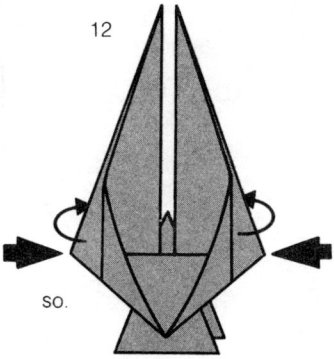
12
so.

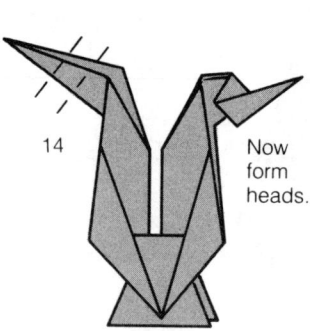
14
Now form heads.

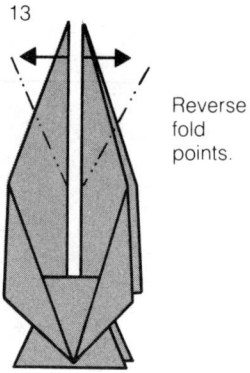
13
Reverse fold points.

PENGUIN 1 *Eric Bird, Leicester, England*

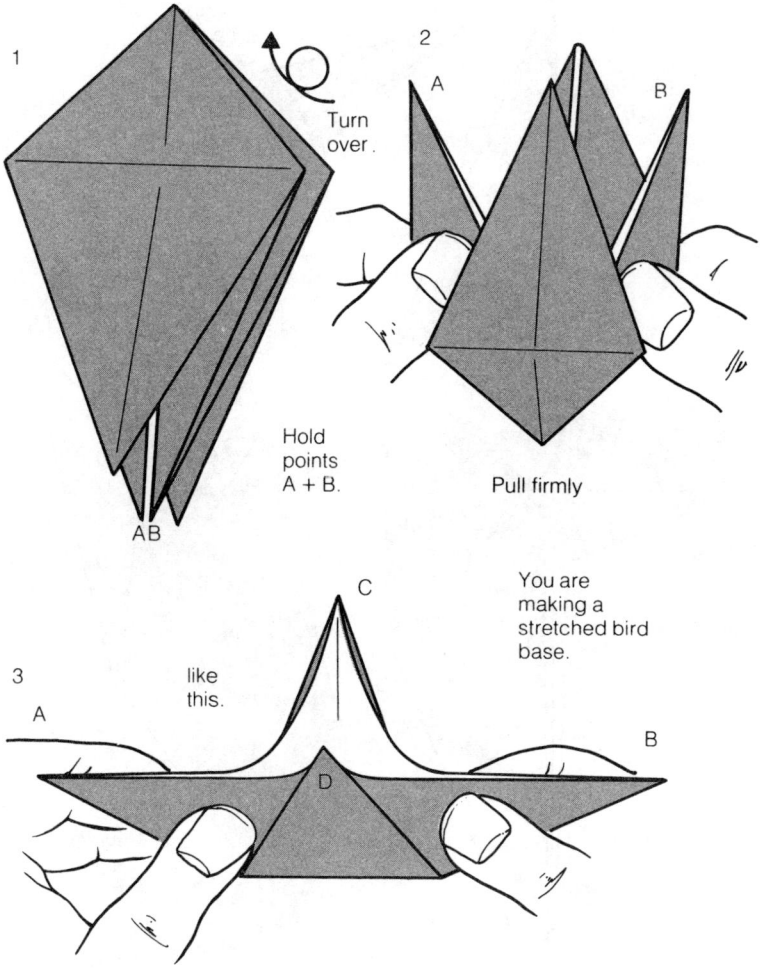

Bring C + D together and press flat.

PENGUIN 1 *This is a stretched Bird Base*

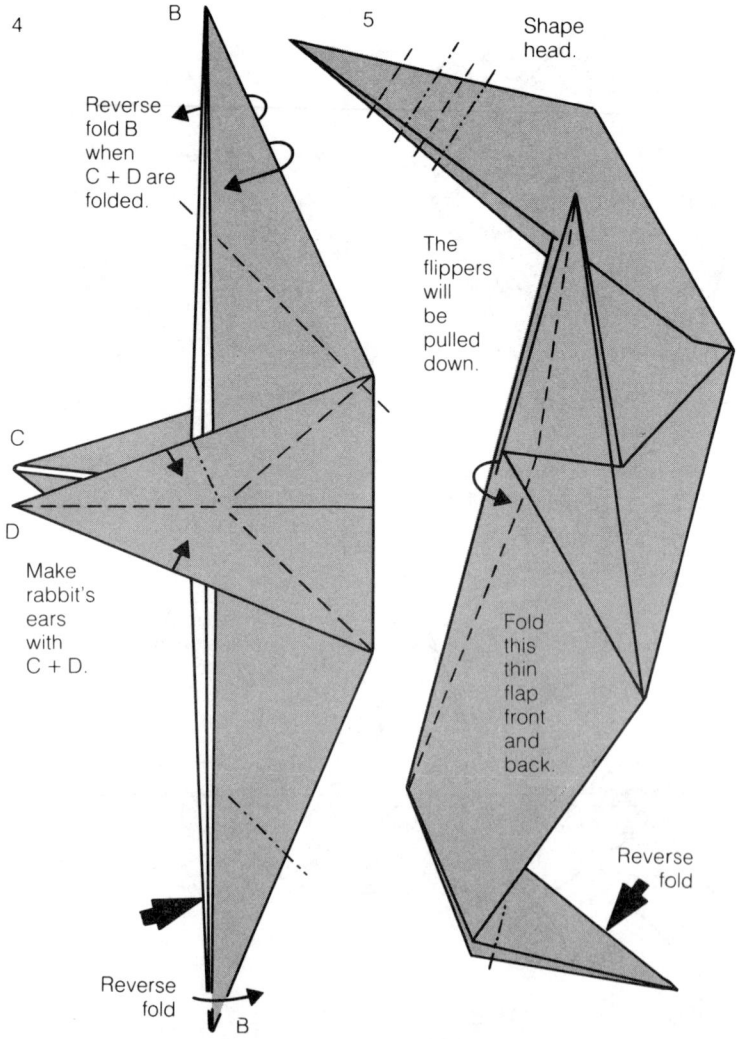

6

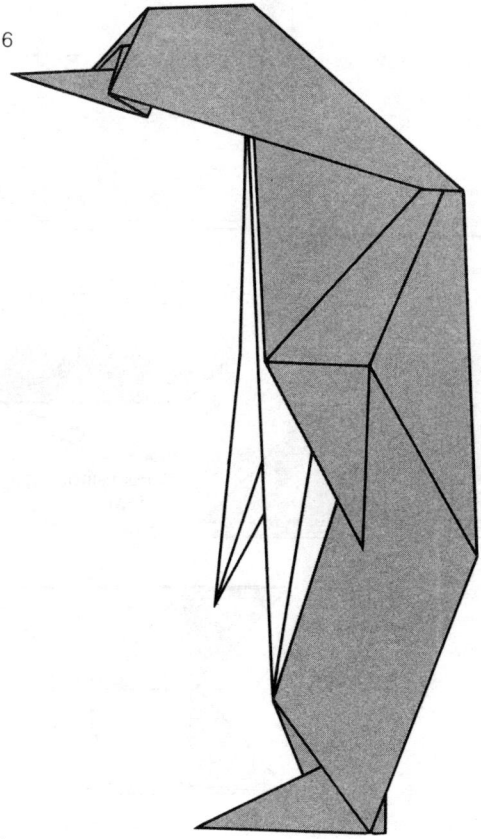

PENGUIN 2 *Robert Harbin, London*

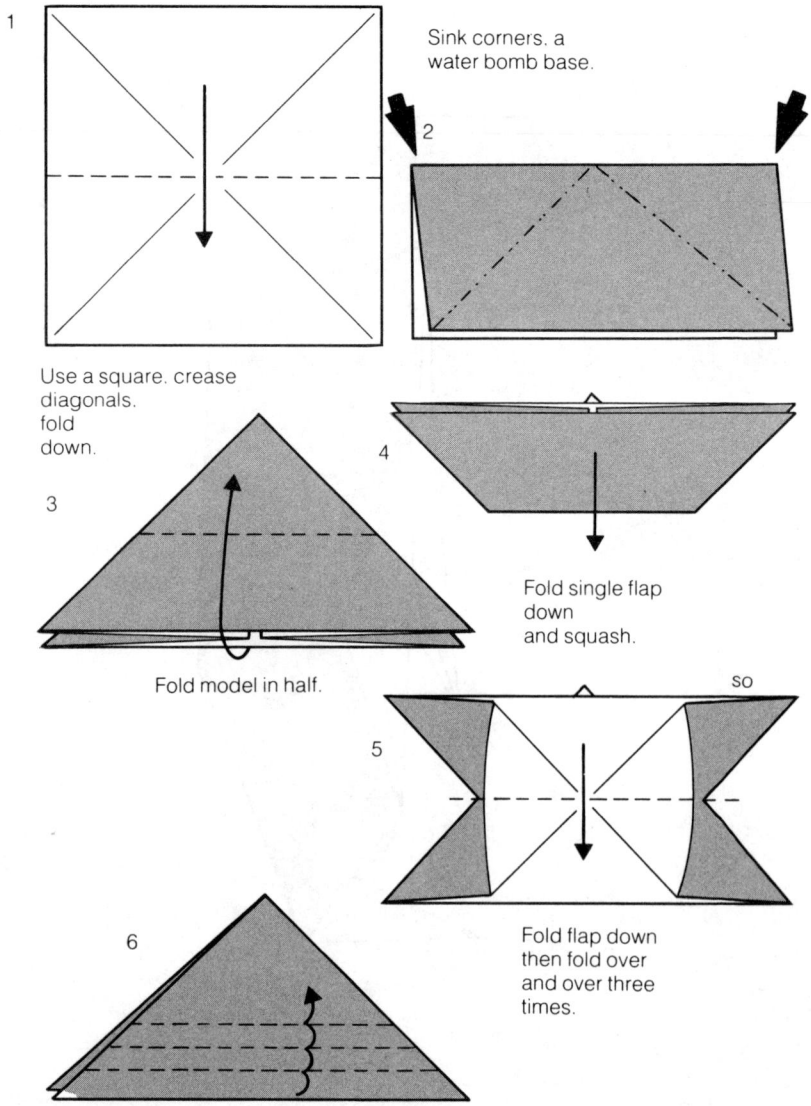

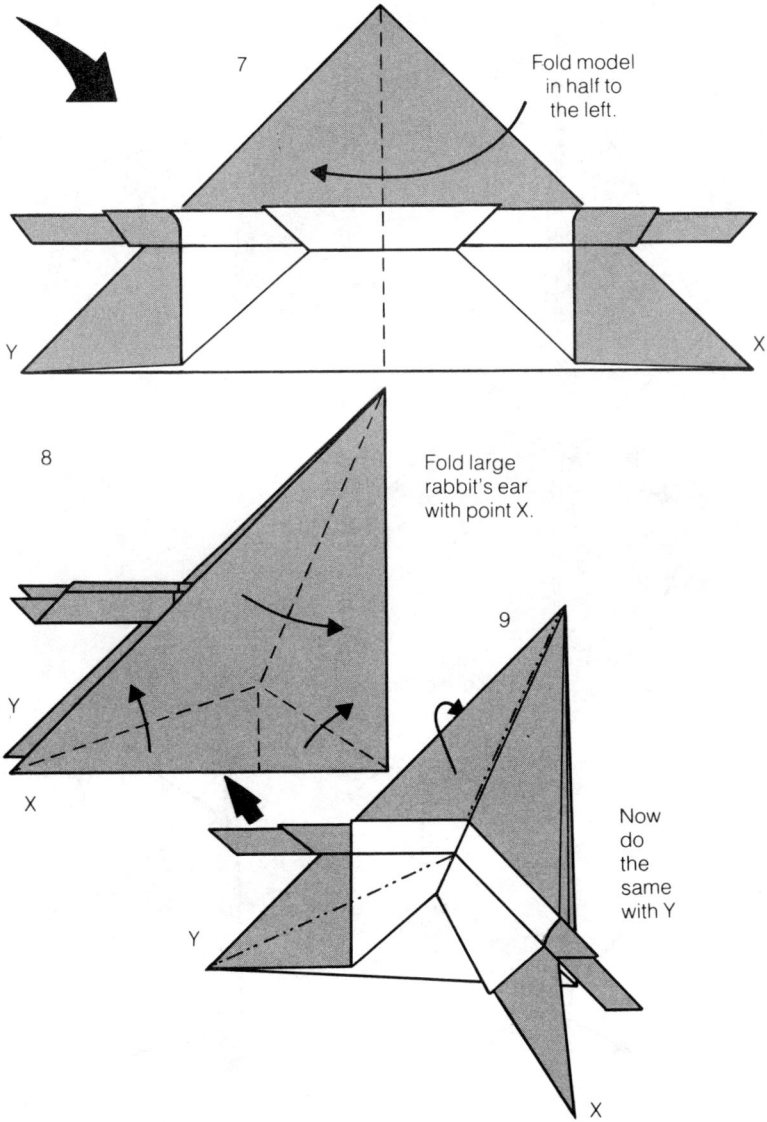
7
Fold model in half to the left.
Y
X
8
Fold large rabbit's ear with point X.
Y
X
9
Now do the same with Y
Y
X

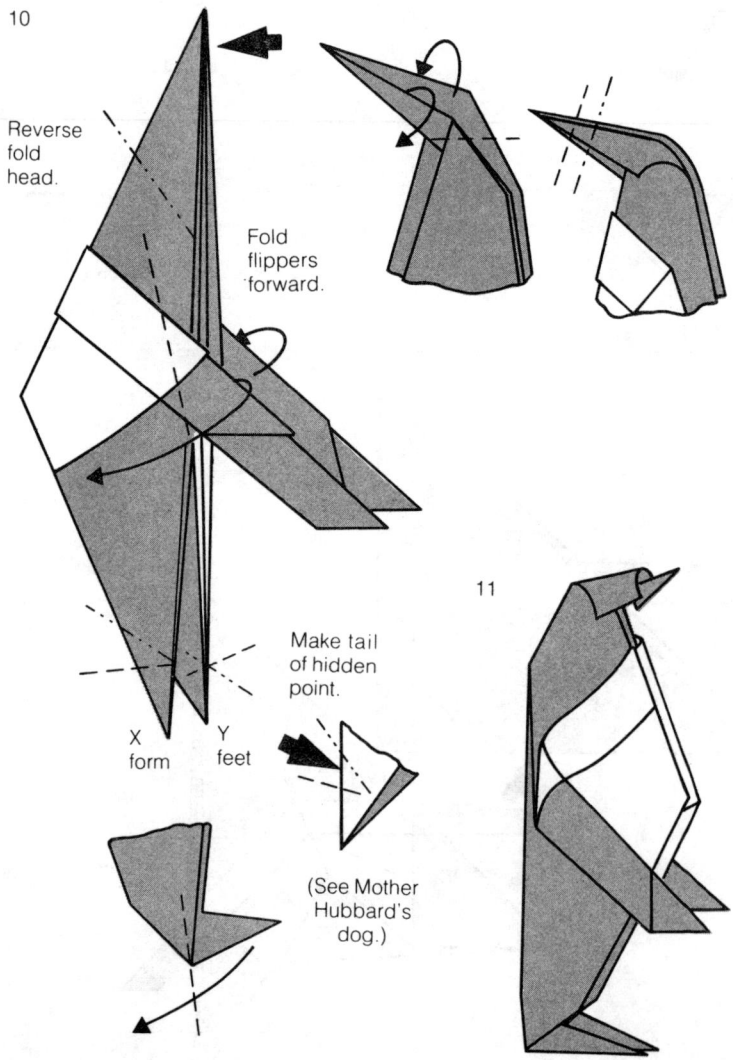
10
Reverse fold head.
Fold flippers forward.
Make tail of hidden point.
X form
Y feet
(See Mother Hubbard's dog.)
11

RABBIT *Michael P. Guy, Birmingham, England*

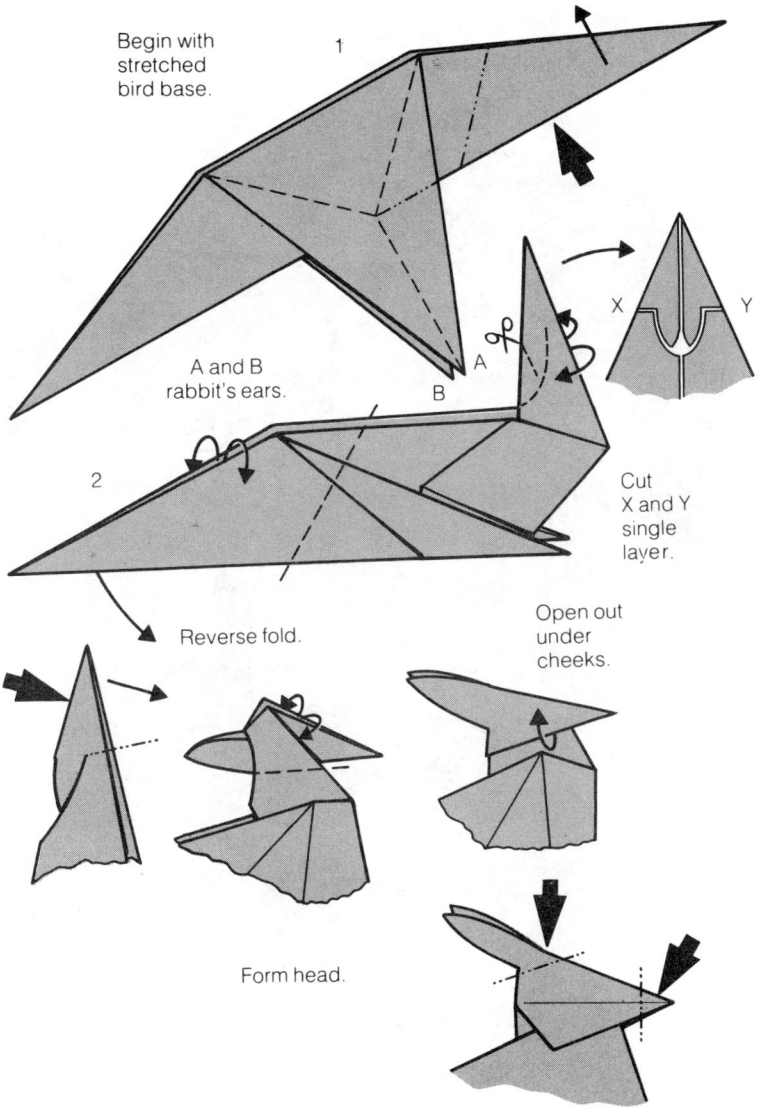

RABBIT *Using stretched Bird Base (see Penguin 1)*

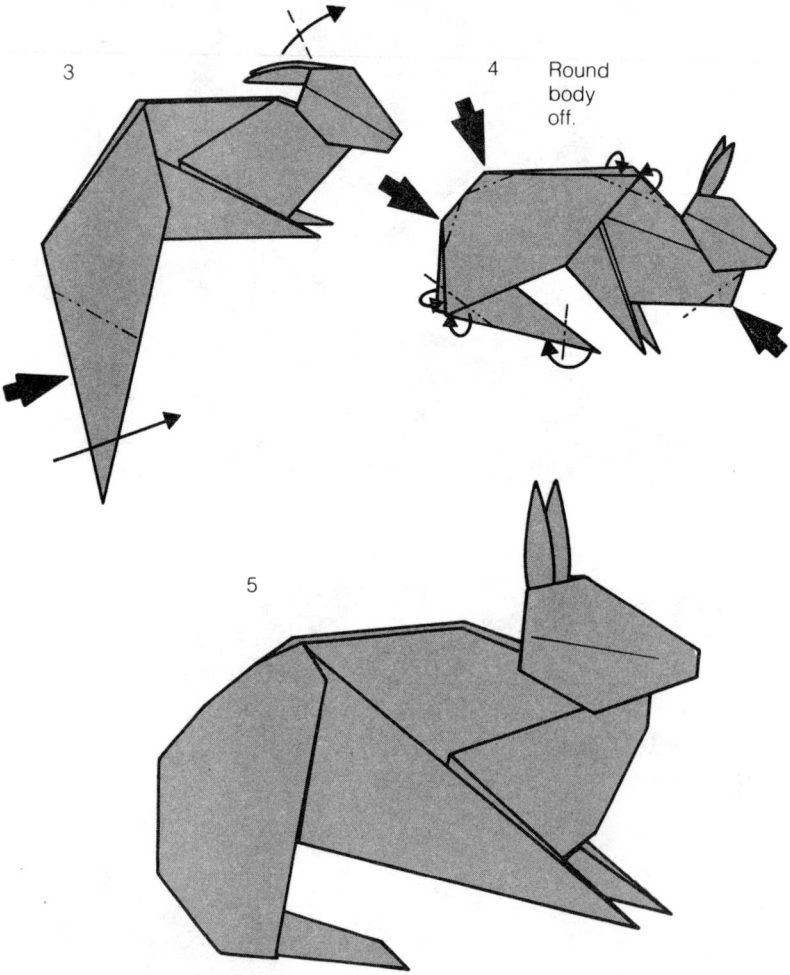

TROPICAL BIRD 1 *Ligia Montoya, Argentina. Fish Base*

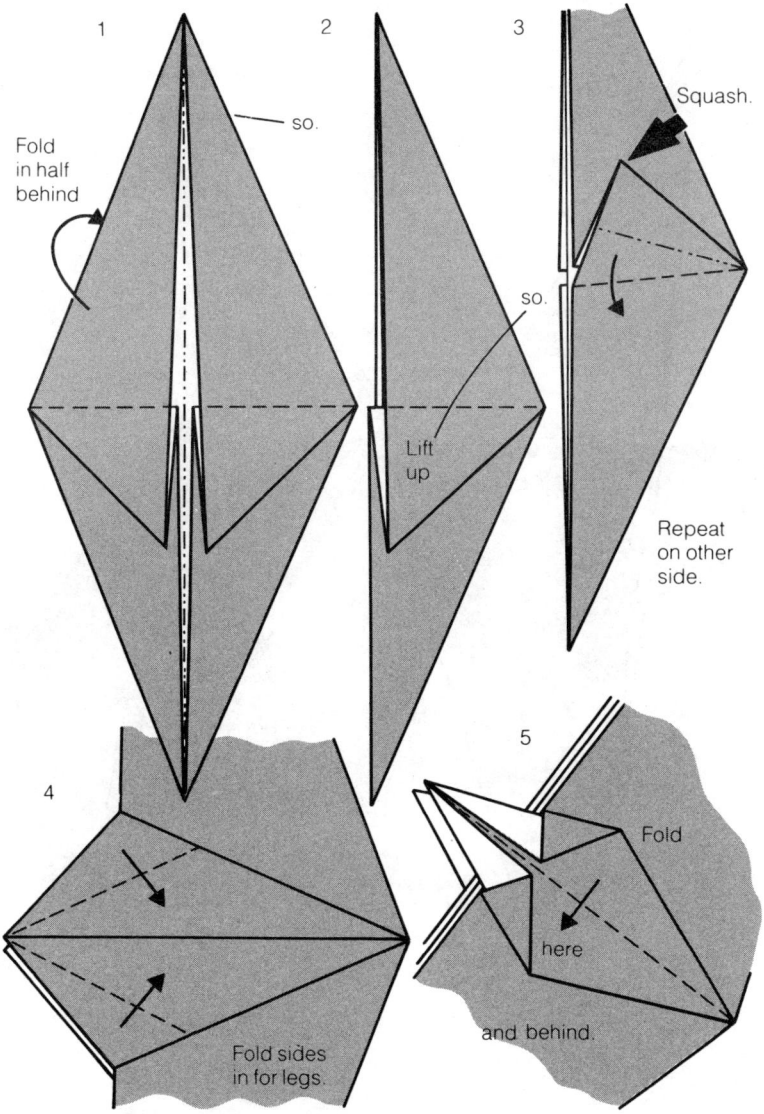

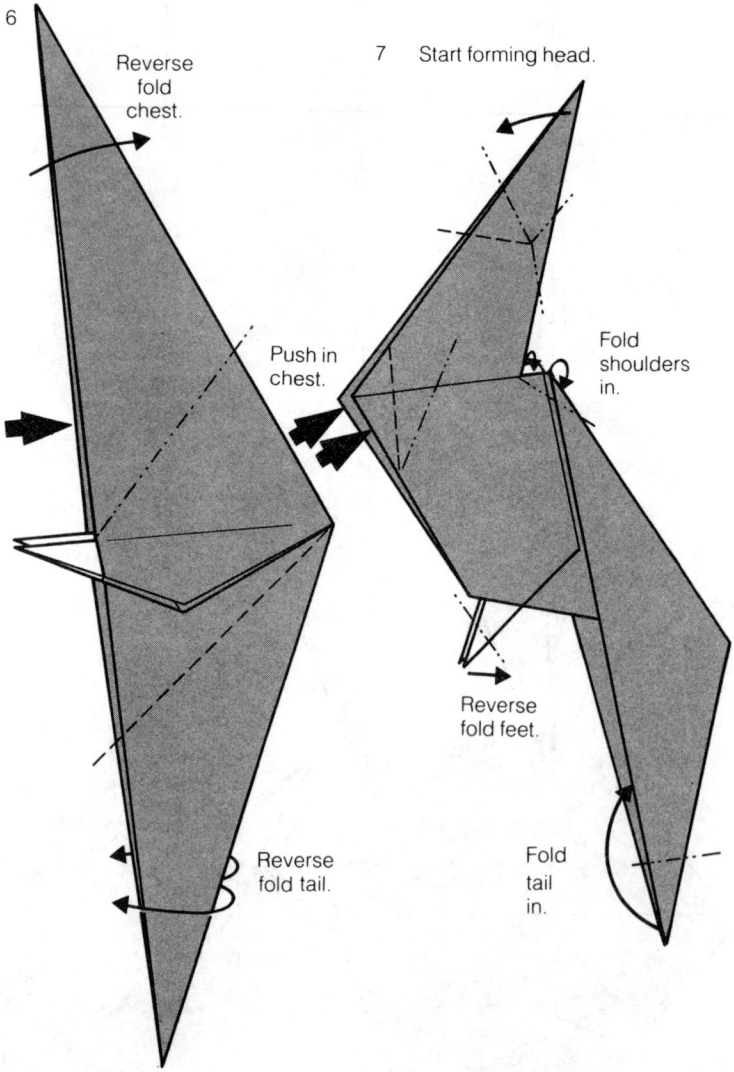
6
Reverse fold chest.
Push in chest.
Reverse fold tail.
7 Start forming head.
Fold shoulders in.
Reverse fold feet.
Fold tail in.

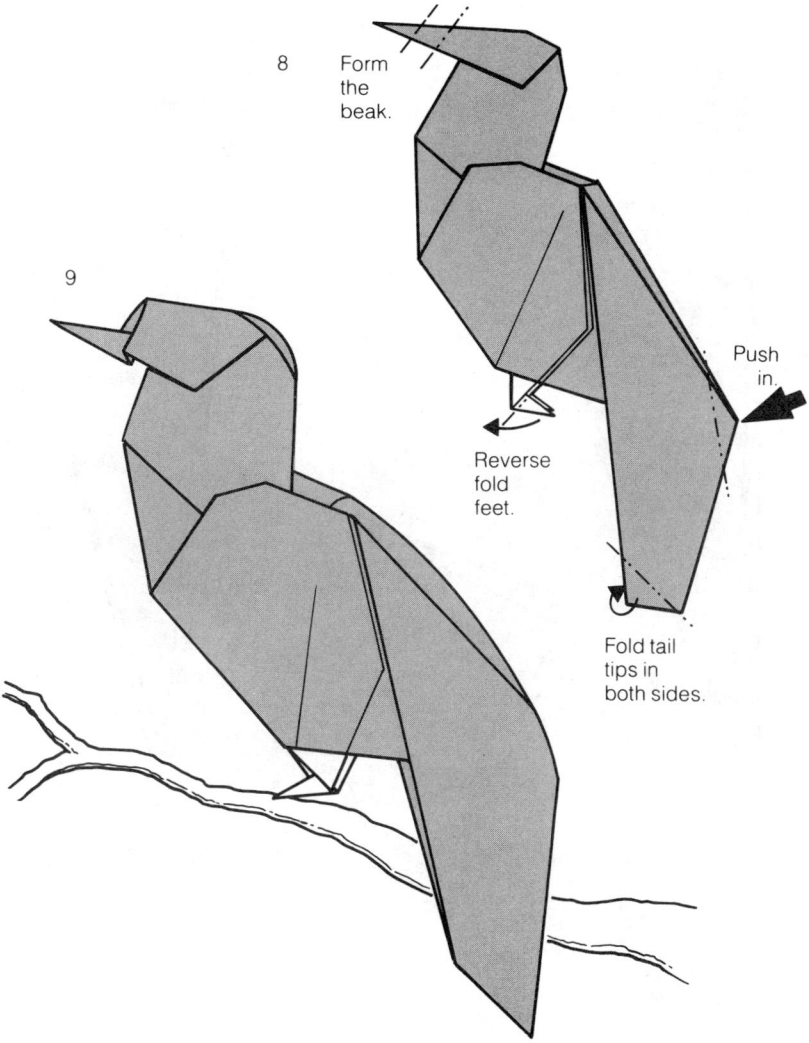
8
Form the beak.
Push in.
Reverse fold feet.
Fold tail tips in both sides.
9

TROPICAL BIRD 2 *Ligia Montoya. Fish Base again*

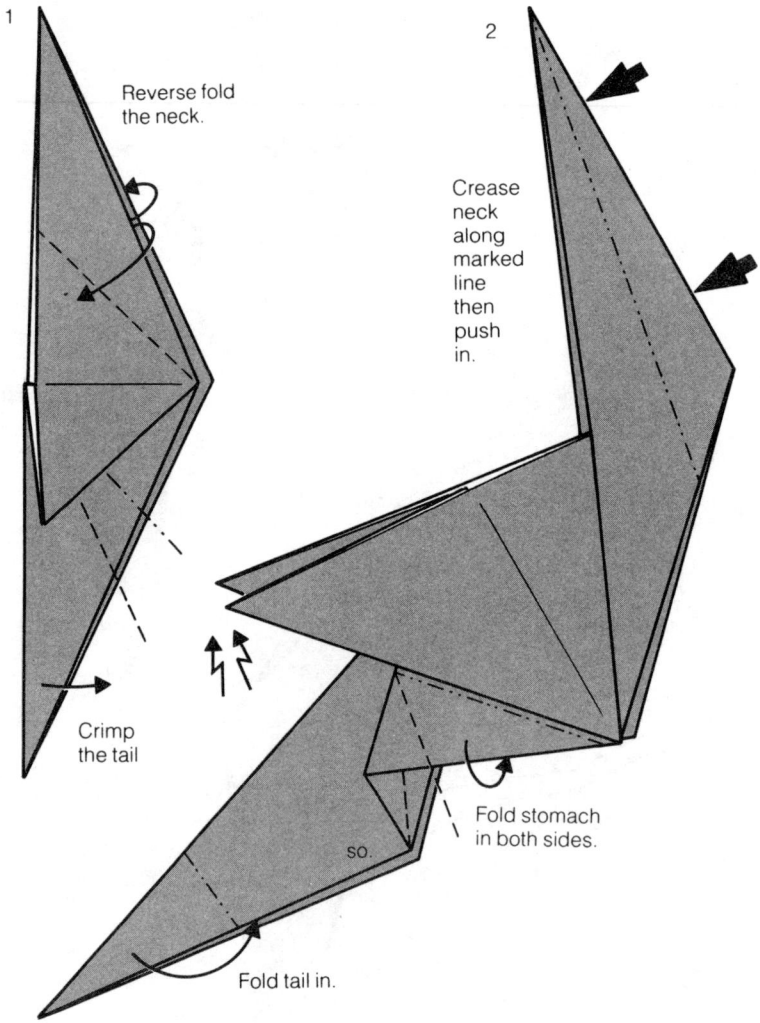

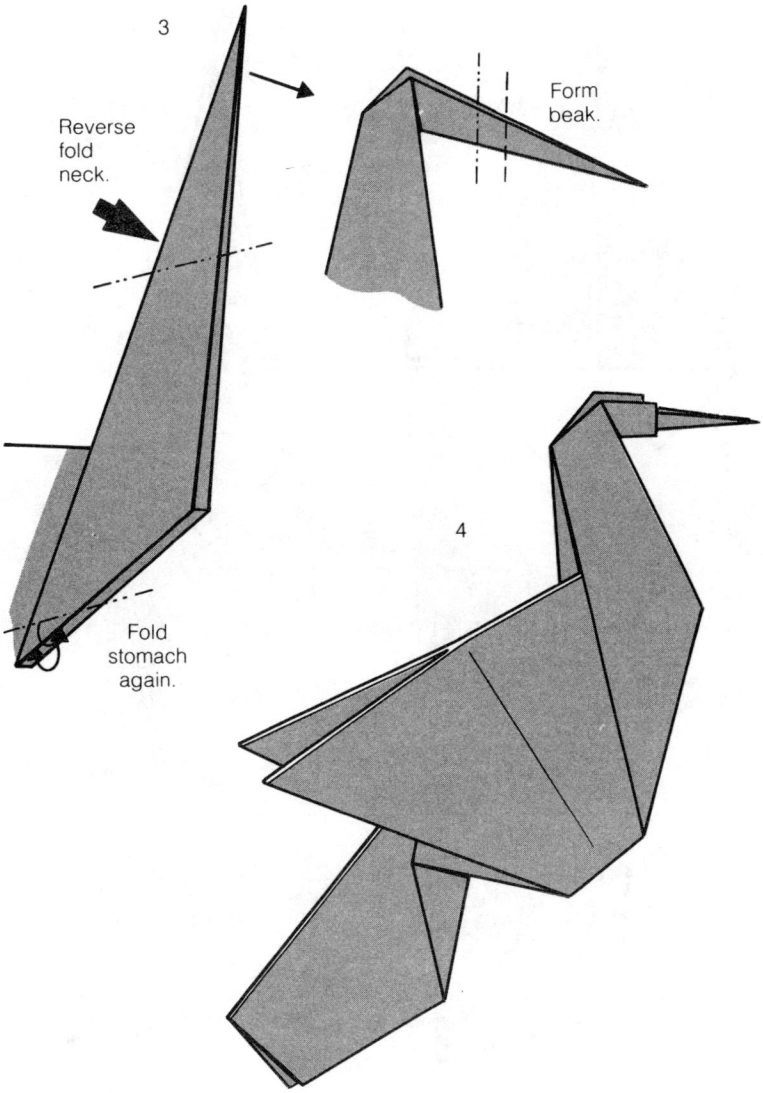
3
Reverse fold neck.
Fold stomach again.
Form beak.
4

XMAS TREE *Robert Harbin, London*

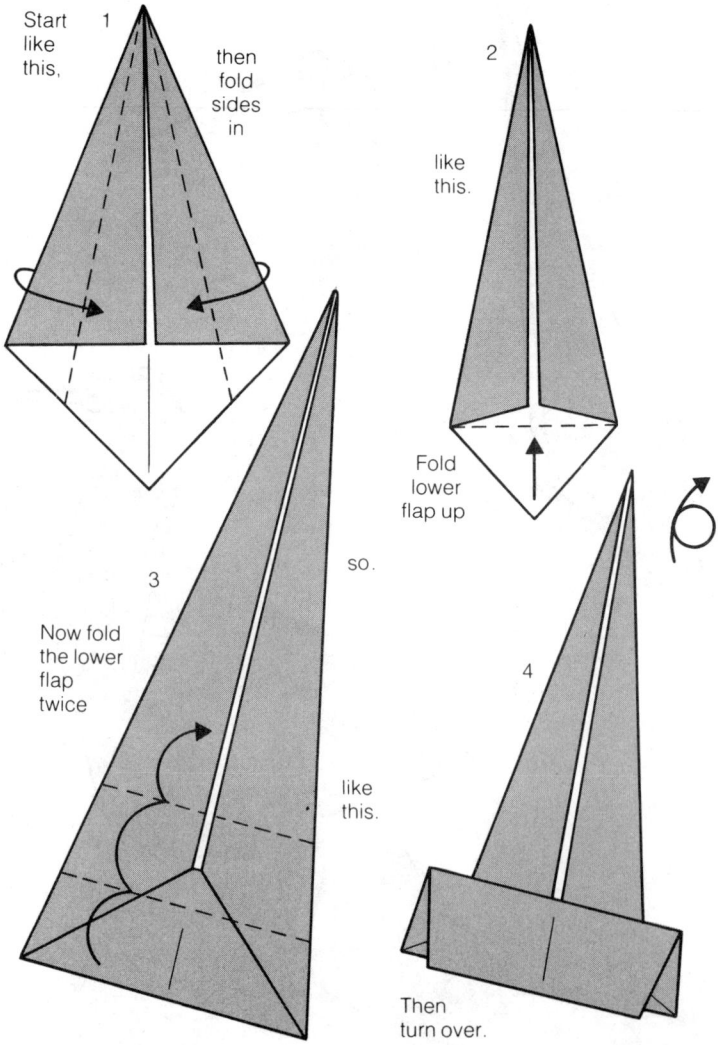

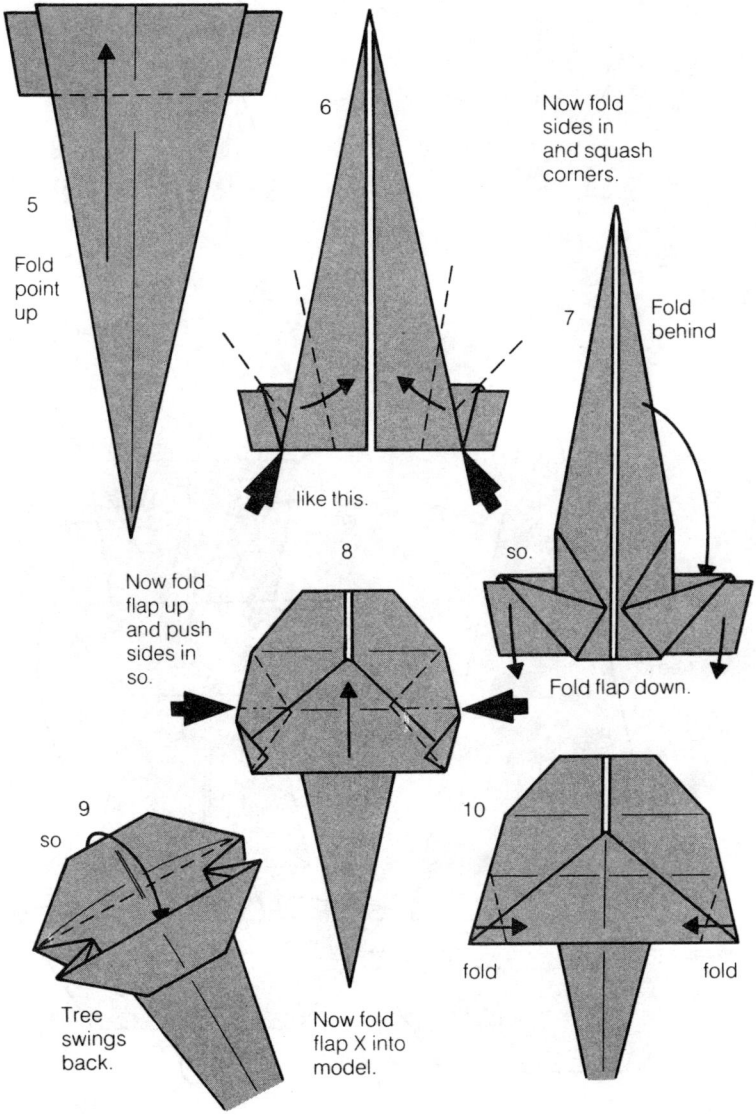
5
Fold point up
6
like this.
Now fold sides in and squash corners.
7
Fold behind
so.
Fold flap down.
8
Now fold flap up and push sides in so.
Now fold flap X into model.
9
so
Tree swings back.
10
fold
fold

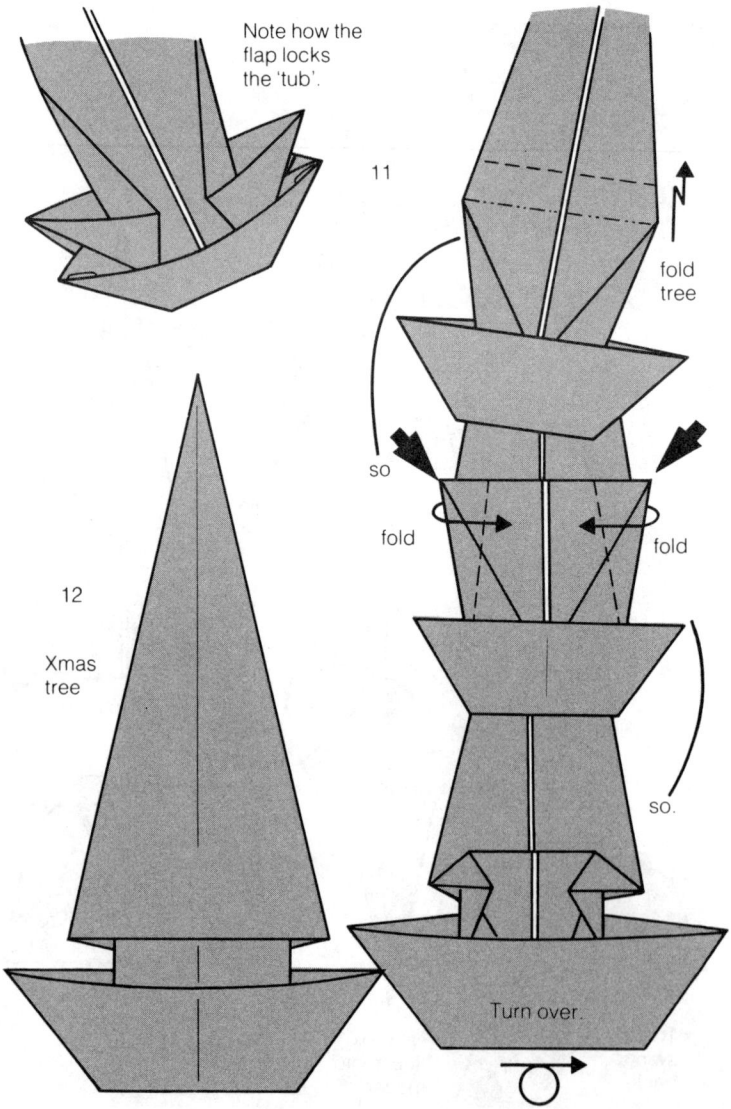
Note how the flap locks the 'tub'.
11
fold tree
so
fold
fold
so.
Turn over.
12
Xmas tree

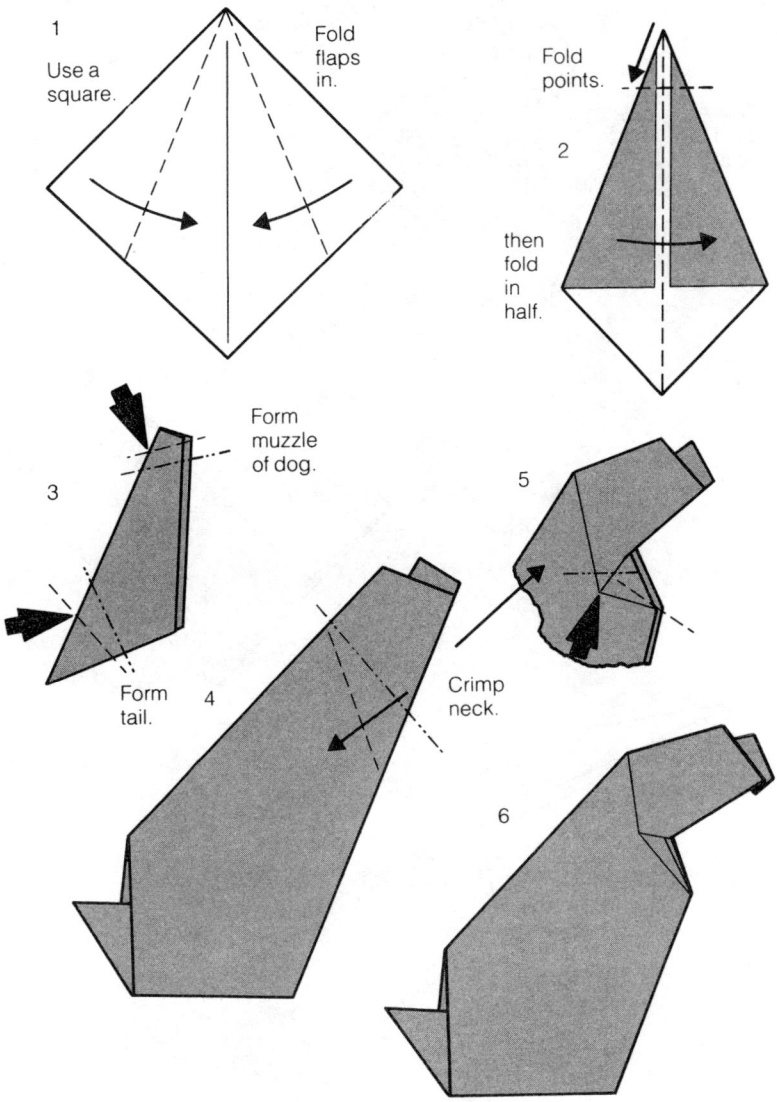
1
Use a square.
Fold flaps in.
Fold points.
2
then fold in half.
Form muzzle of dog.
3
Form tail.
4
5
Crimp neck.
6

MOTHER HUBBARD *Eric Kenneway, London*

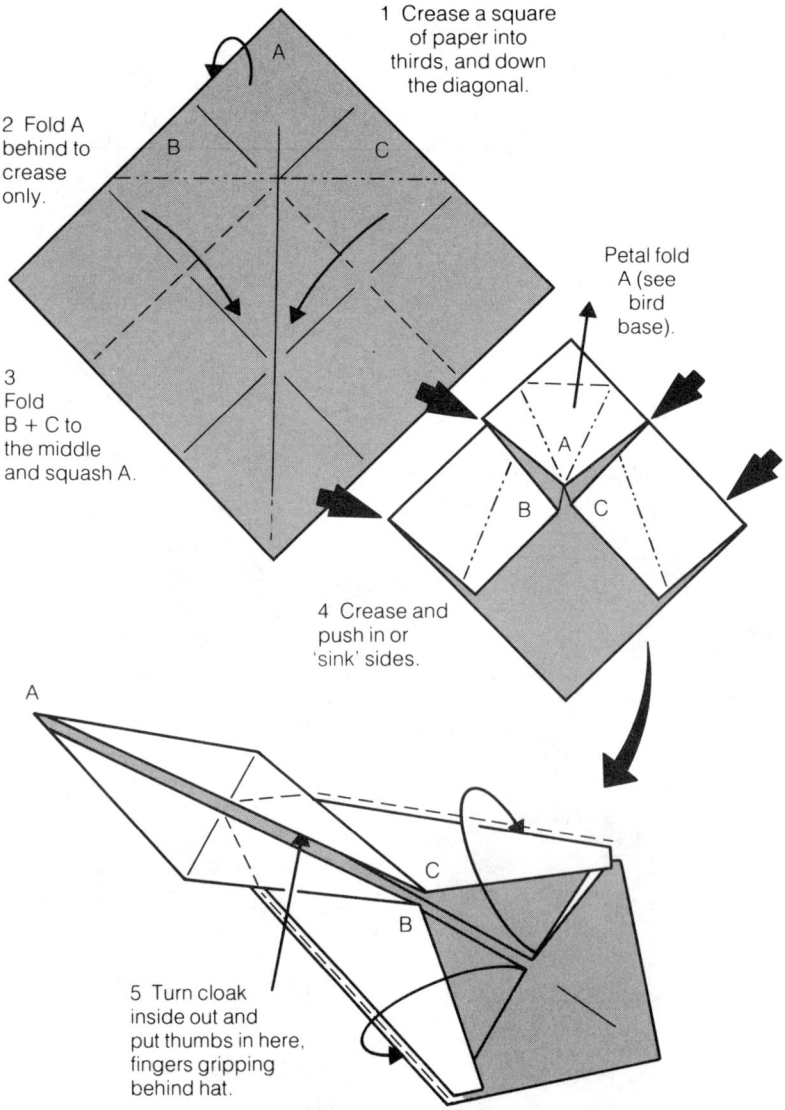

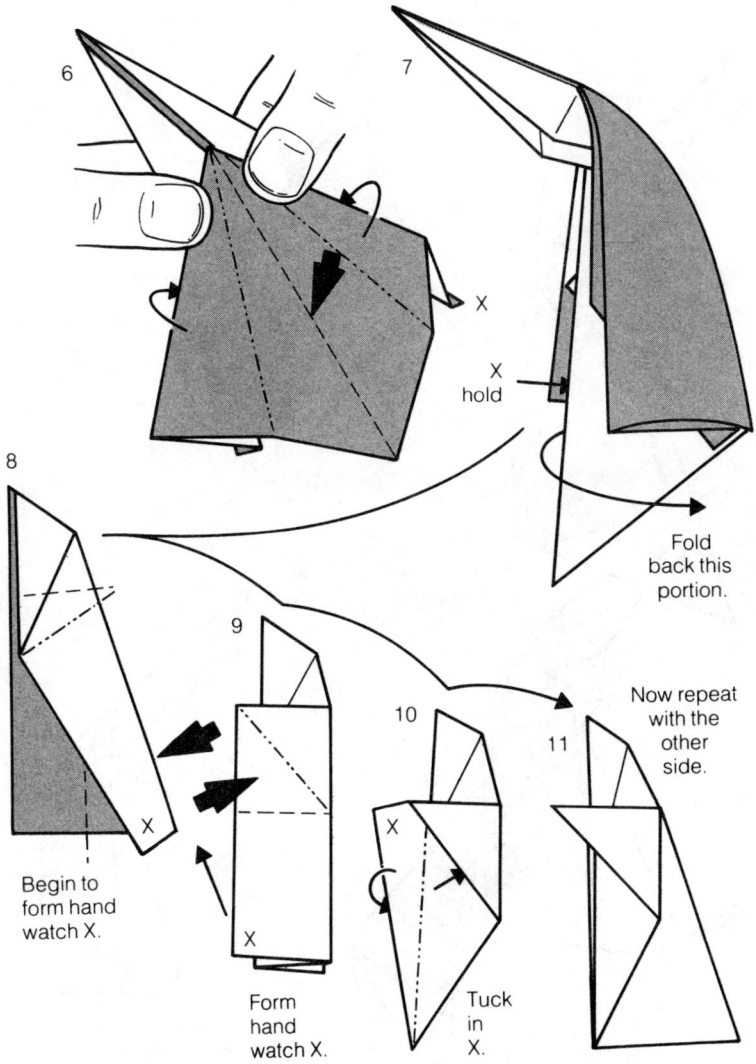
6
7
X
X
hold
Fold
back this
portion.
8
X
Begin to
form hand
watch X.
9
X
Form
hand
watch X.
10
X
Tuck
in
X.
11
Now repeat
with the
other
side.

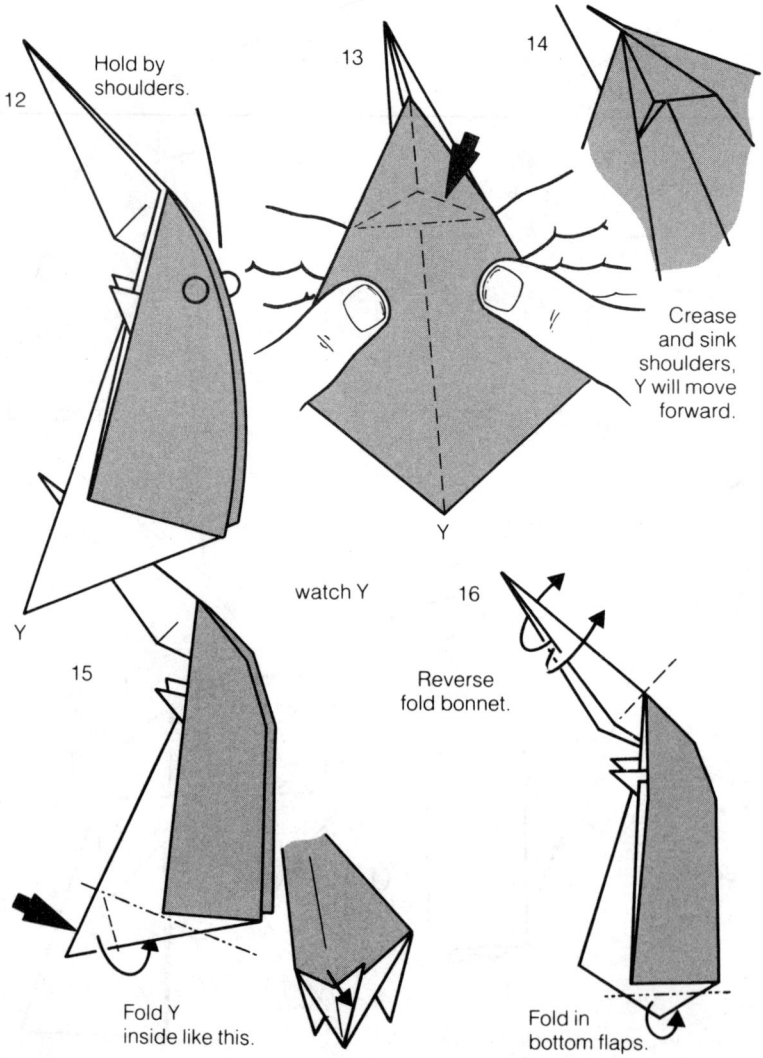
12
Hold by shoulders.
Y
13
Y
14
Crease and sink shoulders, Y will move forward.
watch Y
15
Fold Y inside like this.
16
Reverse fold bonnet.
Fold in bottom flaps.

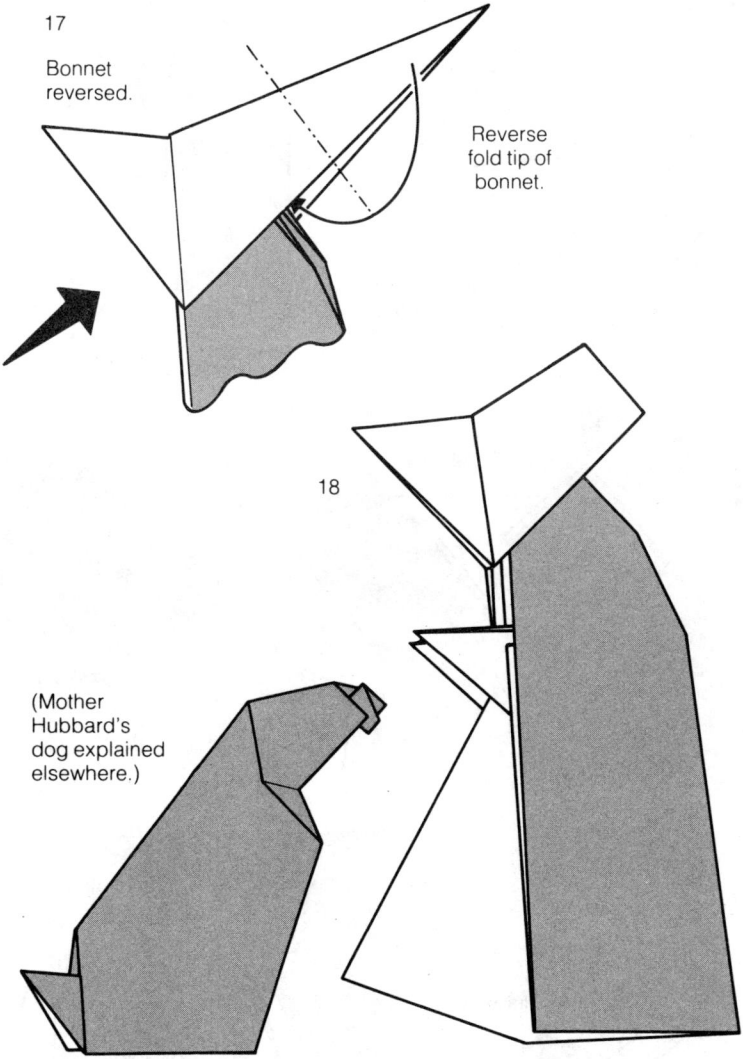
17
Bonnet reversed.
Reverse fold tip of bonnet.
18
(Mother Hubbard's dog explained elsewhere.)

FRIAR TUCK *Eric Kenneway, London*

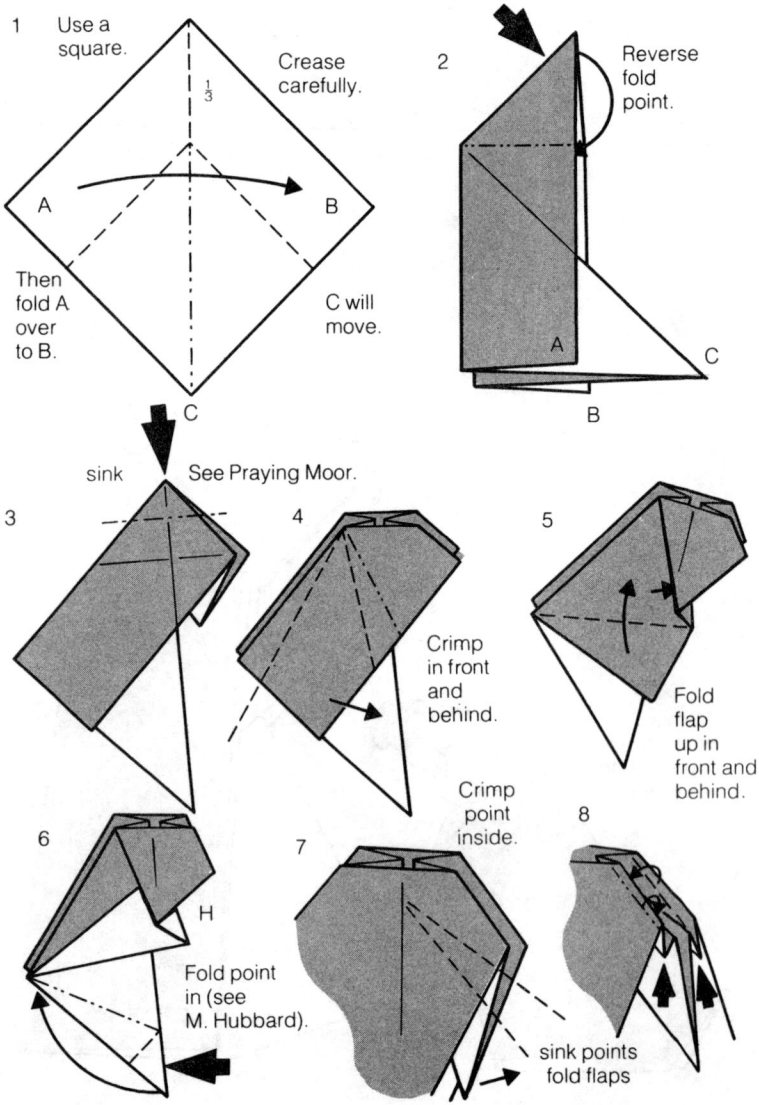

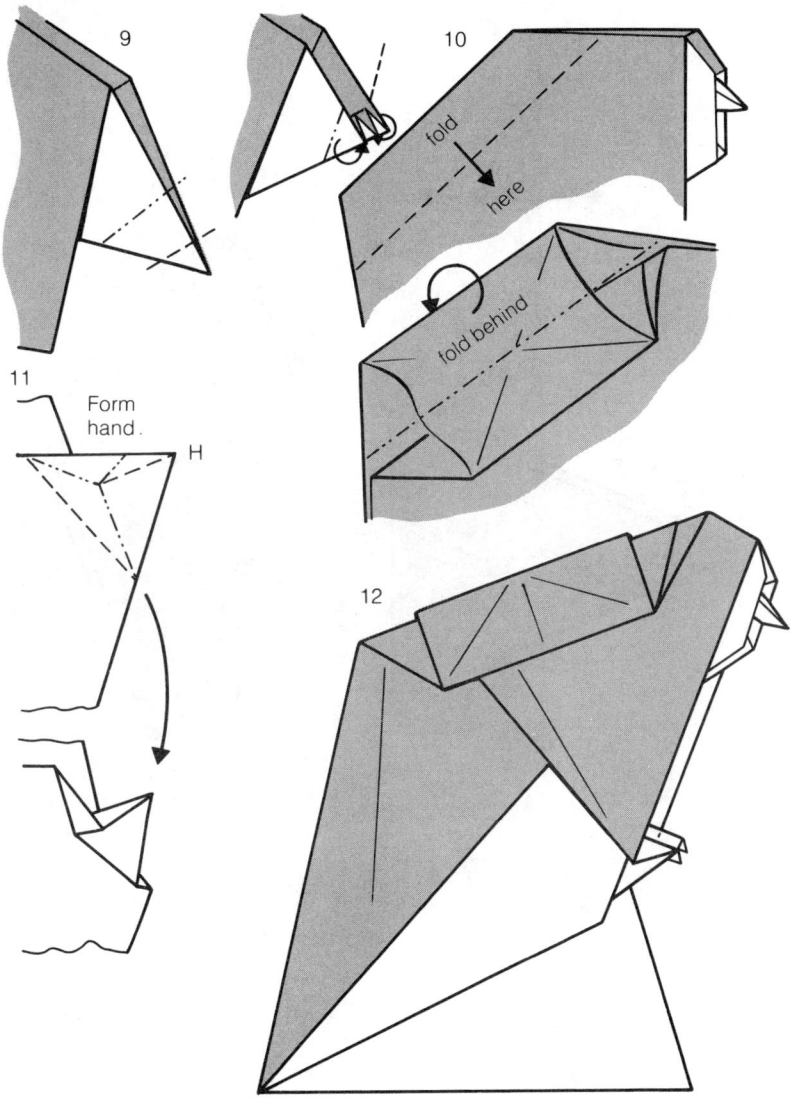
9
10
fold
here
fold behind
11
Form
hand
H
12

SQUIRREL *Merton H. Wolfman, Liverpool, England*

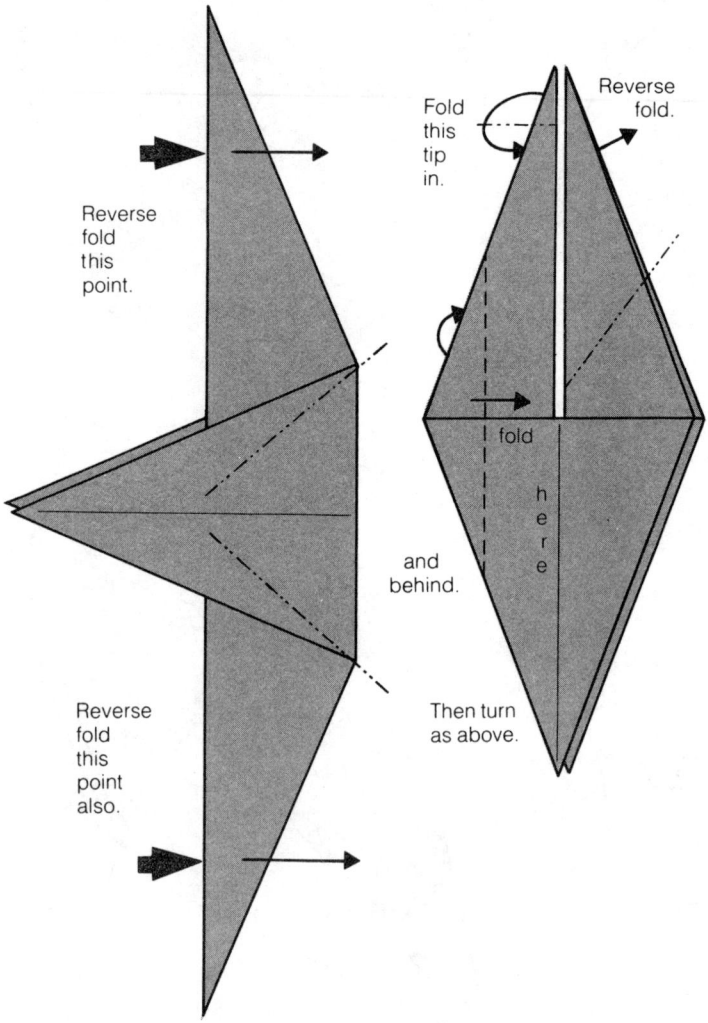

SQUIRREL *Made from the stretched Bird Base*

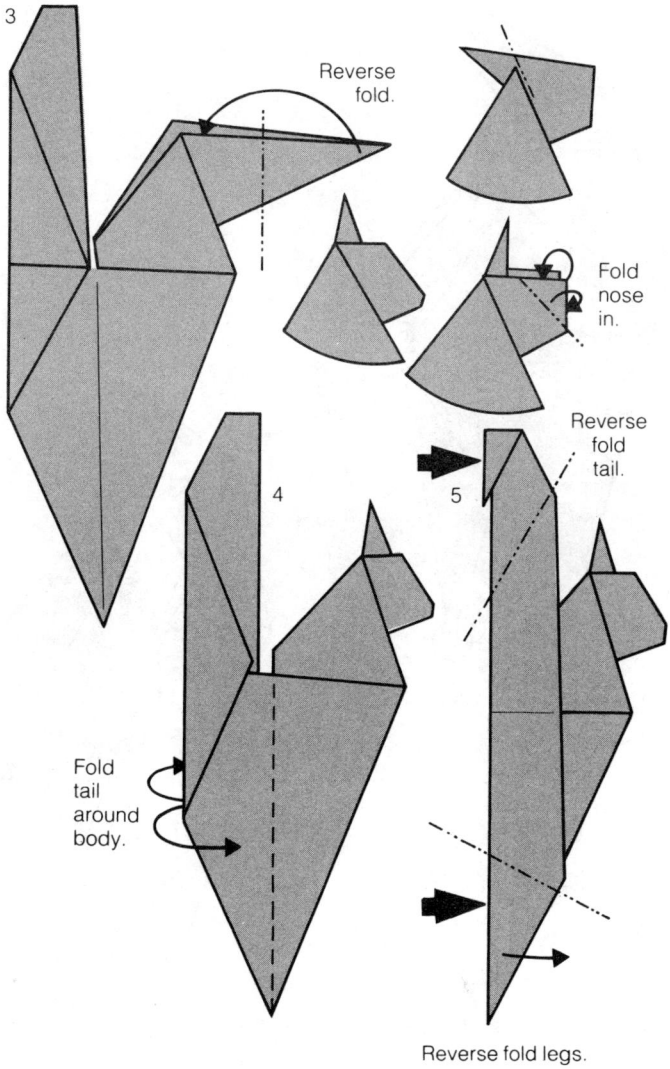

6

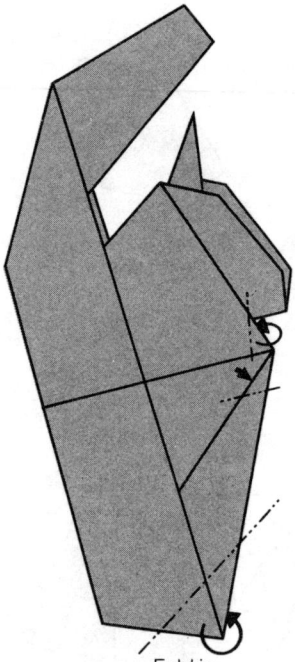

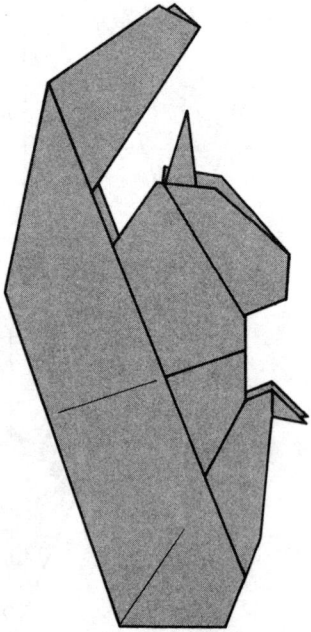

PRINTER'S HAT *Al Koenig and Mike Modrako, USA*

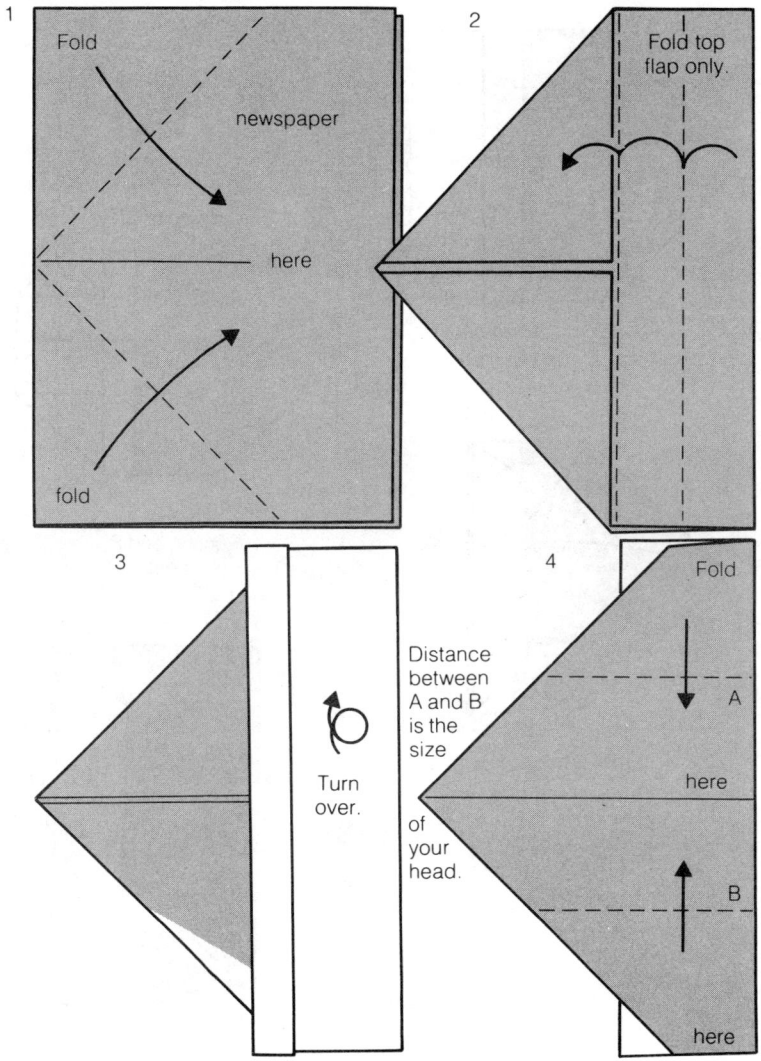

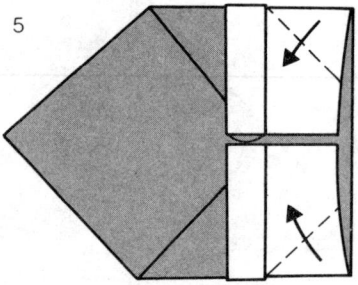
5
Fold corners under.

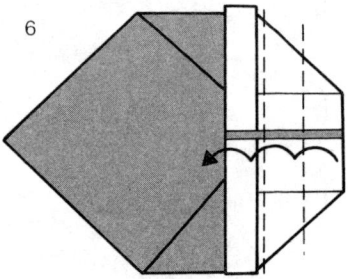
Now fold flap over twice.
6
Open out until A and B meet.

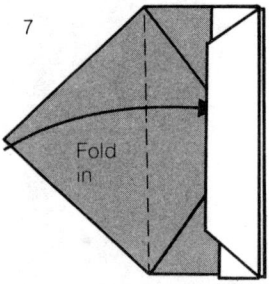
7
Fold in

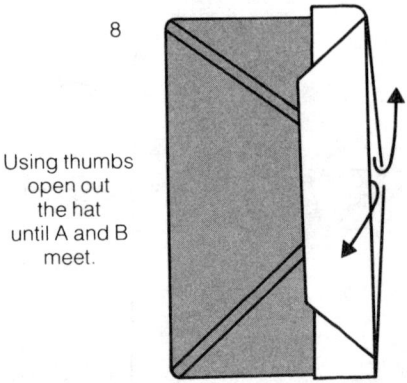
8
Using thumbs open out the hat until A and B meet.

9

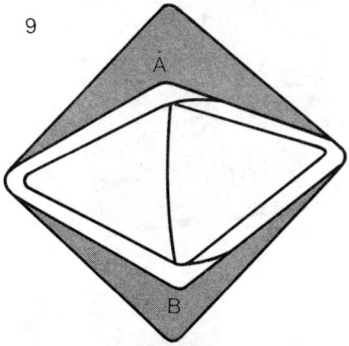

Bring A and B together.

10

Fold in.

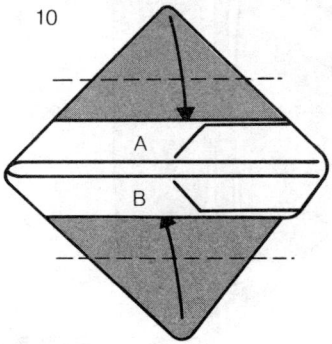

Fold in.

11

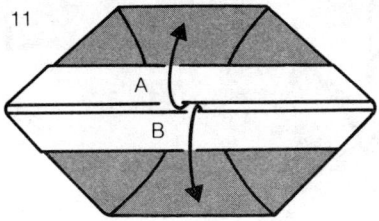

12

Now open out again and put on hat.

DECORATION 1 *Robert Harbin, London, see Multiform*

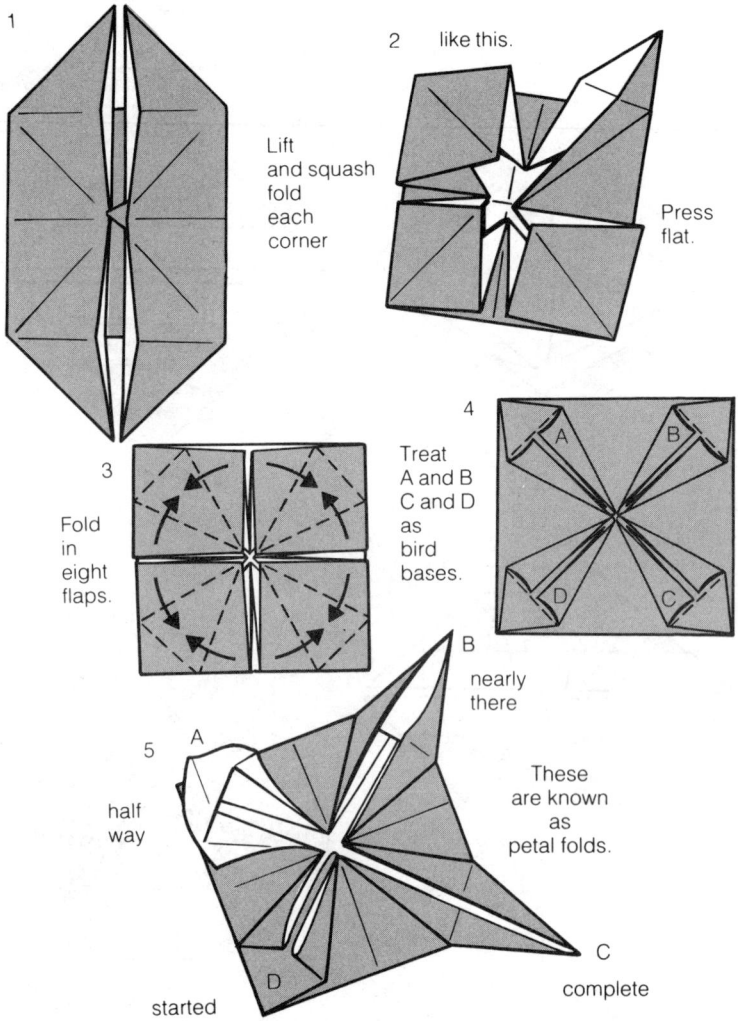

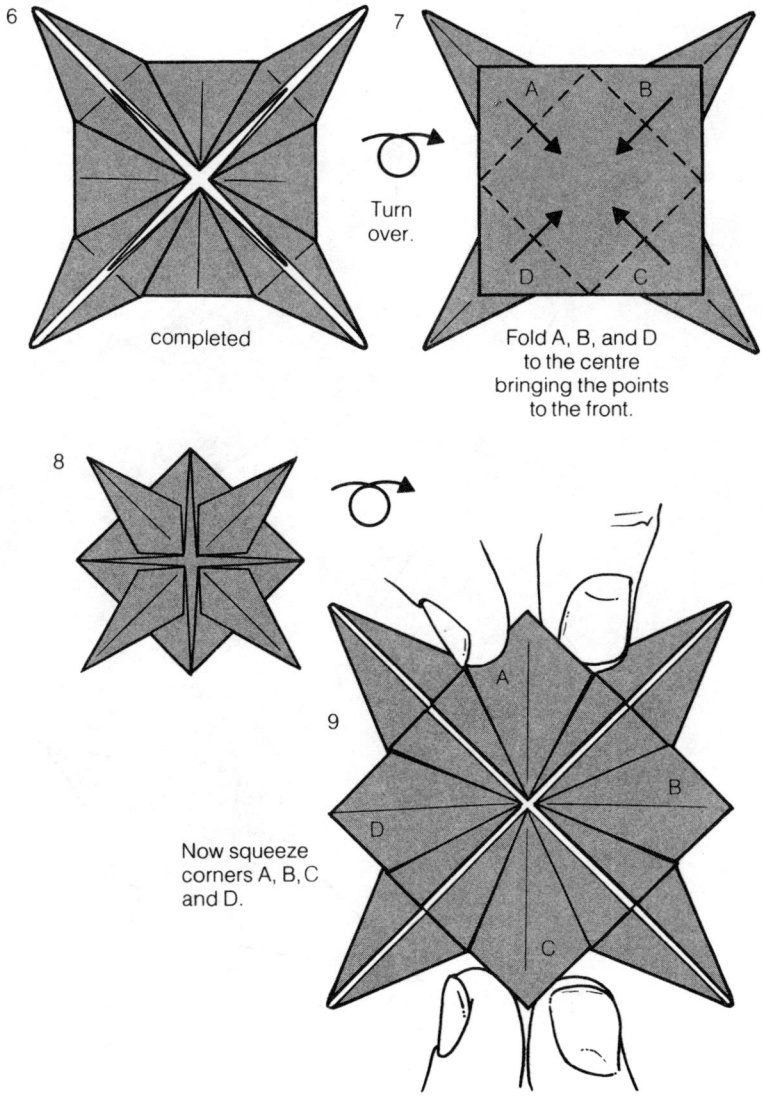
6
completed
7
A
B
D
C
Turn over.
Fold A, B, and D to the centre bringing the points to the front.
8
9
A
B
C
D
Now squeeze corners A, B, C and D.

10

DECORATION 2 *Several Folders discovered this*

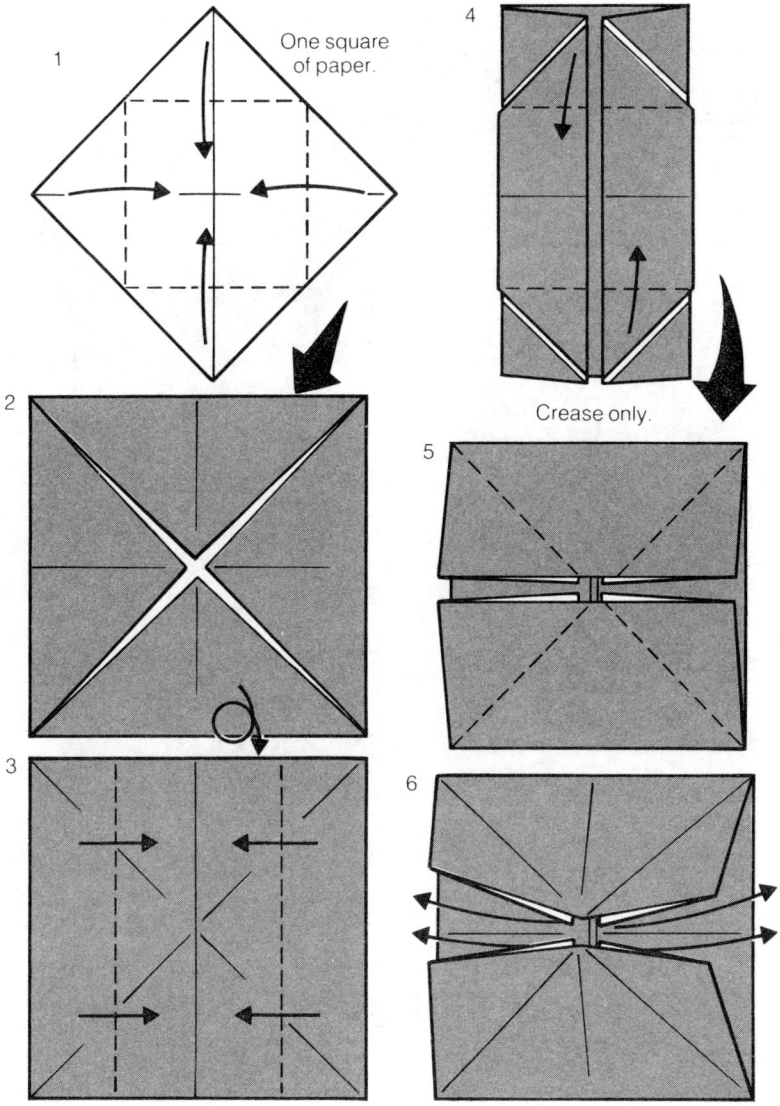

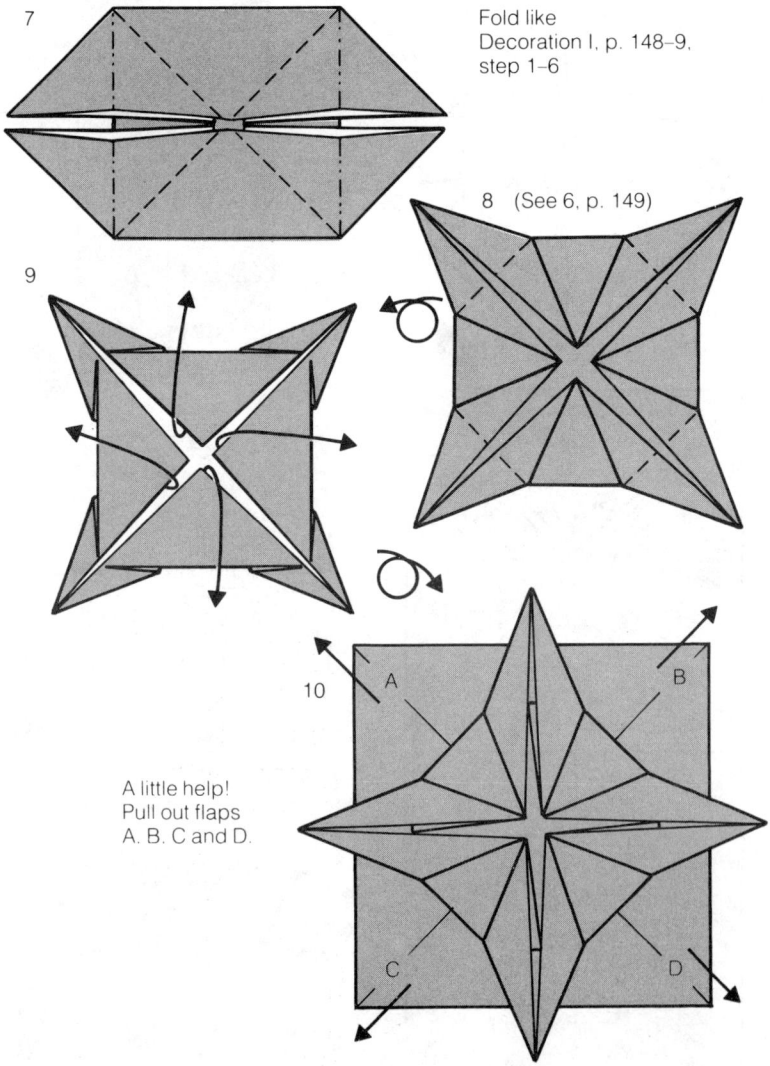
7
Fold like
Decoration I, p. 148–9,
step 1–6
8 (See 6, p. 149)
9
10
A
B
C
D
A little help!
Pull out flaps
A, B, C and D.

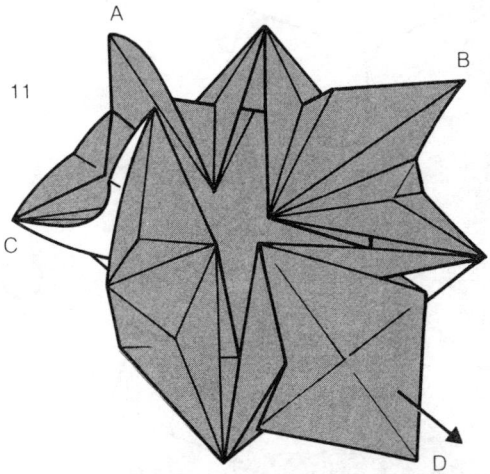
A
B
11
C
D

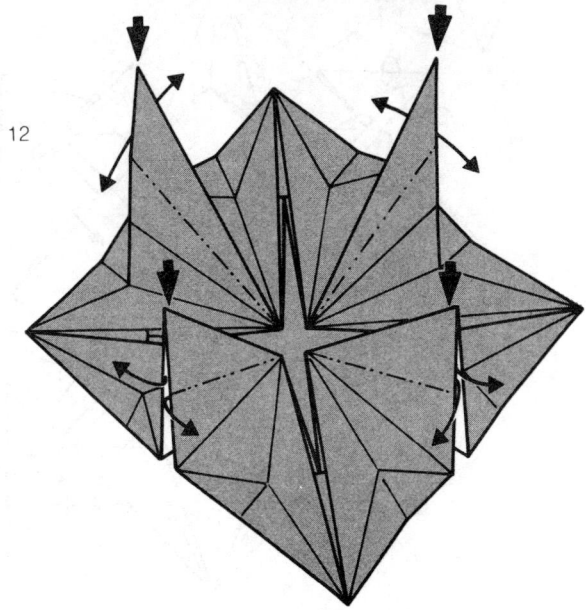
12

13

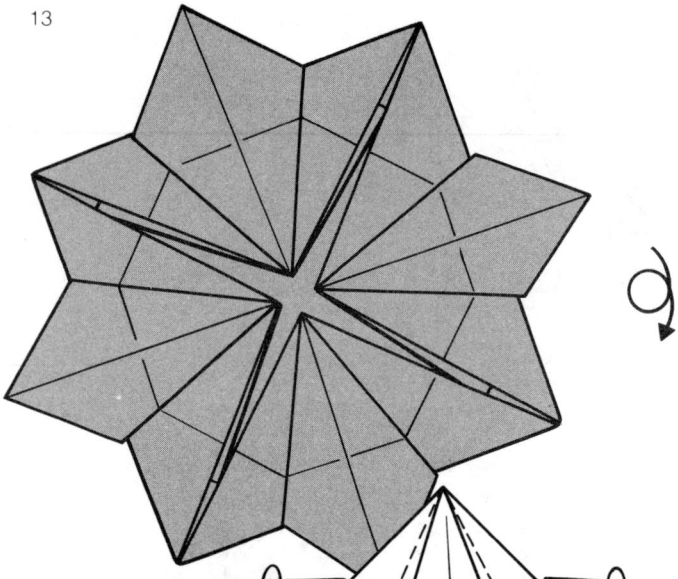

14

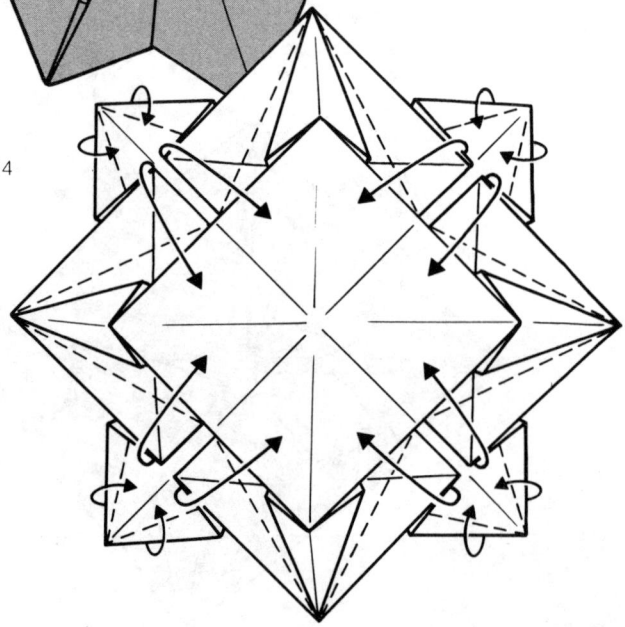

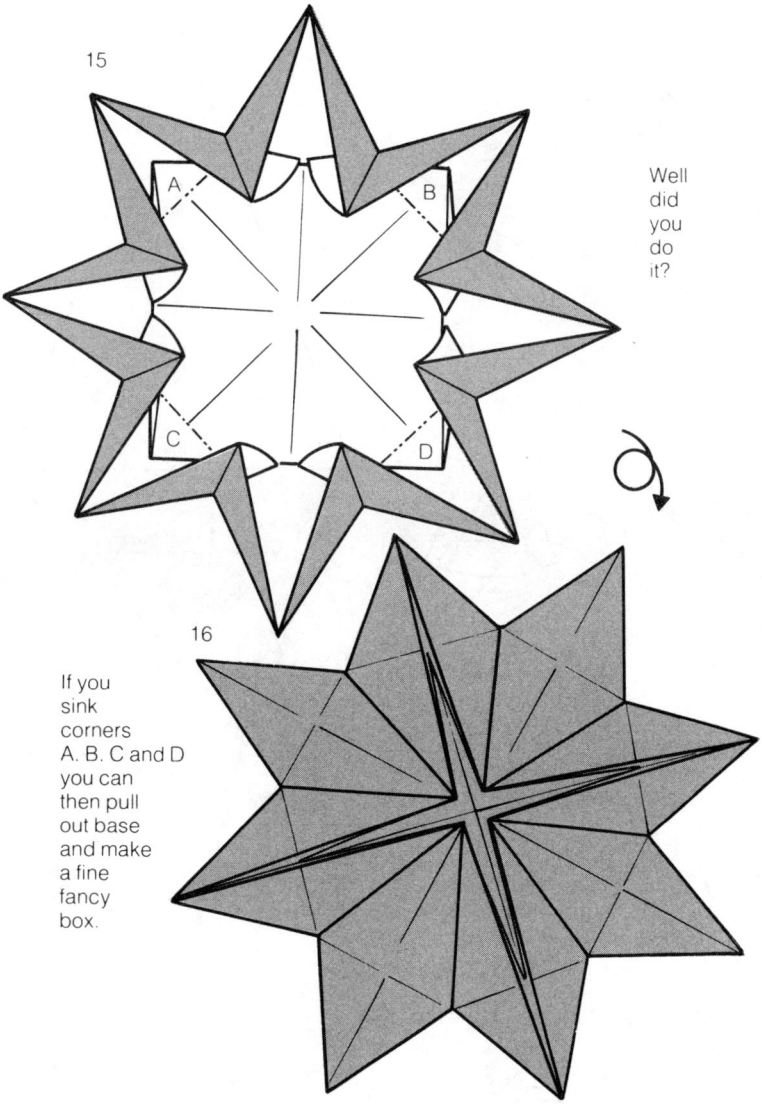
15
A
B
C
D
Well did you do it?
16
If you sink corners A. B. C and D you can then pull out base and make a fine fancy box.

JAPANESE GENTLEMAN *Robert Harbin, London*

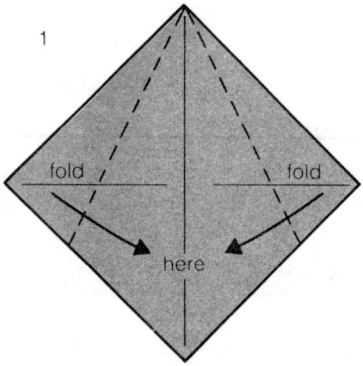

Make diagonal creases.

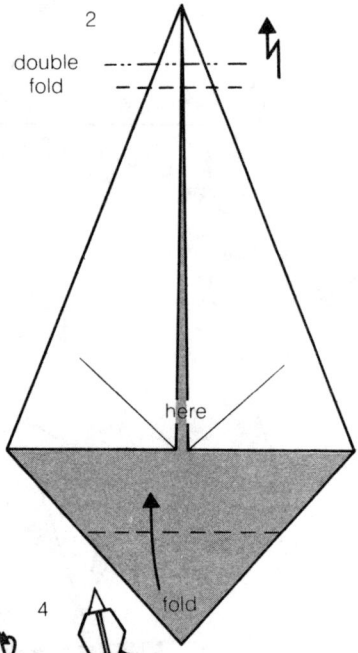

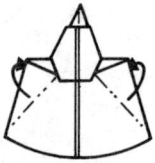

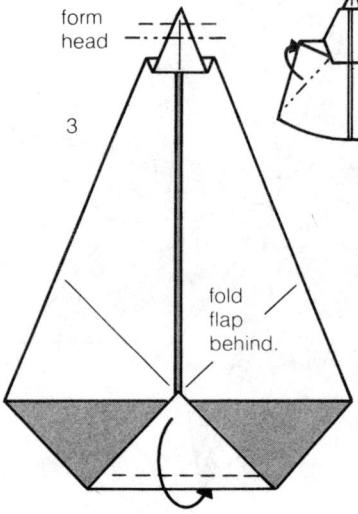

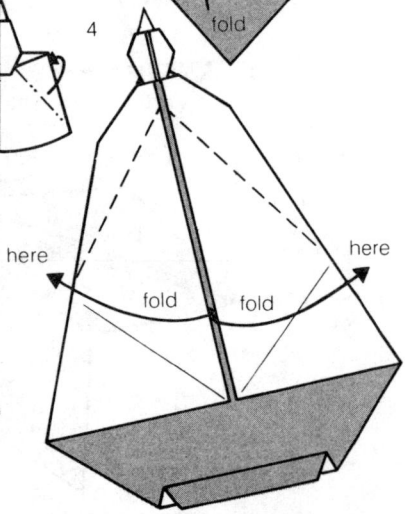

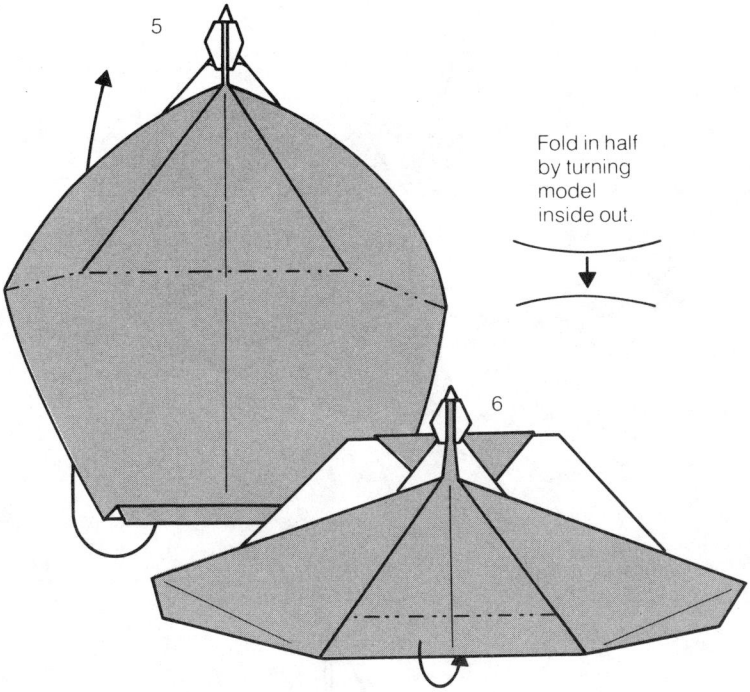

Fold along marked line only.

When you fold flaps.
A and B will move upwards.

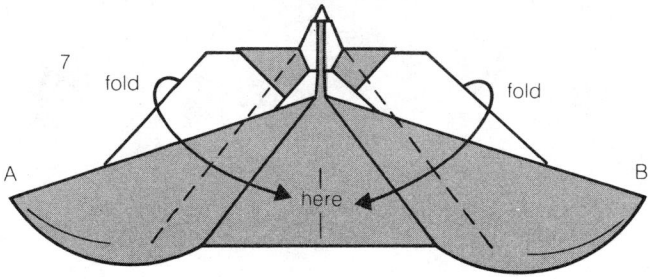

8

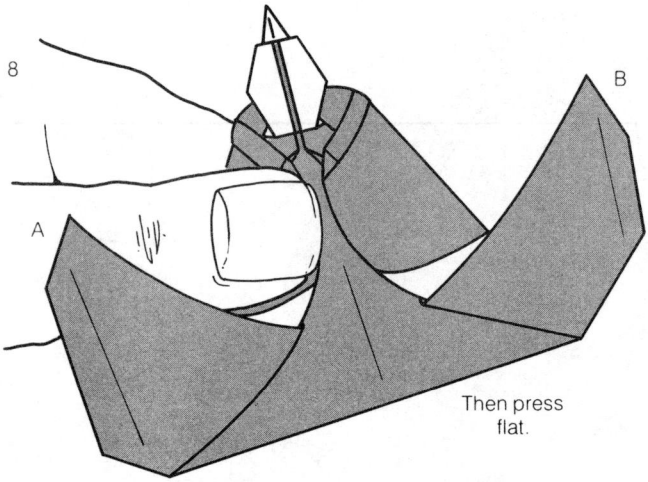

9

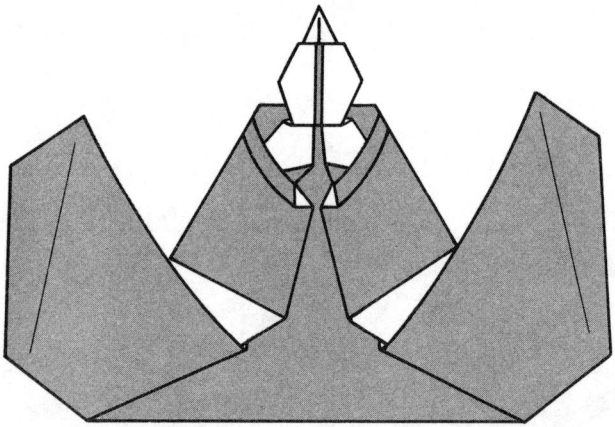

JAPANESE LADY *Begin as for Gentleman*

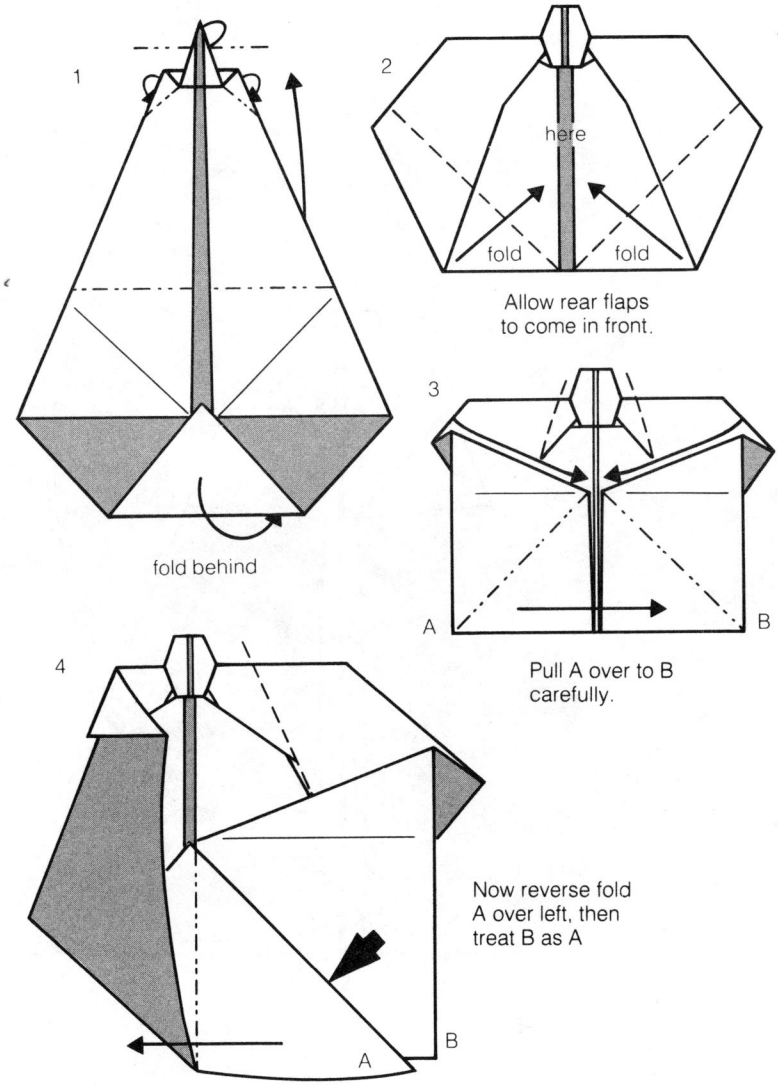

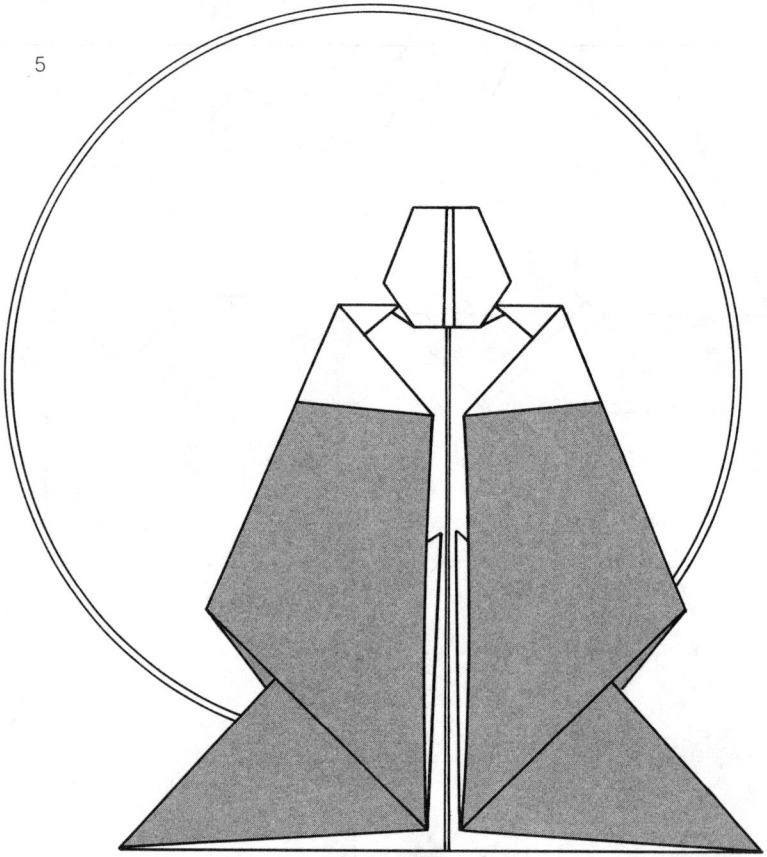
5

FISH *Samuel Randlett, Illinois, USA*

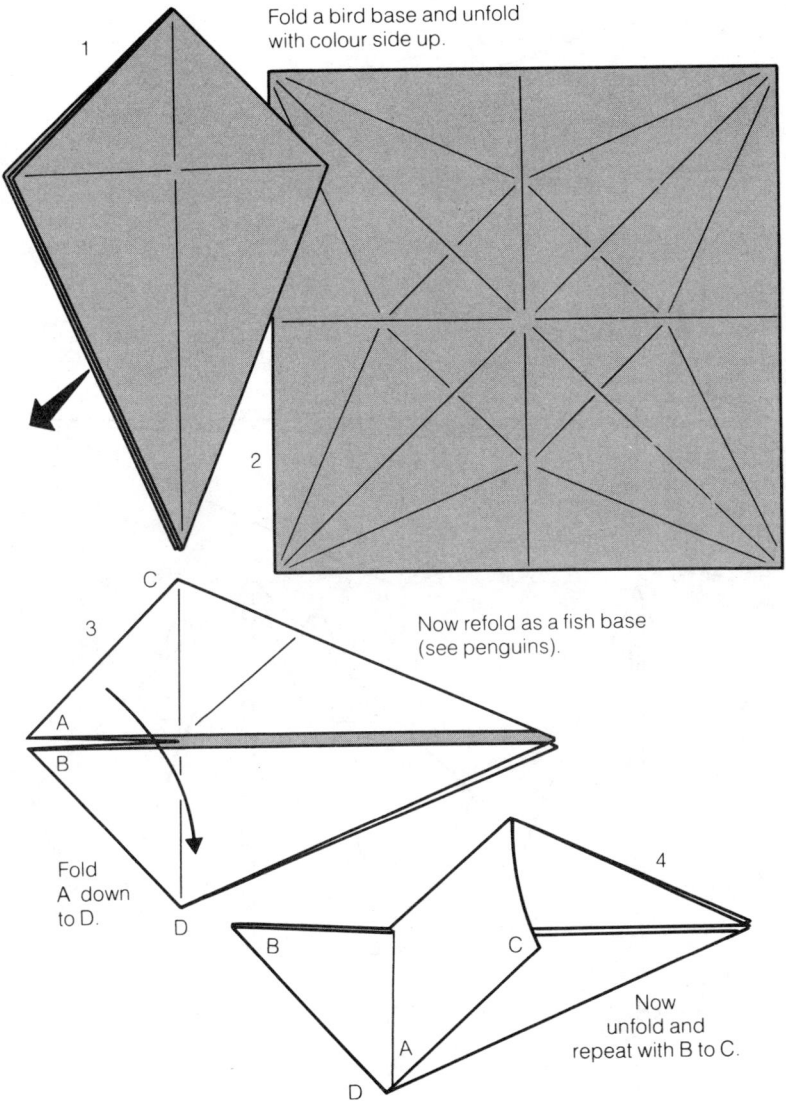

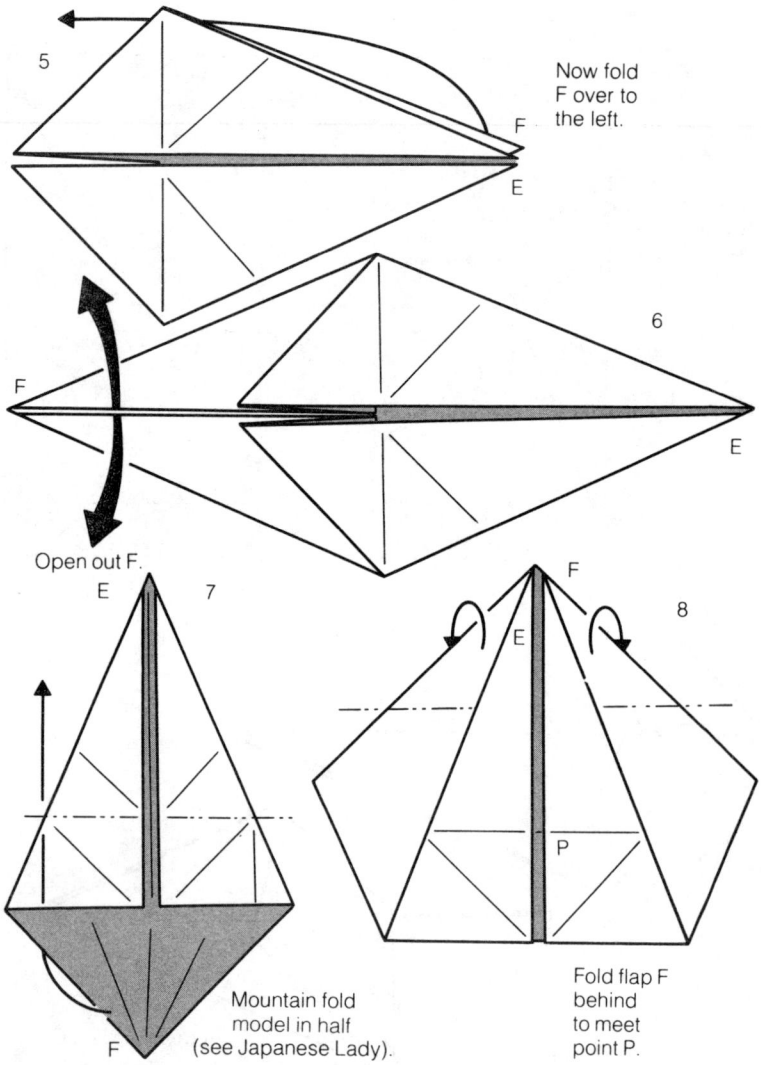
5
Now fold F over to the left.
F
E
6
F
E
Open out F.
E
7
F
8
E
P
F
Mountain fold model in half (see Japanese Lady).
Fold flap F behind to meet point P.

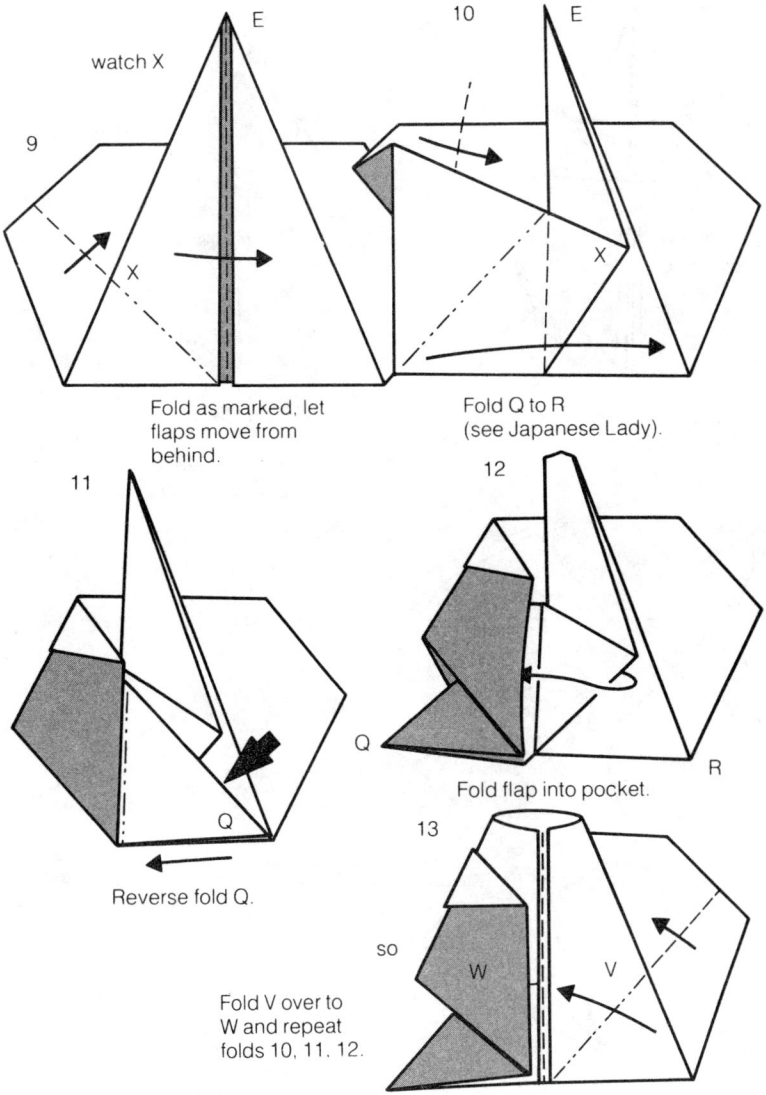
9
watch X
E
X
Fold as marked, let flaps move from behind.
10
E
X
Fold Q to R (see Japanese Lady).
11
Q
Reverse fold Q.
12
Q
R
Fold flap into pocket.
13
so
W
V
Fold V over to W and repeat folds 10, 11, 12.

14
Z
Mountain fold tail
flaps behind.

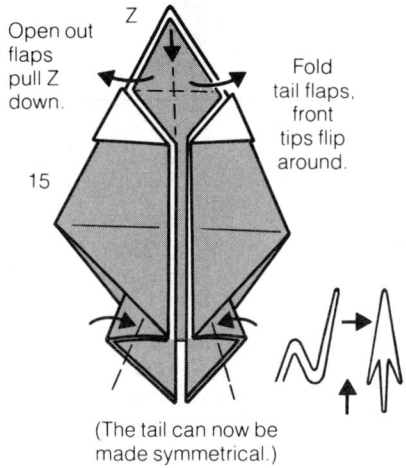
Z
Open out
flaps
pull Z
down.
Fold
tail flaps,
front
tips flip
around.
15
(The tail can now be
made symmetrical.)

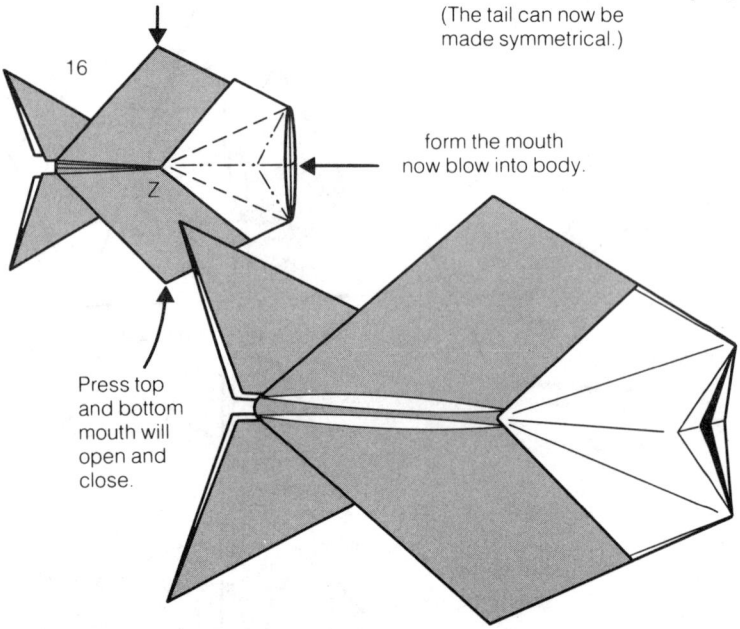
16
Z
form the mouth
now blow into body.
Press top
and bottom
mouth will
open and
close.

ORNITHONIMUS *Sidney French, St. Leonard's-on-Sea, England*

1 Start from white side of paper.

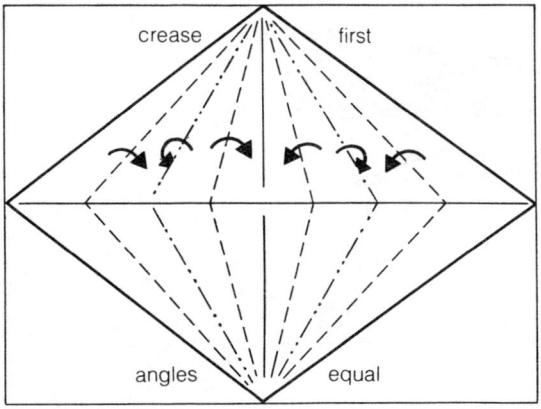

Cut diamond from 4 × 3 rectangle.

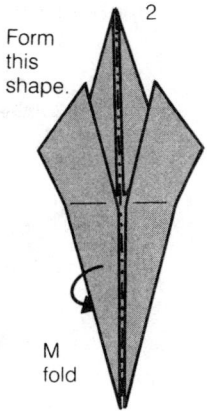

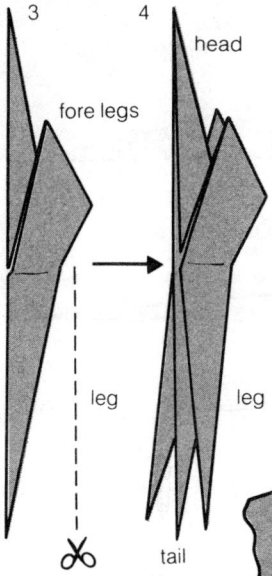

Cut both sides of middle for legs.

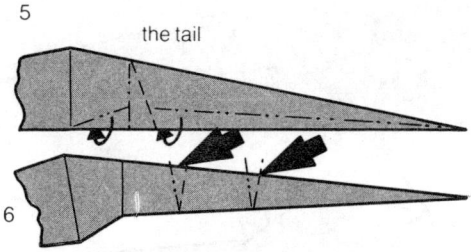

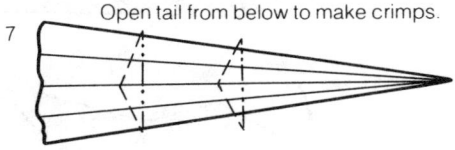

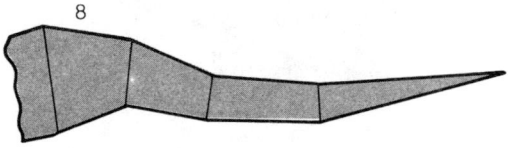

9 The head and neck.

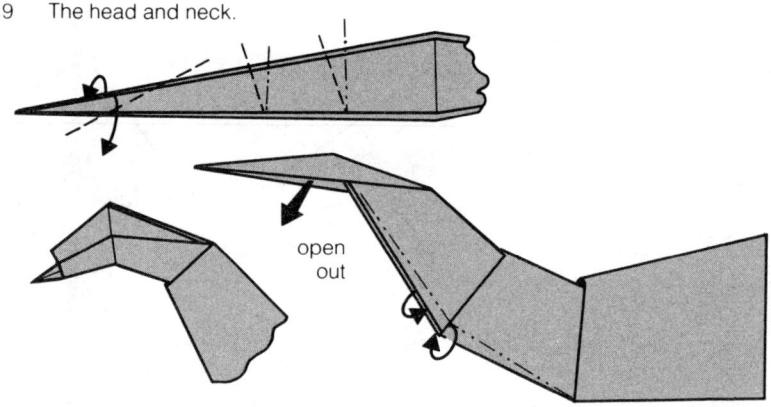

10 back legs

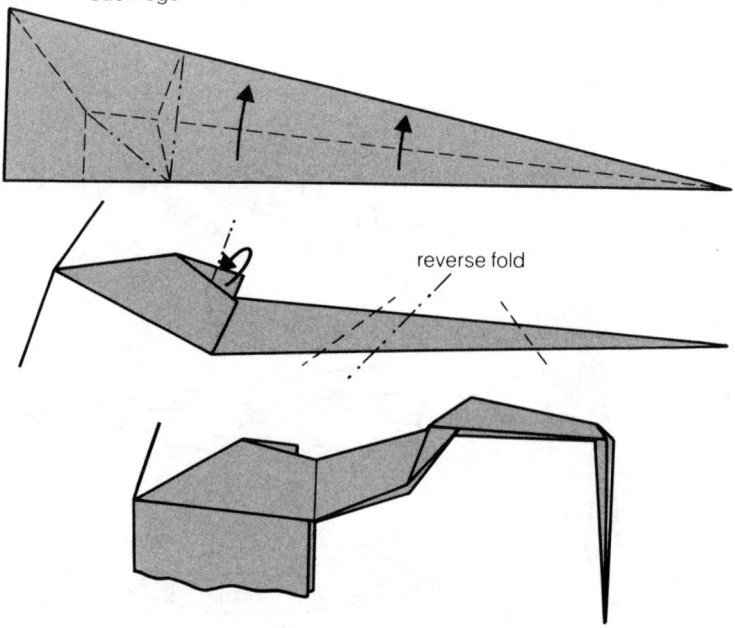

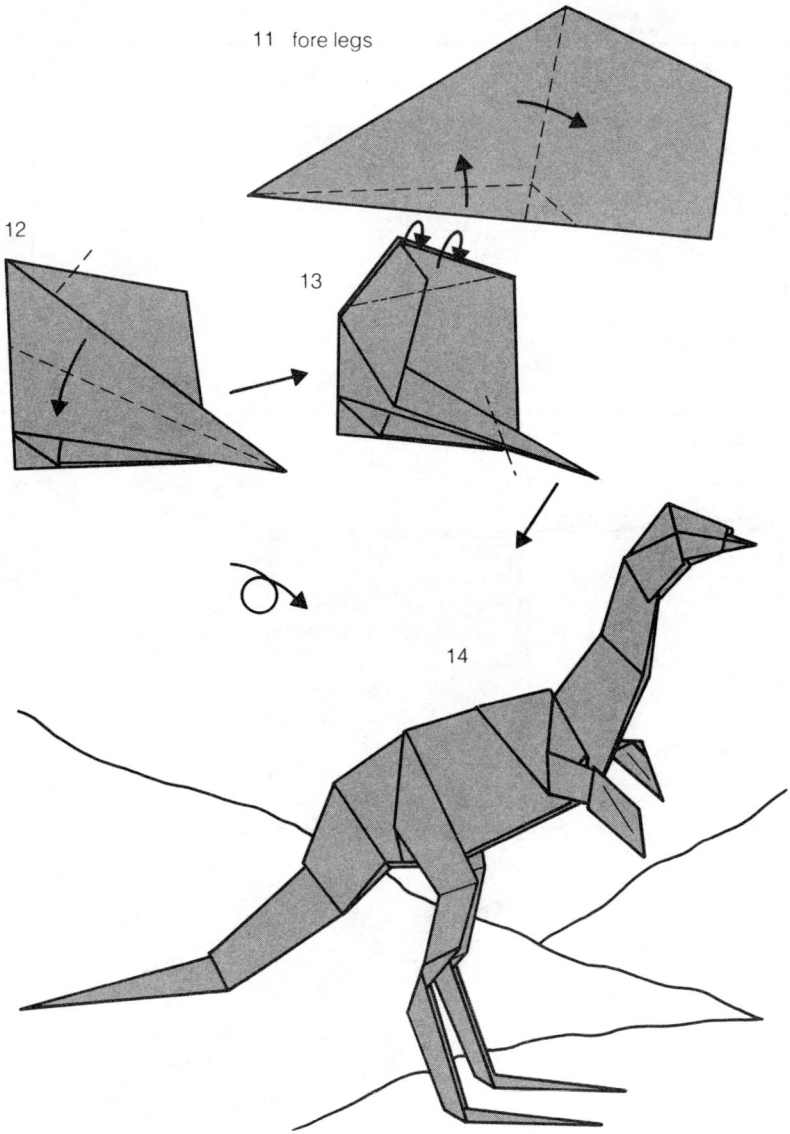
11 fore legs
12
13
14

ALADDIN'S LAMP *Neal Elias, Ohio, USA*

1

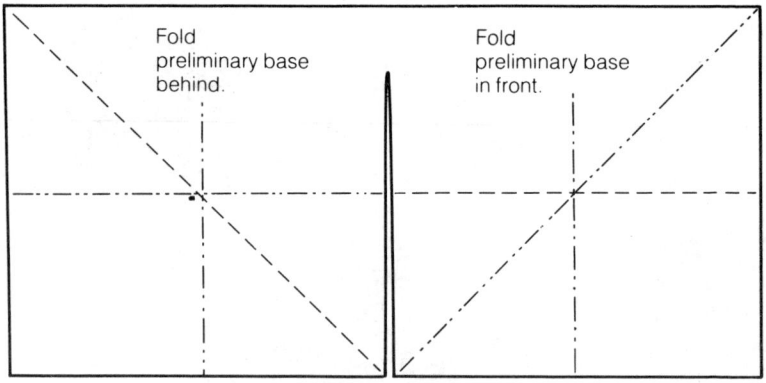

A rectangle cut as shown (gold side under).

2

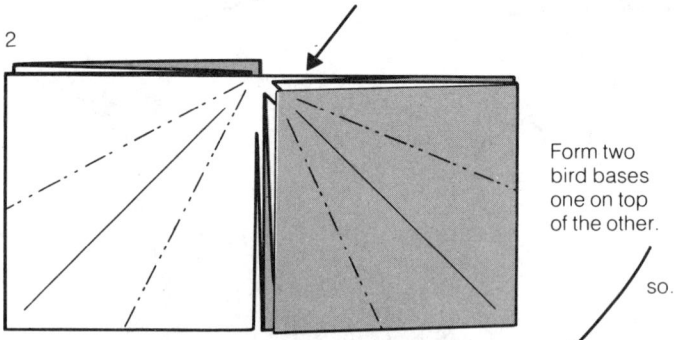

3

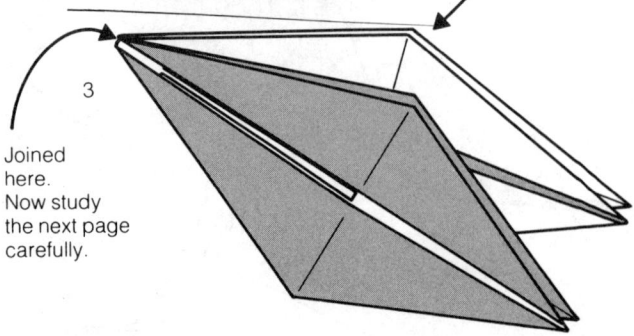

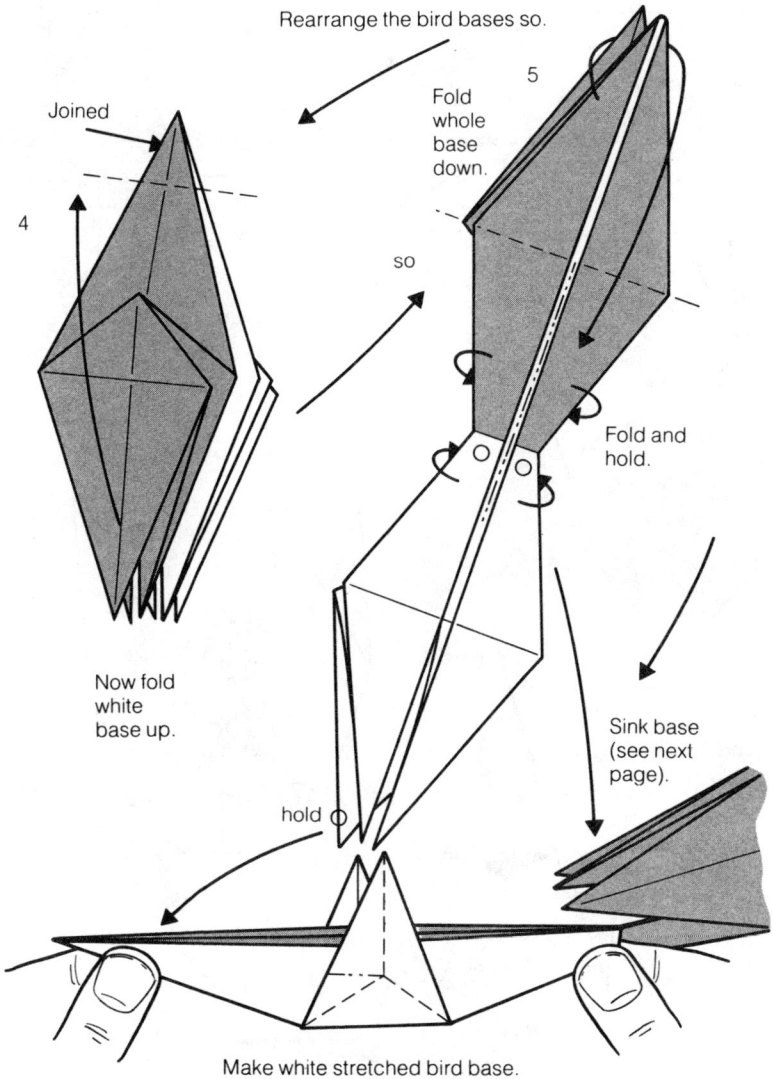

Make white stretched bird base.

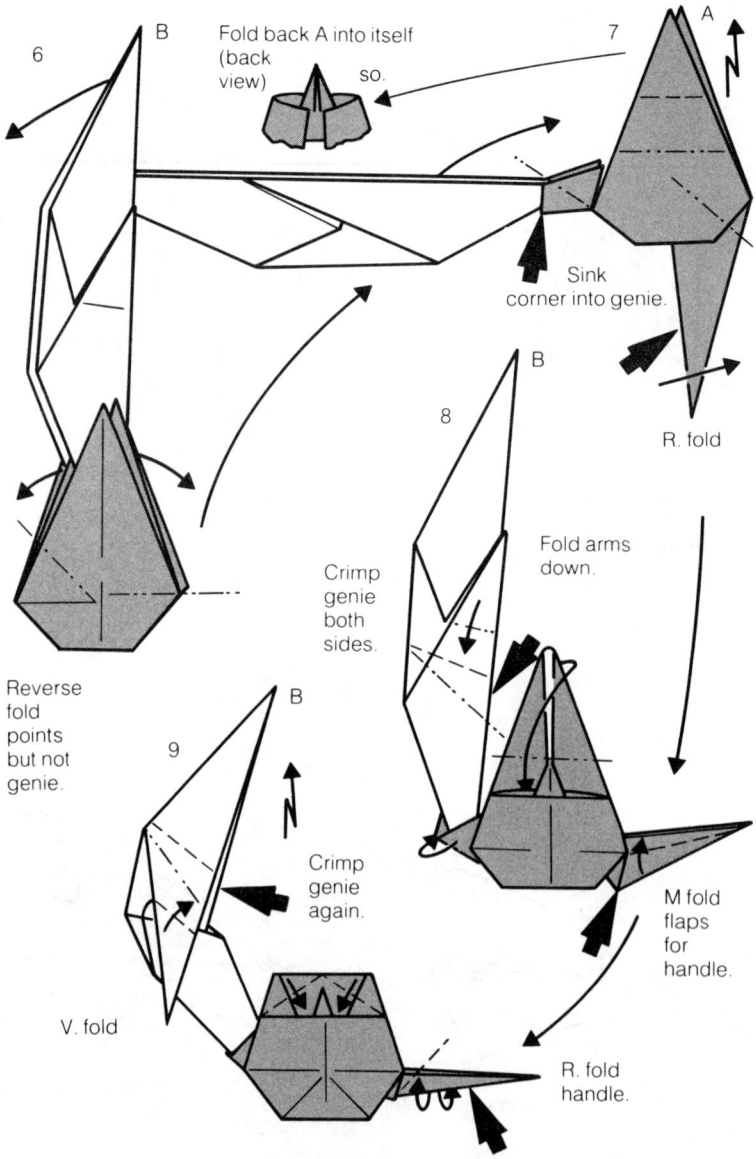
6
B
Fold back A into itself
(back
view)
so.
7
A
Sink
corner into genie.
R. fold
B
8
Fold arms
down.
Crimp
genie
both
sides.
Reverse
fold
points
but not
genie.
B
9
Crimp
genie
again.
M fold
flaps
for
handle.
V. fold
R. fold
handle.

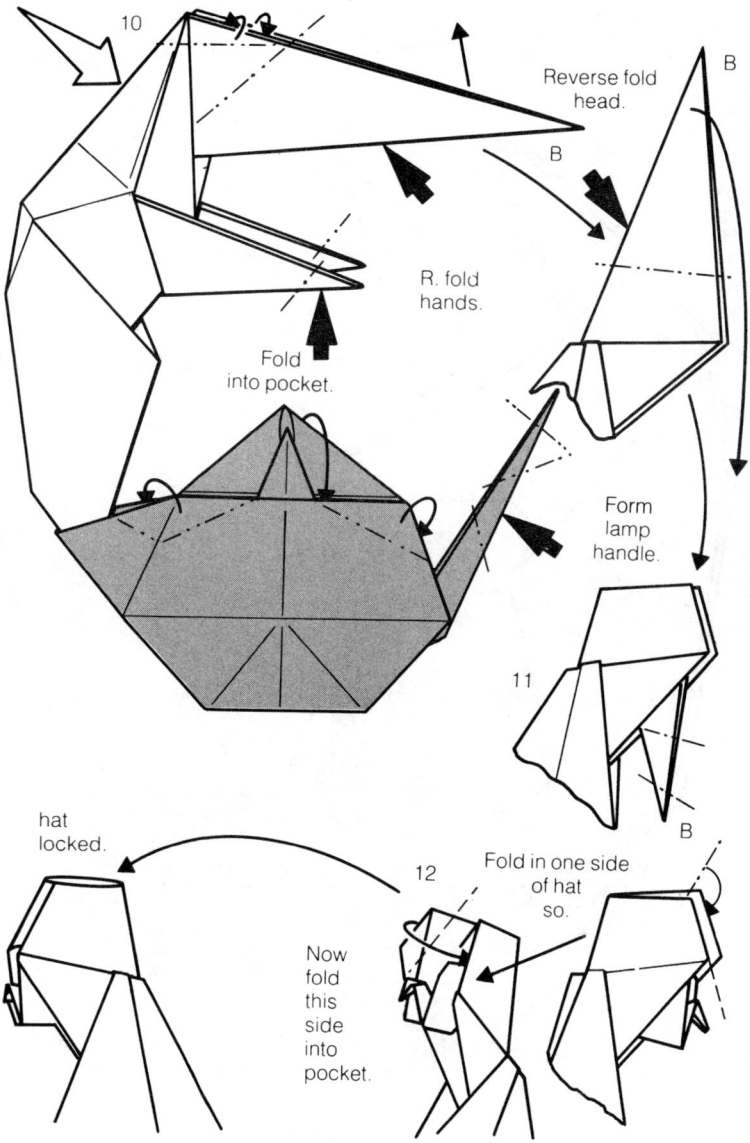
10
Reverse fold head.
B
B
R. fold hands.
Fold into pocket.
Form lamp handle.
11
B
hat locked.
12
Fold in one side of hat so.
Now fold this side into pocket.

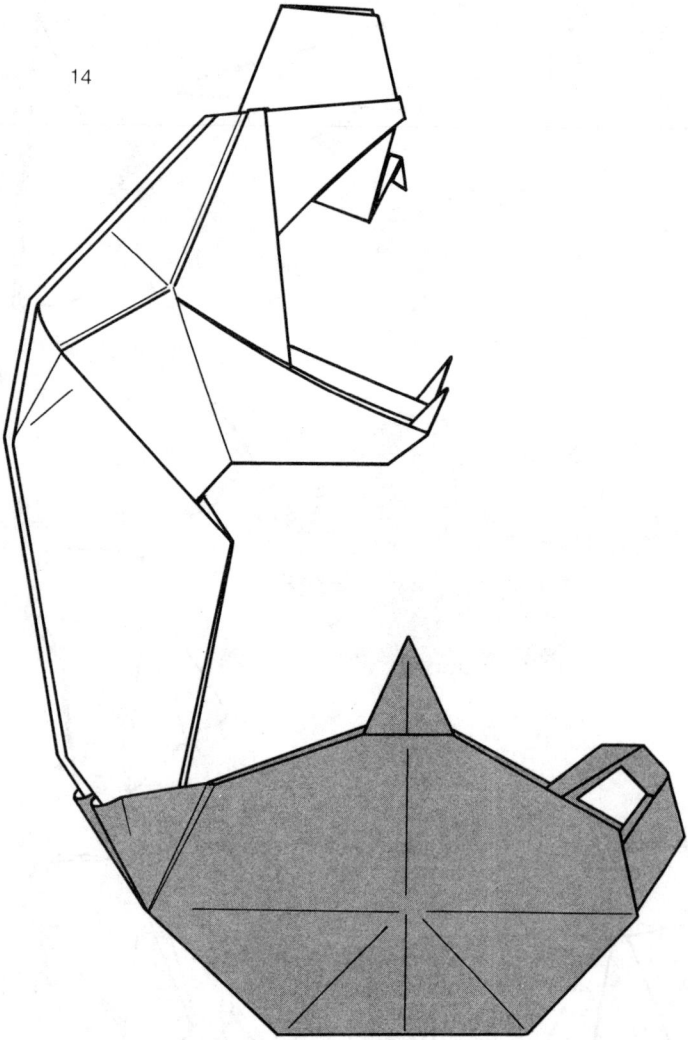
14

OSTRICH *Robert Harbin, London. Begin with Bird Base*

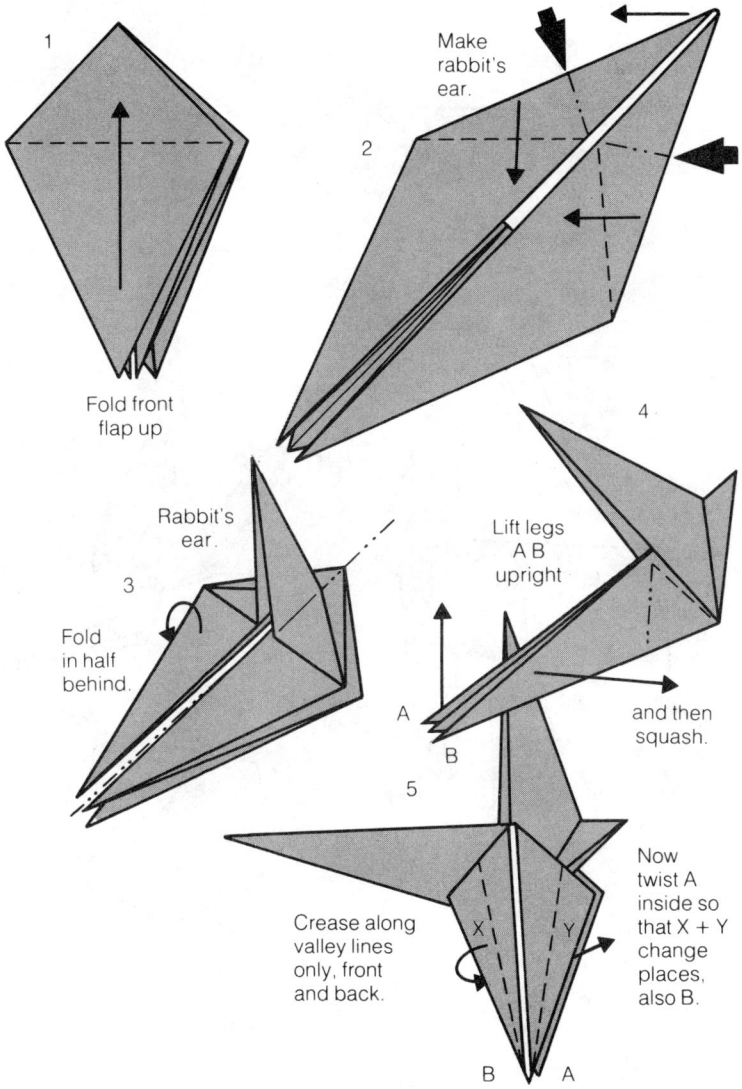

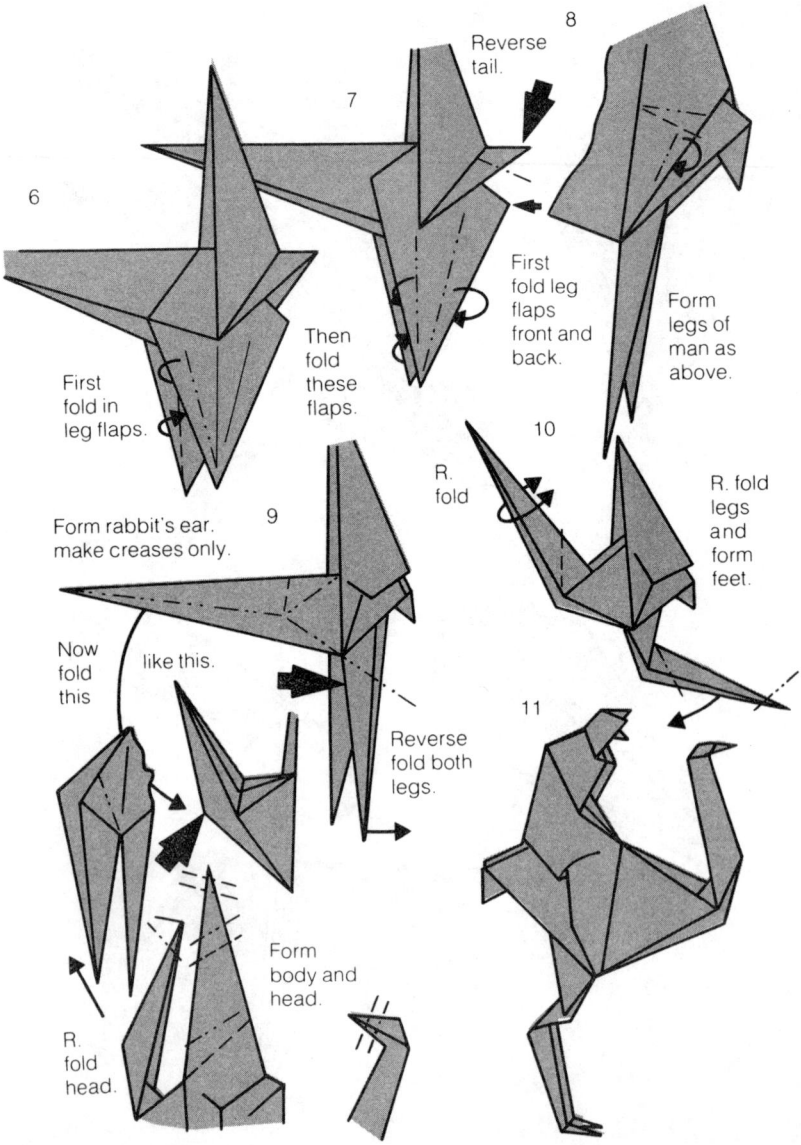
6
First fold in leg flaps.
7
Then fold these flaps.
Reverse tail.
First fold leg flaps front and back.
8
Form legs of man as above.
9
Form rabbit's ear. make creases only.
Now fold this
like this.
Reverse fold both legs.
R. fold head.
Form body and head.
10
R. fold
R. fold legs and form feet.
11

CHURCH *Iris Walker, Hull, England*

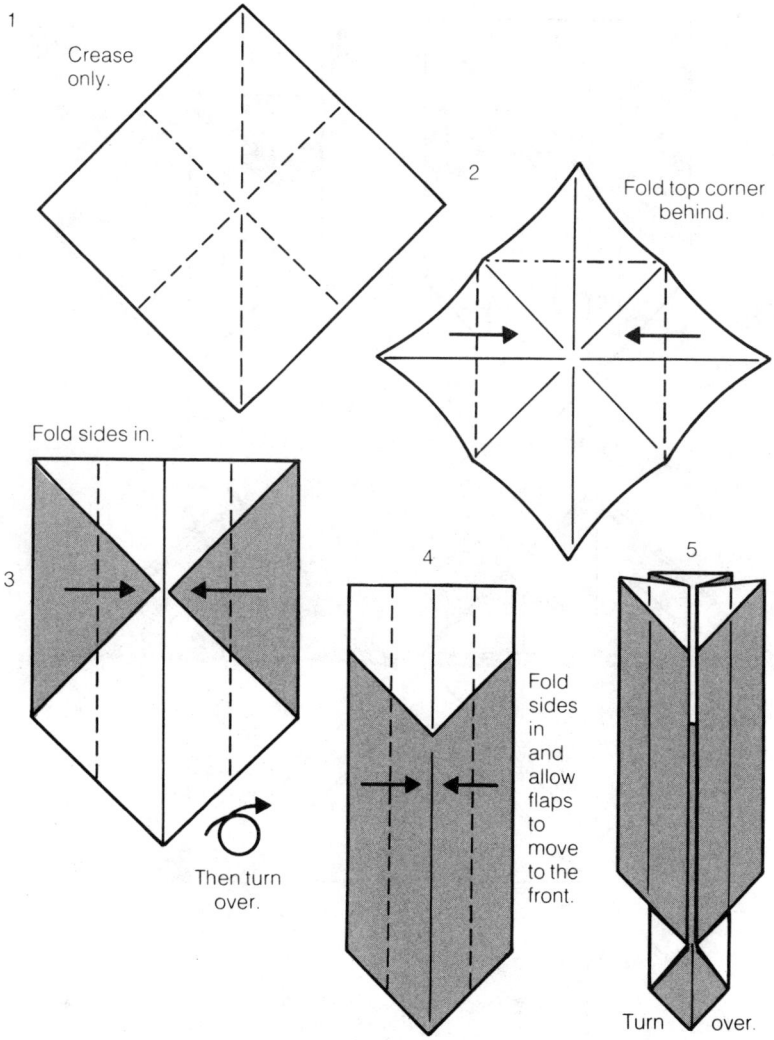

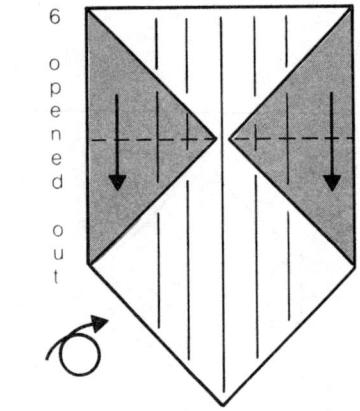
6
opened out
Fold flap down.

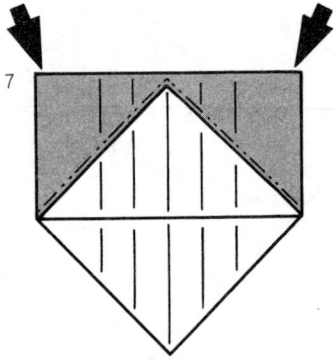
7
Push in corners making water bomb base.

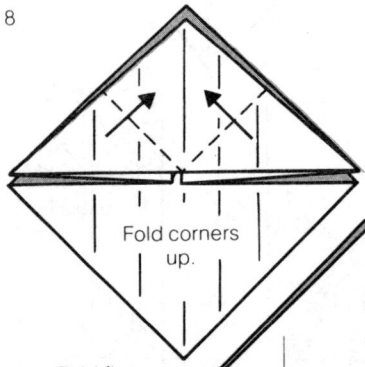
8
Fold corners up.

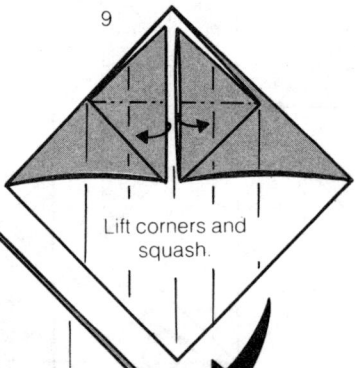
9
Lift corners and squash.

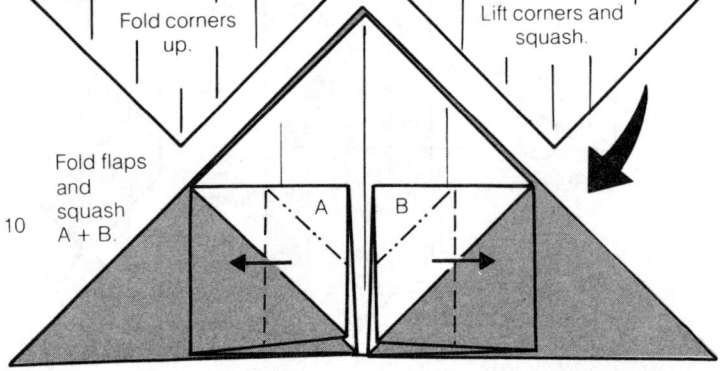
Fold flaps and squash A + B.
10
A
B

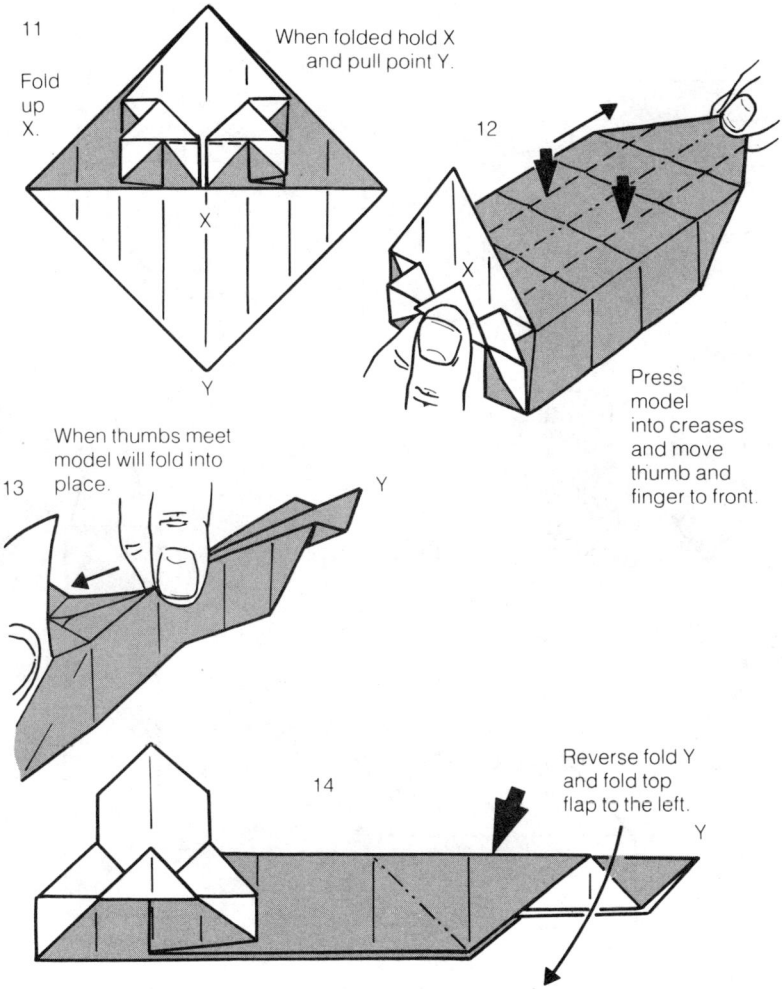
11
Fold up X.
When folded hold X and pull point Y.
X
Y
12
X
Press model into creases and move thumb and finger to front.
When thumbs meet model will fold into place.
13
Y
14
Reverse fold Y and fold top flap to the left.
Y

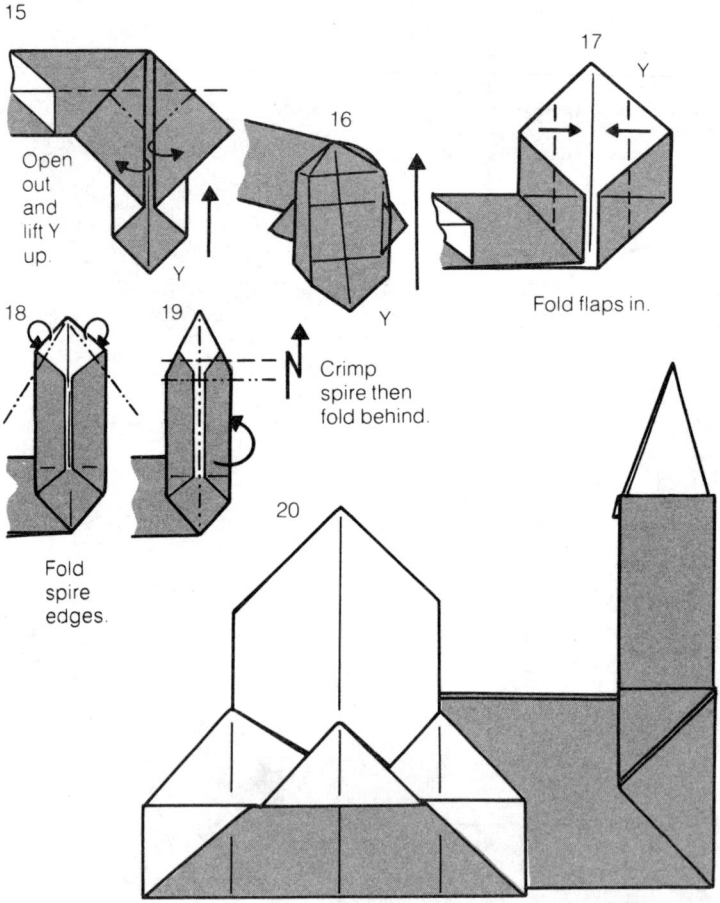
15
Open out and lift Y up.
Y
16
Y
17
Y
Fold flaps in.
18
19
Crimp spire then fold behind.
Fold spire edges.
20

PINK ELEPHANT *Tim Ward and Trevor Hatchett, London*

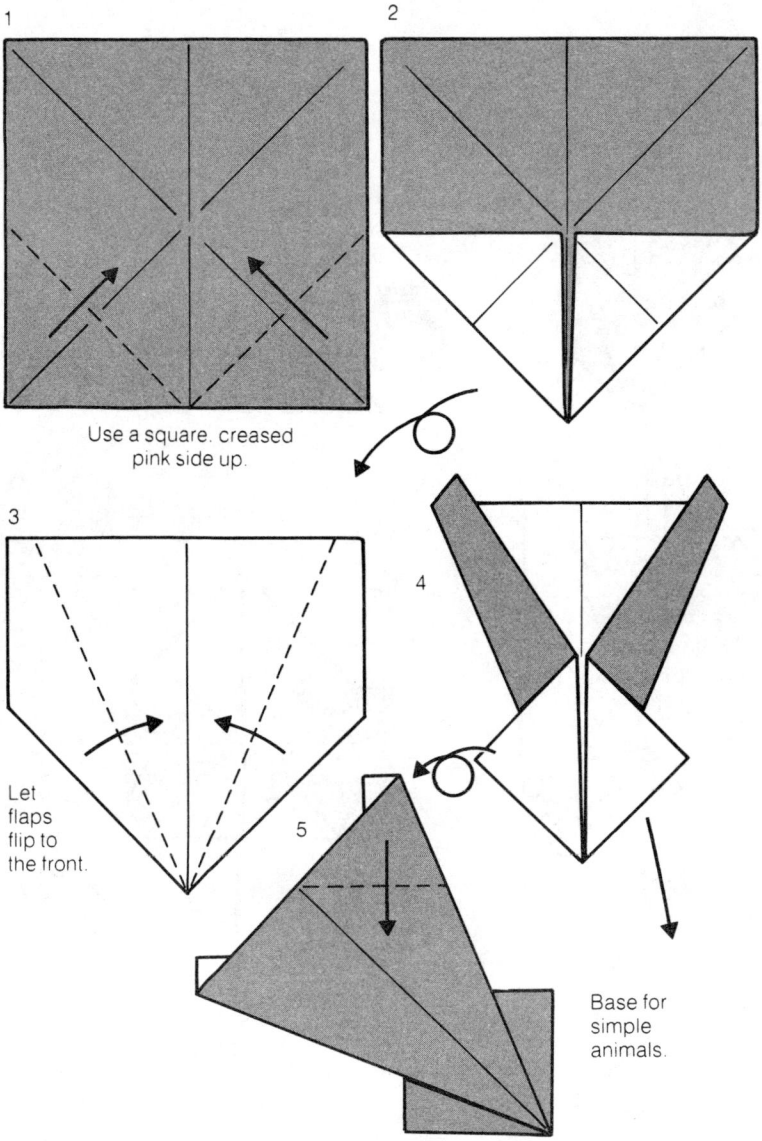

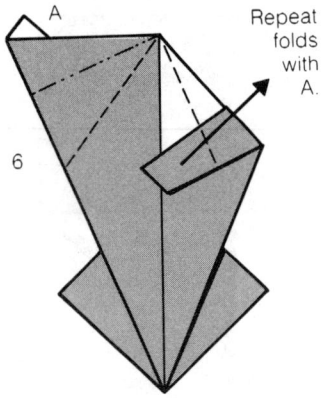

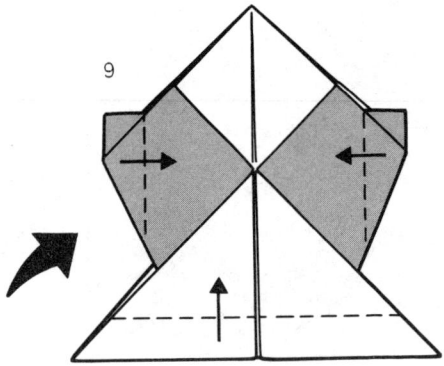

Flap behind flips to front.

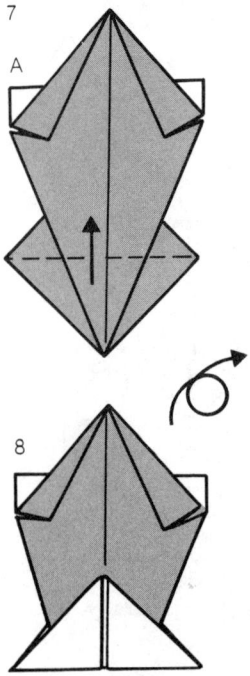

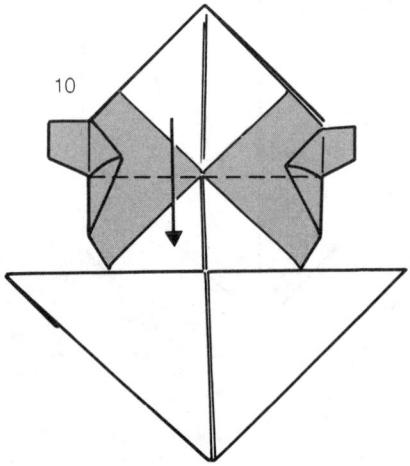

Fold top flat down.

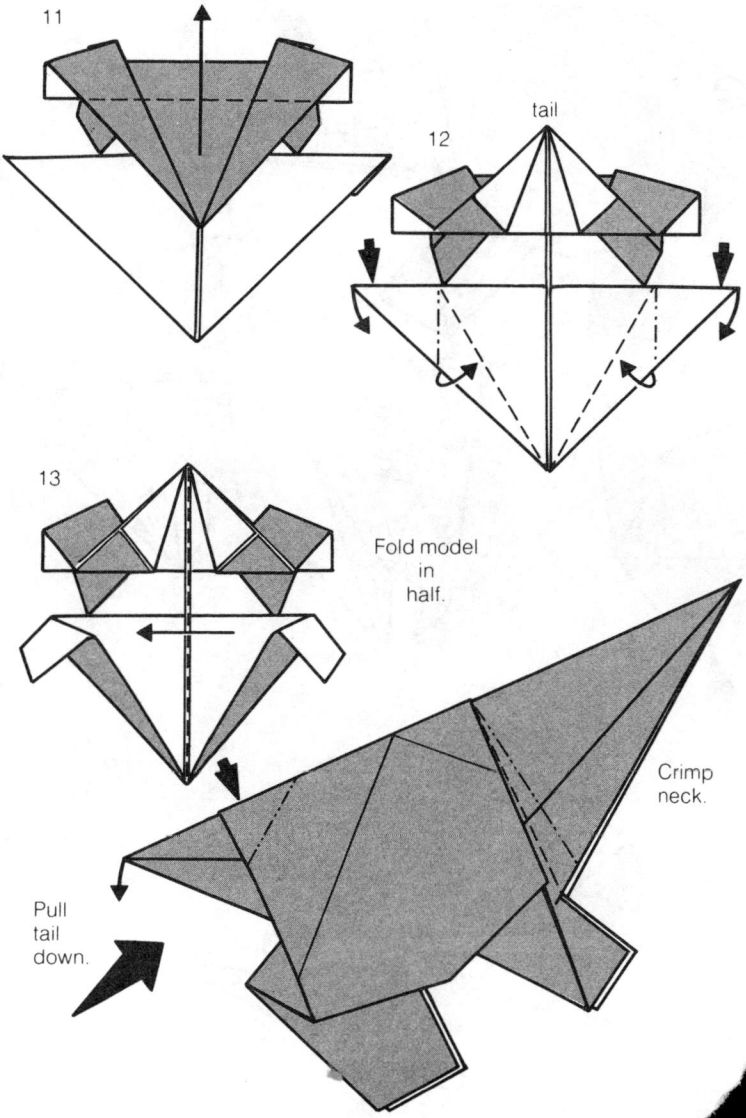
11
tail
12
13
Fold model
in
half.
Crimp
neck.
Pull
tail
down.

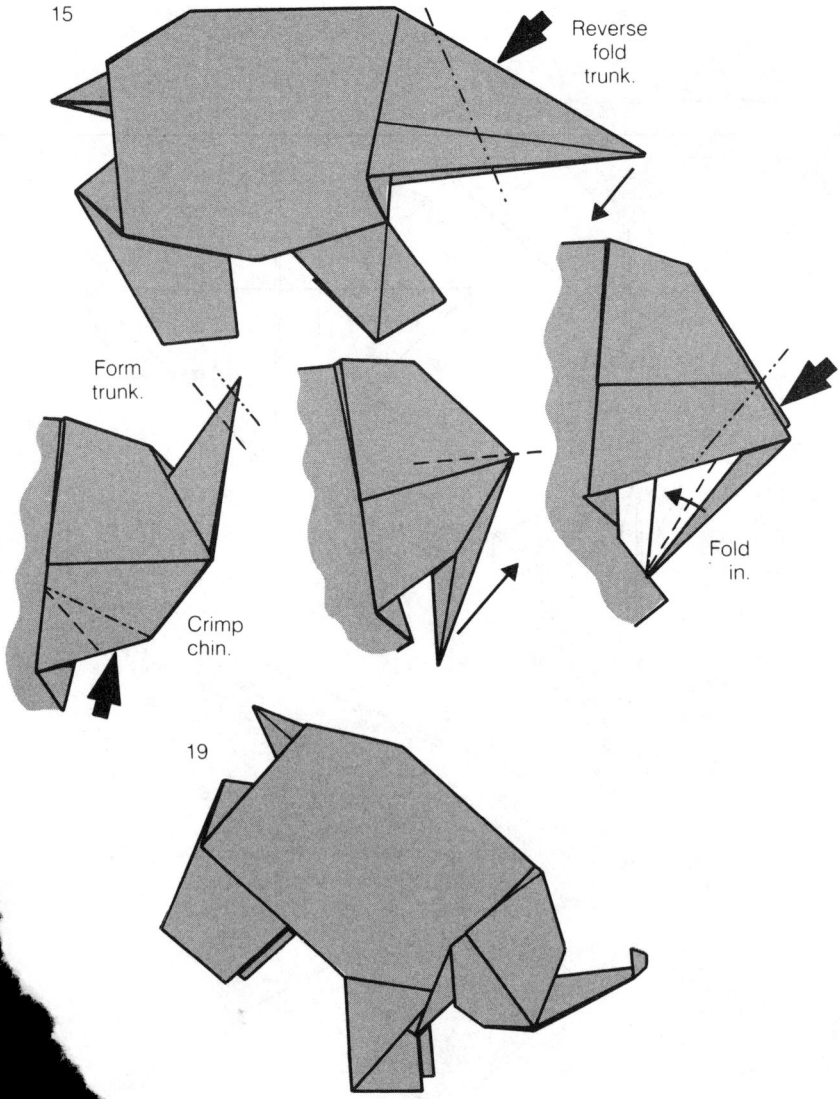
15
Reverse fold trunk.
Form trunk.
Crimp chin.
Fold in.
19

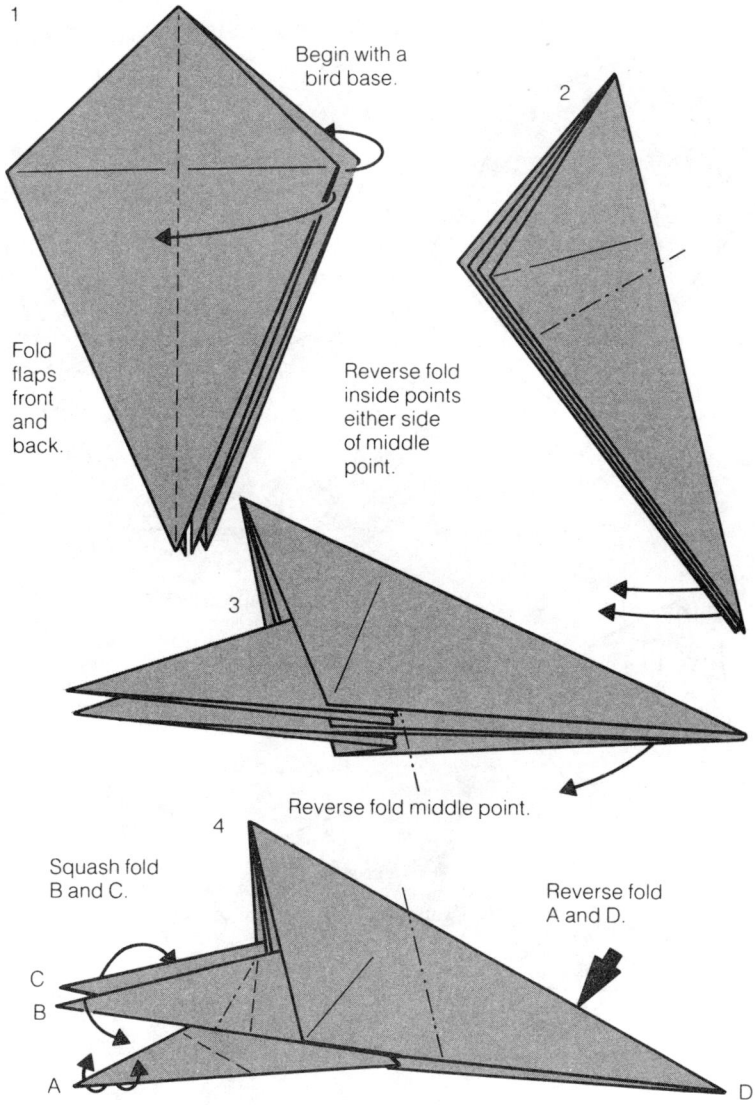
1
Begin with a bird base.
Fold flaps front and back.
2
Reverse fold inside points either side of middle point.
3
Reverse fold middle point.
4
Squash fold B and C.
Reverse fold A and D.
C
B
A
D

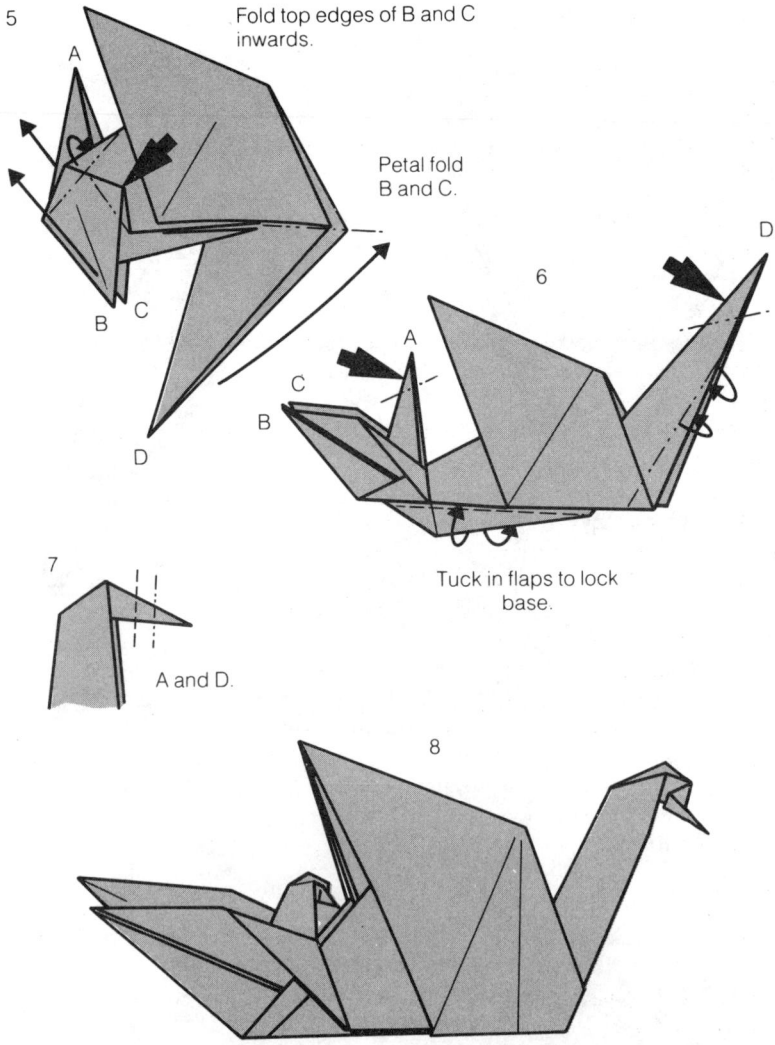
5
Fold top edges of B and C inwards.
A
Petal fold B and C.
B
C
D
6
D
A
C
B
Tuck in flaps to lock base.
7
A and D.
8

Bibliography

by David Lister

Books about origami now number well over a thousand, but many of them are designed for children. The following books include models of a wide range of difficulty and have been selected mainly for their interest for serious folders and because they are likely to be available in bookshops or libraries.

Kenneway, Eric
Simple Origami (1970) Dryad Press, Leicester.
Origami in action (1972) Dryad Press, Leicester.
Origami – Paperfolding for Fun (1980) Octopus Books, London.
Complete Origami (1987) Ebury Press, London.

This last is not primarily a book of instructions, but a delightful encyclopedia of models and numerous unexpected facets of paper-folding.

Temko, Florence
Paper Pandas and Jumping Frogs (1986) China Books, San Francisco.

Jackson, Paul
Origami: a Complete Step-by-Step Guide (1989) Hamlyn, London.
Classic Origami (1990) Quarto Publishing, London.

Biddle, Steve and Megumi
Amazing Origami for Children (1990) Arrow Books, London.
Step-by-Step Origami (1991) Ebury Press, London.

Some books of American 'technical' folding:

Montroll, John
Origami for the Enthusiast (1979) Drew Publications, New York.
Origami Sculptures (1985) Antroll Publishing, Vermont.

Lang, Robert J.
The Complete Book of Origami (1988) Dover Publications, New York.

Montroll, John and **Lang, Robert J.**
Origami Sea Life (1990) Antroll Publishing, Vermont, USA.

Engel, Peter
Folding the Universe (1989) Vintage Books, New York.
(Apart from 227 pages of models, this book contains 81 pages of fascinating serious discussion about many aspects of paper-folding.)

Some books by Japanese authors available in English:

Kawai, Toyoaki
Colourful Origami (this edition 1983) Barnes and Noble, New York.

Nakano, Dokushtei (translated by Eric Kenneway)
Easy Origami (1985) Viking Kestrel, Harmondsworth.

Takahama, Toshie
The Joy of Origami (1985) Shufunotomo, Tokyo.

Kasahara, Kunihiko
Origami for the Connisseur Japan Publications, Tokyo.

Kasahara, Kunihiko
Origami Omnibus (1988) Japan Publications, Tokyo.
(This is a huge collection of every sort of paper-folding.)

Three classic works still in print:

Murray, W. D. and **Rigney, F. J.**
Paper-folding for Beginners (1928, this edition 1960) Dover Publications, New York.

Campbell, Margaret
Paper Toy Making (1937, this edition 1964) Dover Publications, New York.

Harbin, Robert
Paper Magic (1956, this edition 1971) John Maxfield, London.

The first two of these classics were the best paper-folding books published in English before Robert Harbin's *Paper Magic*. They were the books from which Lillian Oppenheimer and Robert Harbin learnt much of their folding. *Paper Magic* took their place and is still an excellent non-technical introduction to the subject.

Three more classics from the early 1960s:

Randlett, Samuel
The Art of Origami (1961) Faber and Faber, London.
The Best of Origami (1963) Faber and Faber, London.

Harbin, Robert
Secrets of Origami (1964) Oldborne Press, London. (Later edition Octopus Books, London.)

Robert Harbin and Samuel Randlett co-operated when writing these three books, which heralded modern paper-folding in the West. Unfortunately they are out-of-print, but they can be found in libraries and secondhand bookshops.

The Japanese output is enormous, both for children and serious folders. The British Origami Society and other paper-folding societies will advise on the best and how to obtain them. Japanese authors to look for include Akira Yoshizawa, Toshie Takahama, Toyraki Kawai, Kumihiko Kasahara, Yoshihide Momotani and Tomoko Fuse.

Language is no barrier to following an origami book because the same symbols for diagrams are used throughout the world. There are many books in Spanish, French, Dutch, German and Italian which are worth having and the origami societies will be pleased to give guidance. Some of the societies themselves issue publications which are not obtainable elsewhere.